9

The Death of Anglo-Saxon England

N.J. HIGHAM

SUTTON PUBLISHING

First published in the United Kingdom in 1997 by
Sutton Publishing Limited · Phoenix Mill
Thrupp · Stroud · Gloucestershire · GL5 2BU

British Library Cataloguing in Publication Data
A catalogue record for this book is available from the British Library

ISBN 0 7509 0885 8

For Naomi
and in loving memory of my grandparents,
Herbert Gowan and Winifred Muriel Higham,
formerly of Battle High Street.

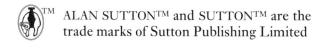TM ALAN SUTTON™ and SUTTON™ are the
trade marks of Sutton Publishing Limited

Typeset in 11/12pt Ehrhardt.
Typesetting and origination by
Sutton Publishing Limited.
Printed in Great Britain by
WBC Limited, Bridgend.

Contents

List of Illustrations

Black and white Illustrations

Maps and Genealogies

Unless otherwise stated, all photographs have been supplied by the author.

Acknowledgements

This volume has grown out of an interest in the crisis of 1066 which stretches back to my days as an undergraduate, when I had the benefit of Mr Eric John's thoughts on several of the issues involved. It has benefited enormously from generations of my own students and discussions over the years with several colleagues, including Professor Jeffrey Denton, Dr David Hill, Dr Conrad Leyser, Dr Alexander Rumble and Professor Don Scragg. It gives me particular pleasure to acknowledge the advice of Dr Simon Keynes concerning the will of Prince Athelstan, and of my colleague Helen Maclean concerning the sagas. The John Rylands University Library and its staff have given me valuable assistance. The staff travel fund of the University of Manchester generously supported study visits to numerous sites in England and Normandy. The staff at Sutton Publishing have been universally supportive and helpful throughout the project. Despite these considerable debts, the views expressed herein are my own, and so too are any errors.

Introduction

Anglo-Saxon England has traditionally been thought of as ending on Saint Callixtus's Day – 14 October – in the year 1066, which was, of course, the date on which Duke William and his conglomerate Norman, Breton and 'French' army defeated and killed Harold II, the last 'English' king of the English. The conflict occurred on Senlac Hill in Sussex, on the site where Battle Abbey was thereafter established by King William. It was certainly a day of great carnage, and not only Harold himself but also the two earls who were his brothers fell on the English side.

The year 1066 is readily examined from the perspective of the military historian, focusing on the several battles fought and tactics used. This is, however, to disregard the political context which set the several armies in motion, and the political consequences of William's unlooked for victory. To look at events from a slightly different perspective, it is surprising that William was crowned king only eighty-eight days after setting foot in England, having won just one major battle and perhaps two lesser engagements, having campaigned only in the extreme south-east and having taken (by negotiation) only one non-coastal town – Canterbury – before the surrender of London. Viking armies a generation earlier had on occasion engaged in far more successful campaigns without anything like such momentous political consequences. The very ease of William's success underlines the significance of the political and even psychological factors at work.

At its most fundamental, this year witnessed a succession crisis of unprecedented scale and complexity in English history and it is this aspect which offers the greater insights into this distant epoch. Within a single calendar year, five separate individuals were recognized as at least *de facto* king within England by some group or other of the indigenous political elite. In that respect, 1066 in English history exceeds even Rome's 'year of the four emperors' – AD 68. As at Rome, the lack of an adult male member of the ruling dynasty was one factor which led to a dogfight for power between men with little dynastic right but the political will to succeed and the military power to back up their several candidacies. That the several claimants offered a bewildering variety of claims to legitimacy as King Edward's heir should not surprise us. The eventual outcome in England, however, brought with it far more substantial changes than had occurred at Rome almost exactly a millennium before, because of William's foreignness, his land-hungry following and the deep-rooted distrust between the victor and the surviving English elite.

William founded and generously endowed Battle Abbey on the site of his great victory over Harold II, staffing it with monks from Fécamp. Little now remains above ground from the Norman period and hardly anything from the first generation of construction, but the late medieval gatehouse still presides over the southern end of the High Street.

There was, admittedly, nothing particularly unusual about a succession dispute in the history of late Anglo-Saxon England. The deaths of numerous English kings had led to some sort of competition concerning the inheritance and there were few clear rules available by which to balance the quality of one claim versus another, such as primogeniture would later provide. The office of king was, of course, gender specific and there was a general assumption that only members of the royal family had any claim to the throne, but there might be more than one such eager for the job at any one time. In practice, all candidates from the ninth century right down to 1066 – when none such was available – were the acknowledged sons of a previous king, so membership of a collateral branch of the royal kin seems to have carried little weight. To be an aetheling – a potential candidate – was normally specific to the sons of a king, yet in the 1060s Edgar Aetheling was a prominent exception to even this generalization, being grandson but not son to a much earlier king of England.

There were several other factors which might come into play. Adults were generally preferred to children or perhaps merely found it easier to press their candidacies to a successful conclusion. Older sons certainly enjoyed advantages over younger, but the superiority of an elder sibling's claim was not beyond question. The names of Aethelred's numerous sons always occur in order of seniority by age when attesting his diplomas and the eldest (Athelstan) had particular reason to consider himself the heir to his father's throne, but it does not necessarily follow that he was recognized as such by his own father. Indeed, it will be argued hereafter that that was not the case. The wishes of the previous king were of considerable significance, and both Edgar and then Aethelred seem to have thrown their weight behind the candidacy of younger sons born of second or third marriages, whose mothers were still politically active at their respective deaths. The king's nomination of his heir was perhaps the most potent single factor in conferring legitimacy on a particular candidate, yet even that did not necessarily guarantee success, as Harold II found to his cost.

In exceptional cases, kings even attempted to establish an order of succession for the entirety of the next generation, as apparently occurred at Aethelwulf's death in 855. His will was considered by Asser to be advisory rather than anything more, and it should be remembered that our knowledge of this document depends on the writings of the self-interested Alfred – who was its ultimate beneficiary – and his favourite bishop and biographer. Even so, Aethelwulf was succeeded in turn by his four sons in age order, each inheriting at a time when any nephews born to their elder brethren were still very young. What is more doubtful is the assumption that Aethelwulf's testament had much influence on the course of events, since the successive tenure of his sons in order of seniority was in any case very likely given the circumstances of their several deaths – again in order of seniority – in comparatively quick succession. Aethelwulf's policy may, in any case, have been a deliberate attempt to minimize disputes at a moment when the West Saxons were experiencing unprecedented Viking attacks, so have been an unusual strategy conditioned by exceptional circumstances. To generalize from his will in search of more general principals regarding the royal succession is inappropriate.

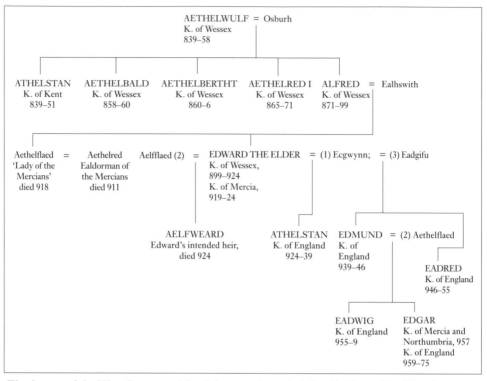

The descent of the West-Saxon and English crown from Aethelwulf, King of the West Saxons 839–58, to Edgar, King of the English 959–75.

Customary inheritance during the Anglo-Saxon period was partible and this certainly impacted on ideas about the descent of the throne. In the past, the kingship of individual English peoples had on occasion been treated as something which was partible, or at least as capable of joint inheritance by two or more successors. After Aethelwulf, a sub-kingship of the south-east shires (Kent and its neighbours) was on occasion held by the next in line, in a manner almost akin to the principality of Wales from Edward I onwards, but this was reabsorbed within the following generation. After the takeover of Mercia by the West-Saxon dynasty, there are signs that kings considered that their new Mercian polity could be detached from the stem of West-Saxon kingship and perhaps even bequeathed as a sub-kingship to some other son; both Athelstan and Edgar reigned as king of the Mercians before being recognized in Wessex. So too did Cnut and then Harold I, but the possibility of a permanent partition never appears to have gathered momentum. Once Northumbria was also incorporated, then all of England, from the Tweed to the Channel, was increasingly being viewed as indivisible, at least from a southern perspective.

There remained some confusion in late Anglo-Saxon England between the personal property of the king and his possessions by virtue of royal office. Alfred's will was clearly concerned only with those estates which he had reserved to himself to bestow as he chose, albeit he recognized himself to be honour bound to look to the needs of several relatives by virtue of his father's earlier provisions. The royal treasure, however, seems to have been considered his to bestow as he wished, and he even established a formula by which to give away more than he had specified in his will, if greater quantities of coin than anticipated should prove to be available when he died. Similarly, Cnut's treasure in 1035 was initially treated as separate from the crown.

The succession was, therefore, a very delicate matter and few candidates could expect to reach the throne without some degree of competition. The individual who was least likely to find himself opposed was one who could bring together a congeries of legitimizing and enabling factors. His cause would be strengthened by being a young adult and an aetheling, descended directly from a recent king – and preferably a king's son. The nomination of the previous ruler carried considerable weight and was normally obtained by a brother or son. Yet he also needed to be acceptable to the wider political establishment. There was a certain amount of somewhat ritualistic acclamation involved in the coronation ceremony but the committed support of the council of the previous ruler and other powerful magnates was certainly important. So too was the backing and approval of the senior churchmen in England, some of whom were central figures in the royal council and whose responsibility it was to undertake the task of coronation. Personal wealth, the support of a powerful faction, large family estates, marriage into other influential kinships were all significant factors.

Strong candidates were not, however, always available. The late Anglo-Saxon period was characterized by succession disputes, minorities and ultimately usurpation or the threat of usurpation from outside the royal kin. This situation even brought about replacement of the dynasty in 1013–14, and then again in 1016, as the Danish royal family competed with ultimate success with the West Saxon and English royal house – the Cerdicings – for the kingship. In some senses, the succession of Edward the Confessor in 1042 was another usurpation, in as much as his paternity lay with the native English dynasty rather than the Danish rulers of the previous quarter century. That foreign dynasties contested the English throne in the eleventh century is one way in which the history of the late Anglo-Saxon state differed fundamentally from that of the England of Alfred's son and grandsons. One important task of this volume will be to identify the root cause of this change, which it will be argued had more to do with the factional politics of Aethelred's England than naked, external aggression.

By 1066, the rights of Alfred's lineage had been too seriously compromised too often to be any longer the *sine qua non* of a candidacy for the succession, as it had been when, for example, King Eadred died in 955. Furthermore, political power had become focused in the hands of a non-royal aristocrat – Harold Godwineson – in a way which had no real precedent in the tenth century, apart perhaps from the position and status of Athelstan Half-king. Members of the royal kindred were few and far between and none was poised to take power. In deciding whom to nominate, King Edward on his deathbed breached previous conventions, which

The making of England – the West-Saxon kings conquered, took over or otherwise acquired royal status throughout England during the period 900–54. Additionally, they periodically established a degree of 'overkingship' over their Welsh or Scottish neighbours.

had invariably run in favour of royal blood, gave priority instead to other factors and supported the candidacy of his brother-in-law, Harold, the earl of Wessex. Harold arguably stood the best chance of protecting England and its current political establishment from attack by belligerent outsiders, all of whom were unacceptable to the opinion formers inside Edward's own court. It was their opinions which presumably swayed the old king, but his support for a dynastic revolution and the consensual processes to which he assented contrast dramatically with, for example, the seizure of the Frankish throne by the Carolingians in the eighth century from the last of the Merovingian line.

Edward the Confessor had ruled England without significant challenge to his kingship – but not his freedom to rule – from 1042 until his death in the opening days of 1066. His kingship was comparatively peaceful. His regime does seem to have had the respect of its neighbours and was certainly well-supplied with arms, ships and fighting men and was not without military kudos. Contemporaries might even have been more able to recognize the figure later conjured up by such as Lord Lytton than the generations which followed the conquest, for whom Edward was primarily viewed as a saintly figure:

> And King Edward looked a king! The habitual lethargic meekness had vanished from his face, and the large crown threw a shadow, like a frown, over his brow. His spirit seemed to have risen from the weight it took from the sluggish blood of his father, Aethelred the Unready, and to have remounted to the brighter and earlier source of ancestral heroes. Worthy in that hour he seemed to boast the blood and wield the sceptre of Athelstan and Alfred.
>
> *Harold, The last of the Saxon Kings*, 3rd edn 1887, p. 82.

The English crown was clearly a highly valued asset. Although he already had a dominant role within the regime, the kingship was something which Earl Harold thought worth some risk taking. The king controlled vast estates and retained a controlling say in the Church, so headed an exceptionally large and rich system of patronage. There was also the kudos of kingship itself and England's was perhaps the most significant among the several thrones along the Atlantic coastline. Harold II took charge of the wealthiest, most centralized and most effective fiscal, judicial and governmental system in Western Europe. He became the head of a nation-state which had some two million or more inhabitants, pretty well all of whom thought of themselves in some sense as English. He and his principal supporters could field armies the equal of any available to potential enemies. It was a state which had been strengthened by an embedded ideology and a close alliance between king and clergy, and was studded with walled towns which had been established with the specific purpose of deterring external aggressors. Furthermore, it had an enviable record of internal peace, and the habit of avoiding civil war by negotiation and compromise – a habit by now a full generation old and designed explicitly to avoid weakening the military potential of the English elite in case of opportunistic foreign intervention such as that which had occurred during Aethelred's reign.

That Harold was by birth half Danish and distantly related to the Danish royal family was of no consequence in this regard. He was considered quintessentially English in the 1060s, when he was the leader of a broad swathe of the Anglo–Danish political establishment then in power in England and emerging as the strongest internal candidate for the succession to the throne of the childless Edward the Confessor. He was in reality a capable politician and a military leader of considerable stature, if not quite the heroic and ultimately tragic figure that nineteenth-century enthusiasts for the gothic were later to invent. Yet we should perhaps be grateful for the interest that that generation rekindled in late Anglo-Saxon England and the Norman Conquest. Today 1066 remains the best-remembered as well as the most famously lampooned date in English history.

On the face of it, Harold's kingship stood a far better chance of survival than, for example, the new Capetan monarchy in Frankia which Hugh Capet established in 987 to near universal disinterest among his new subjects. Yet the Capetan monarchy endured and ultimately prospered, while Harold's kingship was smashed to pieces in battle within the year, leaving many of his supporters dead and his family dispossessed. The consequent death of Anglo-Saxon England was in many ways as strange a phenomenon as the demise of Liberal England during the interwar period. By the Christmas following Edward's death, a foreigner was king and the Norman regime was already in a position to start the process of wholesale replacement of the English elite – both lay and clerical – by immigrants. Within half a decade, that process had become unstoppable. The powerful English state which had driven off the Vikings in the ninth and tenth centuries had succumbed in the space of a few weeks to an unfancied outsider whose candidacy had no significant insular support before his march on London. William's success in having himself crowned king after such a brief campaign is unprecedented. Once he had achieved that coup, his enemies were at a considerable disadvantage – in part because the English had an innate respect for the crown – and could be destroyed piecemeal. The consequences were ultimately far greater than those of the Danish takeover of the English crown a generation earlier, if only because accommodation between the insular elite and the incoming king was far harder to achieve.

It is legitimate in many respects to treat the Battle of Hastings as a marker for the ending of Anglo-Saxon England and the beginning of a new, Anglo-Norman epoch. This is particularly the case as regards the nature of the source materials on which our histories are based, with a decline of written Old English after 1066, a growing body of Latin texts and the appearance of Norman French as an insular, written language for the first time. The chronicle writing which already characterized English approaches to history continued, but to it was added far more narrative-style writing of a thoroughly French kind, after the tradition of the Latin *Deeds of the Dukes of the Normans*, begun by Dudo of St Quentin, copies of which were later obtained and preserved by several of the English monasteries which were heavily colonized by Normans under King William. Twelfth-century copies of the Anglo-Saxon Chronicles would also be annotated in Latin, and in particular be brought up to date with brief notices of key moments in Norman history which pre-Conquest English authors had, unsurprisingly, omitted to mention. Different types of source materials require

Late Anglo-Saxon England was studded with walled towns, many of which had stone defences. The circuit around Wareham in Dorset is among the best preserved in England. Excavations earlier this century have revealed that it has a stone core.

different skills, so there has been an understandable tendency over much of the last century or so for historians to become either 'Anglo-Saxonists' or 'Medievalists' by training.

Yet the subdividing of history into great slabs of time split up by arbitrary events such as battles is now quite properly recognized as a dubious practice. Put simply, the division of one historical epoch from another is a construct of the historian whose privilege it is to look back on events and seek patterns within, and dislocations between, them, and impose his or her own perceptions on the past. The year 1066 is peculiarly susceptible to such patterning – one has only to have regard for the several quite dramatic changes which occurred over the next decade or so to release the juggernaut of historical interpretation down that road. The royal dynasty changed; a new, French-speaking nobility secured the bulk of England and its estates, both lay and clerical; castles were thrown up pretty much for the first time in England; English churches and monasteries were subjected to the most thorough process of building and rebuilding yet seen; the English adopted a radically different set of personal names; the English earldoms were reduced in size and a tenurial revolution occurred. Even if we hold back from the notion that William was responsible for the imposition of 'feudalism' on England, whatever that now means to twentieth-century historians, there is plentiful fuel for the supposition that the Battle of Hastings, in October 1066, was a cusp event of the sort that divides one epoch from another.

This was certainly the view of William's successors. For all the Conqueror's protests concerning the legitimacy of his candidacy, his descendants were counted kings 'from the conquest'. Of all the Old English personal names with royal connections which could have been utilized by them, only Edward ever resurfaced as the name of a king, although Edmund recurred within the royal family in the thirteenth century. William's youngest son, Henry I, married back into the Cerdicings, but no candidate for the English throne ever again claimed by right of descent of the West-Saxon dynasty, bypassing William himself.

This is, however, to take only a retrospective view of events. It must be emphasized that the vast majority of the English population alive in 1065 was still alive, and still active in ways which had altered little if at all, in 1067 or 1070. Indeed, many were still living when William commissioned the Domesday Inquest, at Christmas 1085, and some even outlived the Conqueror himself, who died at Rouen on 9 September 1087. Such men and women lived through a time of considerable change, certainly, but their own perceptions will have contained profound continuities, as did the organizational world of estate, parish, shire and diocese which they inhabited. The English government raised taxes by traditional means after 1066 – albeit in exceptional amounts – and issued instructions to shire-reeves in ways which would have been familiar a generation before. The fabric and practices of government continued, but under new management. A farmer who regularly sold his produce in the markets of, for example, Huntingdon during the early 1060s could well have been still doing the same during the latter part of the decade, and the number of burgesses in that small shire town in the last years of Edward's reign was – according to Domesday Book – still unchanged in 1086. Births, marriages and deaths continued unabated during a period which was characterized by a gradual but significant rise in population which straddled the 1060s, and which the Norman Conquest had power to effect only in very specific localities such as parts of the north and north-west Midlands where the harrying of 1069–70 may have taken a significant toll. But even that is now debated. In many senses, therefore, there was no death to account for, just profound change in the body politic.

What is more, the very terminology which we use is notoriously retrospective. Eleventh-century commentators, whether writing in Old English or Latin, did not use such tautologies as 'Anglo-Saxon England' – their country was England and they were English. It is only later generations wishing to define an epoch which ended at the Norman conquest that have coined the phrase and rendered it a standard term in current historical thought.

We should beware, therefore, glib divisions of history. The current trend is very properly to reintegrate the third quarter of the eleventh century into the broader history of which it is a part and to reassess and revise many of our assumptions concerning the reigns of Edward the Confessor, Harold and William. Scholars have turned their attention in recent years to the late Anglo-Saxon and Norman periods in combination, and stressed the continuities as much as the discontinuities. Their work has produced a spate of excellent monographs and a

St Leonard's Tower, probably begun by Gundulf, the first Norman Bishop of Rochester, provided a focus for his estate at West Malling in Kent. It displays many of the features characteristic of Norman keeps in England, with its considerable height and rectangularity, its shallow pilasters and its first-floor access.

valuable journal in the *Proceedings of the Battle Abbey Conferences*, published as *Anglo-Norman Studies* since 1982. An essential part of this process is attention to the views and expectations of political commentators who were as close as possible to being contemporaries to the events on which they passed comment, and this is perhaps the best antidote to the old tendency of historians to stand back from events and paint broad-brush word sketches of the past.

Yet all that said, 1066 was unique in English history as regards the dynastic revolution that occurred, and its exceptional nature deservedly attracts attention again and again. What followed was, in many respects, profoundly different to what came before. This volume arises out of my own interest in contextualizing the events of that traumatic year, and more particularly the struggle that then ensued concerning the kingship of the English. It does not attempt to handle a very broad range of histories but addresses issues of high politics affecting the royal succession and seeks to explore how kingmaking – and occasionally unmaking – occurred over a period of approximately the last century of Anglo-Saxon England. In so doing, this may appear to many to be a rather traditional work of history: the study of the descent of the crown and the king-centric politics surrounding the succession was a major plank within the writing of medieval history in the late nineteenth and early twentieth centuries and was covered by excellent monographs even in the early postwar era. These include, for example, Freeman's *The History of the Norman Conquest of England*, published

This detail of one of the crosses at Sandbach in Cheshire, carved in about AD 800, illustrates the antiquity of many Christian monuments still preserved and even revered by the English in the eleventh century. In comparison, Christian iconography had to be all but completely reintroduced to Normandy in the tenth and early eleventh centuries.

between 1867 and 1879, Douglas's *William the Conqueror* (1964) and Sir Frank Barlow's *Edward the Confessor* (1970), all of which treat this issue in some detail. Today, many scholars have turned away from the study of kings to the fertile territories of intellectual, social, gender, economic, regional, estate, ritual, settlement, cultural and art histories, to take just a handful, on the assumption perhaps that there is little further to be said on the subject of royalty and the crown. Yet the subject retains an abiding interest, in part at least because kingship was the fundamental catalyst of so many other aspects of history. In addition, a knowledge of the high politics of the period is a *sine qua non* of understanding alternative histories and provides an essential starting point for anyone seeking to pursue an interest in the period, however unfashionable it may appear to professional historians.

To take just one example, Frenchmen of one sort or another were not so very scarce in the England of King Edward, but their integration into English society seems to have been well underway by 1066 – Edward's Norman and French friends were certainly not in any sense then a fifth column operating in William's interest and they were busily becoming English at least until October of that year. It was the violent seizure of royal patronage in England by a Norman candidate with massed Norman and French backing and with vast debts to pay out of the wealth of England which was the fundamental stimulus to profound shifts in ethnic, cultural, social,

*Despite being heavily restored in 1848,
St Andrew's Church, Greensted, Essex is
the only substantial survivor in England
of an important style of pre-Conquest
church construction, with walls of tight-set
vertical posts connected by mortices.
Parallels exist with the stave churches of
Scandinavia.*

economic and even gender histories in the late eleventh century. The arrival of a
Norman king does then matter, whichever type of history is under investigation, and
it was William's seizure of the English throne and the use to which he then put royal
patronage that precipitated the death of Anglo-Saxon England.

The succession to the throne of England was, in addition, the most important
single political issue among the English in 1065–6. It was a matter of importance
too at the courts of Norway, Denmark, Normandy and France, to name but the
most obvious, and arguably had already been so for several years. Indeed, the
future descent of the crown was always something which the landholding classes
had to bear in mind when formulating and pursuing their own political and social
ambitions – their amities, alliances and feuds, their interactions with kings, nobles
and provincial hierarchies, their search for and tenure of office – throughout the
late Anglo-Saxon and early Norman periods. A particular set of unlikely
circumstances merely made the matter of the succession more problematic than
usual in 1066, primarily because of the poverty of legitimate and well-placed
claimants from within the time-honoured lineage of Cerdic and the exceptional
opportunities for personal aggrandizement which this offered to several
prominent men both inside and outside England.

This volume therefore charts the relationship between king-making – and
occasional unmaking – and political power from about 966 up to the end of 1066

By the late Anglo-Saxon period, numerous churches were being reconstructed in stone. Well-built towers often survive from this period, even in places where the remaining fabric has been much altered. An example is All Saints' Church, Hough-on-the-Hill, Lincolnshire, where the west tower has an unusual three-quarter-round western stair turret attached.

in four chapters which are chronologically arranged. Attention must first of all focus on the English crown in the late tenth century, and particularly on the problematic descent of Edgar's kingship to Aethelred. There is then an examination of Aethelred's policies concerning the succession and their fatal interaction with the factional politics and Danish attacks of his reign. The poverty of the royal house in the mid–eleventh century was largely a product of its collapse and dispersal in the period 1010–20. The succession remains the focus of chapters on the descent of the Anglo-Danish crown and on Edward's kingship. Lastly, following a detailed discussion of 1066, is a very brief end-piece, which attempts to tie up various loose ends and particularly to explain what eventually happened to the senior figures who played important roles in the events following Edward's death and yet survived them. There follow some recommendations concerning further reading but these do not constitute a full bibliography, examples of which are widely available in the literature to which reference is made.

This entire work is aimed not at the professional historian but at a much wider market and a more general readership at the level of a first-year undergraduate. It is offered to a readership with an interest in the fundamental question, why did Anglo-Saxon England end? The answers it offers are political ones since the question is itself fundamentally about politics.

ONE

The Making and Unmaking of Aethelred the 'Unraed'

THE LEGACY OF KING EDGAR

If there were any centenarians alive in England in 1066 then they could, perhaps, have recalled the events of 975. Indeed, any such had been born during an era of English history to which their own and then their grandchildren's generations were prone to look back on as a veritable 'Golden Age'. The next such period was deemed to have been in the reign of Edward the Confessor, at least in the opinion of nostalgic English writers after the Conquest and of the anonymous author of Edward's *Life*, written shortly after his death.

In the spring of 975 Alfred's great-grandson, King Edgar, was on the English throne. He was in his prime, aged around thirty-one or thirty-two, and had been undisputed ruler of all England since the death of his brother Eadwig, King of the West Saxons, in 959. Indeed, Edgar was the first such to be accepted universally without open resistance and he presided over what looked to be one of the most powerful states in western Europe. His magnificent coronation (or perhaps recoronation) in 973 and the subsequent demonstration of the power of his fleet in the Irish Sea as far north as Chester emphasized his quasi-imperial position as the dominant ruler within the British Isles.

Looking back on his death with all the benefits of hindsight, the antecessor of the Peterborough and Worcester manuscripts of the Anglo-Saxon Chronicle recorded the opinion that: 'There was no fleet so proud, nor raiding-army so strong, that fetched carrion among the English race, while the noble king governed the royal seat.'

Perhaps none tried but a powerful contrast would later be drawn between Edgar's reign and that of his youngest son and eventual successor – Aethelred 'the Unready' – which was to be beset by raids. So too did the chroniclers particularly remark the appearance of a comet at harvest time following Edgar's death, and the assumption would seem to be that this, like Halley's Comet in late

King Edgar carried out a far-reaching reorganization of the English coinage in about 973, establishing central control of dies and licensing coiners at about sixty different centres to produce a voluminous but standardized coinage. This silver penny minted by a coiner called Aethelsige at Shrewsbury carries the legend EADGAR REX ANGLO (rum) – Edgar king of the English. Such legends advertised the universality of Edgar's rule.

April 1066, was a portent of disasters to come. Such retrospective observations had, of course, the comfort of being already fulfilled by events when written, but there is an instructive parallel as regards the credulity of contemporaries when provided with the opportunity to interpret portents.

In contrast with his forebears over the previous four generations, Edgar is never known to have led his armies or fleet into battle. The reason is simple: his reign coincided with a total absence from England of raiding fleets from the Viking world. Potential enemies were perhaps sufficiently impressed by the defences of the war-hardened English state, and its renowned and oft-victorious kings and ealdormen, to seek softer targets from which to secure booty. In any case, the Vikings had their own affairs to mind and wars in Scandinavia and Germany were absorbing much of their energies. Edgar was 'the Peaceable' therefore less by choice than in the absence of enemies, since without external Viking involvement there was certainly no king within the British Isles who was eager to come to blows with his forces.

A younger son of King Edmund, Edgar had achieved power only by posing as the candidate of several powerful figures who were less than satisfied with the policies of his brother as king and he reigned first exclusively in Mercia. Following Eadwig's death he reversed his brother's patronage in various respects but also sought to heal the wounds that competition for the crown had opened. Although he did promote Dunstan to Canterbury as Archbishop, Edgar was probably no more than a luke-warm enthusiast for his ideas concerning monastic reform until his elevation of Abbot Aethelwold of Abingdon to the rich and influential see of Winchester. It was primarily the alliance and friendship between Edgar and his new bishop which pushed forward the aims of sections at least of the reform party within the English church, for which the king subsequently received considerable credit.

Edgar's reign certainly coincided with the reform, refoundation, or foundation from scratch, of numerous communities of regular monks and nuns. In many instances these overturned existing communities of canons and excluded the

King Edgar with the saints Dunstan and Aethelwold, from an eleventh-century copy of the Regularis Concordia, *the monastic manual drawn up in Edgar's reign and associated with Bishop Aethelwold. Two generations later, Edgar's rule was recalled by the English as a golden age and successive regimes borrowed from it to reinforce their own legitimacy.*

established interests of sections of the regional community, with some potential to create resentment. Yet many leading noble families joined in the rush towards monastic patronage and several gave substantial resources to their foundations, even while on occasion opposing the similar activities of their rivals. Men clearly anticipated spiritual rewards in the hereafter but they also sought, and often found, favourable political and social outcomes in the here and now. Monastic reform should not, therefore, be viewed as something which was divorced from other political considerations at the time. Rather, it was integral to wider processes and was just one theatre for the interplay of the conflicting interests of different sections of the elite.

Beneath the king, Athelstan Half-king's family were perhaps the best-known patrons of the reformed church but they were less influential in government in the 970s than in recent decades. During the reigns of Kings Edmund (939–46) and Eadred (946–55), Athelstan and his two brothers had ruled half England as ealdormen and were by far the most influential family at court, allied to the young Dunstan and deeply involved in the seminal reformation of Glastonbury to become England's first Benedictine monastery for many generations. However, the accession of the young Eadwig – Edmund's elder son – in November 955 brought to the throne a king committed to making his own appointments and challenging those whose influence had grown great during the reign of his sickly uncle. Eadwig has received a poor press from monastic authors writing after his eclipse by his brother. His exile of Ealdorman Athelstan's close associate, Dunstan, was singled out for hostile comment and the young king portrayed as the very mirror of both immorality and incompetence, but this vision is at the very least overdone. His purpose was arguably in part to reduce the power of Athelstan's faction to manageable proportions and balance it with his own friends. He set about driving back the limits of his ealdordom by establishing new and unrelated figures in power within Mercia. Athelstan himself responded by retiring to Glastonbury and he became a monk there in 956. He may have been forced into retirement but he had presumably already negotiated the succession to his offices, since his son Aethelwold obtained the ealdordom of East Anglia and a close associate, Byrhtnoth, took over Essex. This looks, therefore, like an honourable settlement of the differences between king and ealdorman which conserved the core offices of Athelstan's family while at the same time reducing their wider influence and gave the king increased control over royal patronage.

The principal new appointment by Eadwig was Ealdorman Aelfhere of south-west Mercia. Aelfhere was the son of Ealhhelm, one of several ealdormen within Mercia under Eadwig's father, King Edmund, but of ultimately West-Saxon origin and a distant relative of the royal line. Aelfhere's (probably older) brother, the wealthy and well-connected Aelfheah, was also prominent at Eadwig's court and perhaps served as his seneschal. Aelfhere's appointment was probably intended by Eadwig as a counterbalance to the influence of the house of Athelstan Half-king in central England and he certainly had the necessary personal status and family connections.

Nonetheless, this compromise – supposing, that is, that such was agreed by king and ealdorman – and the quiet departure of Athelstan himself, failed to reconcile Athelstan's following to Eadwig's kingship. Rather than accept their loss of influence across half of the Midlands they and the Mercians withdrew allegiance from King Eadwig. Edmund's younger son, Edgar, had been fostered by Athelstan's wife so was foster-brother to Aethelwold, and it was surely he and his associates – including Bishop Oswald at Worcester – who encouraged the Mercians to break away from Eadwig in 957 and recognize Edgar as king in his place. The entire faction can reasonably have expected that their interests would be better served by a king of their own choosing and one who had such powerful, pre-existing ties to their own leaders. They were probably correct in this calculation, for when Edgar succeeded to Wessex after the premature but apparently natural death of his brother in 959, all Athelstan Half-king's surviving sons were prominent members of his court.

Their rival, the newly appointed Ealdorman Aelfhere, survived this crisis, having preserved his own interests by also declaring for Edgar in 957 when all Mercia slipped out of Eadwig's control, and Aethelwold's death in 962 significantly weakened the Half-king's family. Athough he was succeeded by his youngest brother Aethelwine in East Anglia, his death denied the family the opportunity to regain the West-Saxon ealdordom which one of Athelstan's brothers had previously held and this went instead to Aelfhere's brother Aelfheah.

During the 960s, therefore, these two families were evenly balanced, each having effective control of two ealdordoms. Their competition for power centred on central and south-eastern Mercia, that is territory which had historically been Mercian but which had been attached for a generation to the East-Anglian ealdordom. Aethelwine cannot be blamed if he hankered for the return of patronage and lordships which had been his father's, nor Aelfhere if he defended his tenure of parts of this territory with vigour. By the late 950s Aelfhere was the premier ealdorman – merely on the basis of primacy of appointment – and his brother was often the second lay nobleman named in witness lists. The latter's death in about 971–2 seems not to have much altered the balance, since no new appointment was made to Wessex. Rather, Edgar is thought to have moved towards a four-fold division of England under his own ultimate authority, with superior ealdordoms in overall control of Mercia and East Anglia, and an earl in Northumbria, all subject to his own kingship centred in Wessex. Each of these great lords then delegated power and responsibilities to subordinate ealdormen, in an orderly hierarchy organized regionally but focused on the person of the king.

In some senses Edgar's recognition of such paramount regional rulers represents the resurrection of what look suspiciously like the principal kingdoms of pre-Viking England. They were, of course, to be under the overall rule of the West-Saxon kings and there is no hint that any regional ruler was to be acknowledged as a king. Nor were they in theory hereditary posts, although the retention of the East-Anglian ealdordom by Athelstan's family under Eadwig and Edgar certainly underlines a tendency throughout the late Anglo-Saxon period for kings to allow what amounts to succession to such posts to favoured, or very powerful, families.

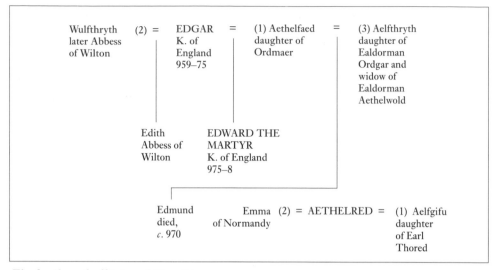

The family and offspring of King Edgar.

If this is fair comment then it marks a significant break with the efforts of Alfred, his son and grandsons to integrate Mercia, particularly, into a single, enlarged, English state, ordered in ealdordoms, shires and dioceses, and suggests that Edgar's policies had more in common with those of contemporary Frankia – where substantial counties were becoming ever more independent of the crown – than had his predecessors. This was, therefore, a period which witnessed some resurrection of regional identity *vis-à-vis* the overriding kingship of the English, and this process certainly played an important role in the organization of power over the next century or so and influenced the course of the Viking wars which beset Edgar's son Aethelred.

Like several of his ancestors, Edgar's marital affairs were sufficiently unconventional to be condemned by later clerical commentators. His first wife was Aethelflaed Eneda, 'the white duck', daughter of a Hertfordshire landowner called Ordmaer, and this perhaps ties in with his fosterage as a child by the wife of Athelstan Half-king, with whose family Ordmaer was connected. This marriage predates Edgar's acquisition of the English throne and his eldest son, Edward, was its product. Thereafter Edgar married Wulfthryth, the daughter of an important West-Saxon nobleman with whom he apparently allied himself as part of a strategy of reconciliation with the aristocracy of his new kingship soon after his brother's death. This marriage produced a daughter, later St Edith, but Wulfthryth had become Abbess of Wilton by about 965. While Wulfthryth was still alive, however, Edgar remarried in 964–5 Aelfthryth, the daughter of Ordgar, a Devonshire landowner, but also the widow of Ealdorman Aethelwold, so daughter-in-law of Athelstan 'Half-king'. Aelfthryth bore him Edmund, who died in 970, and Aethelred.

By 975, therefore, Edgar had, by three different mothers, sired three living offspring, two of whom were male but none of whom were yet adult. Edward's date of birth is unknown, but he was then in his mid-teens and obviously the eldest. It seems, however, to have been Edgar's intention to have passed his inheritance not to his eldest son but to his heirs by Queen Aelfthryth, since her name and that of her first born preceded that of Prince Edward on a grant of privileges to New Minster at Winchester, drawn up by the queen's ally, Bishop Aethelwold. By 975, Edmund's claim had been transposed to the aetheling Aethelred, who was barely nine years old in this year. Edward's legitimacy as a potential king was in doubt, due perhaps to some distant blood relationship between Edgar and Queen Aethelflaed or the fact that she, unlike Aelfthryth, is not known to have been crowned as queen. Whatever the facts of the matter, Edward was probably already falling foul of the ambitions of his step-mother to secure the throne for her own son, and she was clearly a redoubtable figure and had wide connections among the elite, both lay and clerical, and particularly among the court.

At this stage, tensions over the succession and between rival sections of the regional nobility were more implicit than otherwise, since the king was himself still a young man in overall control of his own regime and the patronage it wielded, without obvious rival and likely to rule for many years to come. The climate of political solidarity proved illusory, however, when King Edgar died on 8 July 975 of unknown causes, and his death removed the controlling hand of effective and unchallengeable kingship from the political arena.

EDWARD THE MARTYR

With the kingship in sudden crisis and without an adult claimant to the throne, the various, pre-existing political tensions between the ealdormen of Mercia and East Anglia naturally – almost predictably – developed into a struggle to control the succession. These divisions in turn encouraged outsiders to once again consider England an attractive target for raids, although there is no guarantee that they would have thought much differently even had Edgar survived for another decade or so. The disasters which the comet of late summer 975 had seemed to augur began the very next year with a great famine, but worse was to follow at the end of the decade, when the Vikings returned to England once more.

There was nothing unusual about a disputed succession to the English throne. Such was a periodic hazard of politics which contained both dangers and opportunities, and it was one that could be anticipated and prepared for by interested parties. Alfred's inheritance had been contested in 899 and his son had to fight for his crown. Edward the Elder's inheritance was perhaps disputed between the sons of his own several marriages in 925, and certainly Eadred's was to be in 955. The timing of Edgar's death may well have surprised many of the political classes but they will not have been entirely unprepared for the dangers it posed and the opportunities it offered.

It was not Aethelred who immediately succeeded his father but the elder aetheling, Edward, around whom Archbishop Dunstan, Ealdormen Aethelwine of

Silver penny of King Edward the Martyr, minted at Lincoln. Edward's coinage continued the general design of his father's, advertising his legitimacy as heir to the throne.

East Anglia and Byrhtnoth of Essex, Bishop Oswald of Worcester and others rallied. Edward's mother had come from a family with whom Aethelwine was connected, but Aethelred's mother had been his own sister-in-law, and had produced the family at least one son. On that basis, Aethelwine's faction might have chosen to support either of Edgar's sons. The decisive factor influencing their choice for the succession is likely to have been the close association already existing between Queen Aelfthryth, Bishop Aethelwold of Winchester and Ealdorman Aelfhere. If Aelfhere backed Aethelred, both Archbishop Oswald – who was also Bishop of Worcester – and his close friend and political ally Aethelwine would automatically have been prejudiced against Aethelred. Bishop Aethelwold's aggrandizement in favour of such Fenland houses as Peterborough and Thorney also had considerable potential to antagonize Aethelwine, as well as both archbishops, neither of whom had enjoyed similar levels of support from Edgar. To Edward's advantage was also his seniority over Aethelred and the shorter length of time which would elapse before he became an effective, adult king – and his earliest and most committed supporters can have expected to gain considerable influence at their rivals' expense from their support.

Furthermore, Archbishop Dunstan is reported to have censured Edgar's association with Aelfthryth as adulterous – presumably on account of the continuing survival of Wulfthryth – and the consequent bad blood between him and the dowager queen may well have determined the attitude of the senior archbishop in this crisis. The support of the two archbishops and a significant faction containing two senior ealdormen was sufficient to obtain Edward the throne, but he was necessarily the candidate of only one clique – a powerful one – within the political elite.

Edward's reign displays all the symptoms of a disputed succession and a royal minority, with a vicious struggle for power breaking out between his supporters and their opponents. Monastic writers – and particularly Oswald's hagiographer at Ramsey – lamented the suppression of monasteries and eviction of their inmates by the laity, and particularly accused Ealdorman Aelfhere of the

Mercians. Aelfhere has no contemporary apologists but the simple depiction of him as an enemy of monasticism and Ealdorman Aethelwine as its protector is a thoroughly misleading representation of events. Both were active monastic patrons and both were also remembered by different houses as their despoilers. Aethelwine took the opportunity offered by the succession crisis to recover lands from Ely, despite his acclamation as the saviour of the monastic movement by Oswald's monks at Ramsey. Their enemy, Aelfhere, had shown himself in the past a generous patron of Glastonbury, which was the earliest and in many respects the most prestigious of the English houses to be reformed by Dunstan, and he was well enough regarded to eventually be buried there.

What is particularly noticeable is Aelfhere's failure to endow any of Oswald's foundations, and this arguably reflects the ealdorman's hostility towards Oswald's houses in western Mercia, both in terms of their estates and their new-found regalities. He had himself probably been required to disgorge the estates of Evesham when that house was reformed. The creation of what amounted to a great clerical fiefdom at Worcester through the separation of the triple hundred of Oswaldslow from the ealdormanry was necessarily at the expense of Aelfhere's own influence within the core of the old Mercian state, centred as that had eventually come to be on Gloucestershire and Worcestershire. Although he was a witness to the royal charters and diplomas conserved at Worcester, Aelfhere cannot have welcomed the endowment of his principal rival's favourite clerk in his own backyard. Oswald thereafter built up an estate administration and group of tenants centred upon himself and at odds with the rest of the local elite. Many local families within Aelfhere's ambit arguably felt aggrieved at Oswald's reformation of local minsters such as Pershore, Westbury and Winchcombe which had hitherto lain under their own influence. The ealdorman was presumably under some pressure to respond to their needs. His resentments had been restrained while Edgar still lived but the succession crisis offered him the opportunity to overturn a series of policies which were opposed to his own interests, in the heart of his territory and generally unpopular among his followers.

Aelfhere's dispute was not with the church *per se*, therefore, but with Bishop Oswald and his allies, who had attached themselves to the young King Edward. Oswald's association with Ealdorman Aethelwine of the East Angles was particularly close – the two had co-operated in the foundation of Ramsey Abbey, near to Aethelwine's principal seat at Upwood, as recently as 971. In that same year Oswald was himself promoted to the archdiocese of York, which he thenceforth held in plurality with Worcester, and his administrative energies are evidenced there as well, in reclamation of lands from the laity for the church and other actions unlikely to have endeared him to sections of the local elite.

There broke out in 975, therefore, a struggle for power within the national and provincial elite. This was in part a regional struggle between Ealdorman Aelfhere and Archbishop Oswald, with the ealdorman taking the opportunity to regain influence, property and patronage lost during Edgar's reign in consequence of royal backing for the bishop's activities. It was in part a far wider struggle for power between Aelfhere – the premier ealdorman of Edgar's reign – and the

Glastonbury was the earliest English monastery to be reformed (in Edmund's reign) and attracted the patronage of numerous members of the elite. Largely as a result of its consequent wealth, little now remains above ground of the comparatively small buildings of this period, but archaeological excavation this century has confirmed the general layout and exposed the foundations of successive Anglo-Saxon churches.

political heirs of Athelstan Half-king, who recalled the greater influence of their own connection in the recent past. It was also a contest between Queen Aelfthryth – supported perhaps by Edgar's favourite cleric, Bishop Aethelwold – and Archbishop Dunstan – backed to some degree by Oswald. Such tensions enabled many lesser men to pursue their own grievances: 'Widows were robbed', the chroniclers protested, as royal oversight of judicial processs fell into temporary abeyance.

At the same time, Edgar's ealdorman of Northumbria since 963, one Oslac, was banished, presumably ousted by enemies within his ealdordom. Northumbria was perennially the most difficult province to govern, owing to its Scandinavian complexion and the lack of royal assets there, and it should not surprise us if the men of York took the opportunity offered by a temporary hiatus of royal authority to oust an ealdorman who had been foisted upon them by a southern king from (apparently) the east Midlands. West-Saxon authority over the north was only two decades old at this date, and many of the Northumbrians may even have still entertained separatist ambitions. Oslac was presumably unpopular, in addition, as the power behind their aggressively reformist new archbishop and he was not as well protected as the latter by the authority implicit in his office. Oslac's roots suggest that he was also perhaps an associate of Aethelwine, in which case his exclusion was a success for the enemies of his connection and Edward's court.

There emerges at this point some potential for an alliance of sorts between the most powerful group within Northumbria – that is, the Anglo-Scandinavian community centred in Yorkshire – and the leaders of western, English Mercia. This is worth noting not because it produced any coherent policy – rather, their respective aims may have been very different – but because such combinations were a recurring factor in the politics of late Anglo-Saxon and early Norman England and would later exercise considerable but sporadic influence on events at the centre. The English political community exhibited a tendency to break along the fault line of the ancient West Saxon–Mercian frontier, with East Anglia sometimes attached to the former and sometimes to the latter. Edgar's early backers had exploited this fact and such was to be the case again during the succession crisis of 1035, when Cnut died, and then again in 1065 and again in the northern rebellions against William in the late 1060s.

The early running in this instance was, however, made by Aethelwine's party. The co-operation of the two archbishops with this group ensured that they were able to place their own candidate on the throne and so obtain the crucial advantage of speaking for the king. It is not recorded where or when Edward was consecrated, but it seems very likely that his backers would have hurried this ceremony through so as to reinforce his position and he certainly thereafter acted as if he had been crowned.

Edward made several new appointments to ealdordoms early in his reign, appointing Aethelweard to western Wessex, Aethelmaer to central Wessex and Edwin to Sussex – and presumably Kent and Surrey – apparently with the intention of strengthening his position by building up a group of noblemen who depended heavily upon his own kingship. Eadwig had done much the same in 956 and there are some connections between the two. Edwin was probably a West

Saxon or southern Mercian, since he was eventually buried at Abingdon, but he is otherwise obscure. Aethelmaer left lands within his ealdordom when he died but also in Rutland, which may imply that he was a member of Aethelwine's eastern Mercian affinity. Aethelweard was a descendant of King Alfred's elder brother, Aethelred I, so distantly related to the royal family, and was also close kin to King Eadwig's widow. That same family had provided Edward the Elder with his second wife in Aelfflaed, his own second cousin, soon after his succession and all three instances look like attempts to stabilize tenure of a disputed crown by securing the support of a well-connected and wealthy West-Saxon family of distinguished lineage.

Edward's dispositions overturned Edgar's comparatively hands-on approach to Wessex, but it also threatened any ambitions which Ealdorman Aelfhere may have entertained to regain control of his brother's West-Saxon ealdordom. It additionally promoted an associate of both Queen Aelfthryth and Bishop Aethelwold, in the person of Aethelweard. This policy was perhaps intended to be conciliatory, but was somewhat dangerous, although his high birth and kinship with Edward himself presumably warranted his advancement.

Both sides were presumably very conscious of the precedents offered by the succession crisis of 956–9, and Edward even seems to have consciously moulded himself on Eadwig, the elder of Edmund's two sons. Then the stresses underlying royal minority had found ultimate expression in recognition of two different heirs to the throne in Wessex and Mercia respectively, and the tension between them had been resolved only by the premature death of the elder.

Aelfhere's appointment as an ealdorman had been under Eadwig's patronage, of course, and his struggle for power in 975–8 with Ealdorman Aethelwine and St Oswald stems from these earlier conflicts, but the separatist solution adopted by Eadwig's opponents in 957 was less accessible in the 970s, owing to the commitment of the leading Mercian and Northumbrian cleric – Oswald – to Edward. Ealdorman Aelfhere now apparently found himself in some difficulty. He was not short of associates and sympathizers and he had an alternative candidate to Edward, but there was no obvious means by which he could both safeguard his own position and promote the interests of the young Aethelred against an alliance of Edward, the archbishops and a substantial noble faction with a controlling influence in eastern Mercia and East Anglia. Once Edward should emerge as an adult king – and that was imminent by 978 – he could presumably be expected to throw his full weight behind Oswald and Aethelwine, to the detriment of Aelfhere's interests. Aelfhere's party, therefore, had a vested interest in pre-empting his emergence to effective power. The realities of contemporary power politics necessitated that the issue be decided by a struggle for the throne itself, in circumstances which have some parallels with the better known dynastic contests of the fifteenth century.

In a sense, events played into the hands of Edward's opponents. The Peterborough version of the Anglo-Saxon Chronicle refers to four events in succession during these years, which culminated in regicide:

The 'Gap' at Corfe, Dorset where Edward was killed was probably the narrow valley between Nine Barrow Down and the Purbeck Hills, immediately behind Corfe Castle.

1   Aelfhere's attack (in 976) on the monasteries;
2   Ealdorman Oslac's expulsion from England (also in 976), which removed a long-serving and very senior figure from the royal council and perhaps freed the Northumbrians to align themselves against the court;
3   The disaster at Calne in 978, where the royal council met in a first storey room, the floor of which collapsed beneath them causing numerous injuries and deaths;
4   The murder of King Edward at Corfe, on the evening of 18 March 978.

If the chronicler was correct in his ordering of these events, then the court party was seriously weakened in the spring of 978 by its failure to sustain its own clerical allies, enforced departures and a clutch of accidental injuries and deaths among its inner core. The opportunity was there for a coup against the young king to place Prince Aethelred on his father's throne, and many stood to gain thereby. Not only was he much younger than his brother – offering the prospect of weak and factional royal government for considerably longer – but Aethelred's debt to those who had cleared his way to the throne might have been expected to give them continuing influence even after his majority.

It is not certain who was responsible for Edward's murder. Bishop Aethelwold is most unlikely to have condoned violence against the king, despite his apparent preference for Aethelred over Edward, but the dowager Queen Aelfthryth had a vested interest in Aethelred's succession and either she or her own close kin may have been involved in her stepson's murder, which one contemporary certainly blamed on her 'nobles and chief men' and which occurred while the king was her guest. It seems very probable, therefore, that Aelfthryth played a role not dissimilar to that which Shakespeare wrote into his character of Lady Macbeth, as opposed to the eleventh-century historical figure on whom she was based. If she was responsible, this would not be the only time that a dowager queen would intervene in high politics during the late Anglo-Saxon period. Indeed, Aethelflaed, the 'Lady of the Mercians' and Queen Eadgifu had already provided well-known precedents by this time. Yet no one individual was ever prosecuted for the act of regicide, the culprits presumably sheltering behind the moral responsibility of the queen herself, whose arraignment thereafter would have been too embarrassing to be seriously contemplated by her son. Aelfhere was suspiciously prominent over the next few years, but his removal of Edward's remains from Wareham – where they had been deposited unceremoniously in 978 – to Shaftesbury and more honourable burial in 979 may signal a desire to distance himself from more guilty associates. On balance, he seems unlikely to have actually done the deed, although he may well have been party to the plot and certainly profited by it.

Whereas a succession crisis was unexceptional, regicide was not a normal part of political behaviour in tenth-century England. The only comparable incident in recent years was King Edmund's murder in a brawl in 956, but this seems to have been entirely unpremeditated and devoid of political purpose. Edward's death was very different and was known so to be at the time, as his rapid transition to the status of a popular saint and martyr demonstrates.

AETHELRED: THE FOUNDATION OF KINGSHIP

It was in this inauspicious manner that Aethelred came to the English throne, being crowned in haste within the same year as his brother's murder at Kingston-on-Thames – the site where his uncle and Aelfhere's earlier patron, King Eadwig, had been crowned in 956. King Eadred before him had likewise been consecrated there in 946, following the untimely murder of his brother and Aethelred's grandfather, King Edmund. The ceremony of Aethelred's consecration as king was, therefore, charged with the recent history of his dynasty and redolent with precedents for those attending. Those precedents did not, however, give grounds for believing that the collapse of the English state and the rule thereover of Cerdic's line were likely to occur during the reign which was just opening.

Aethelred became king aged about twelve, so his reign opened with a comparatively long minority. The dowager queen seems to have been a power at

Following his assassination, Edward the Martyr was hastily buried at nearby St Martin's Church, Wareham, before being reinterred at Shaftesbury. St Martin's retains many pre-Conquest features despite the addition of a north aisle and much alteration to the south doorway.

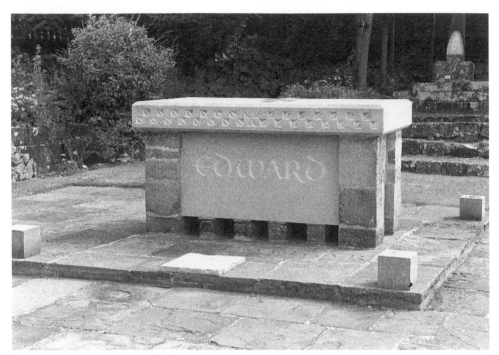

The nunnery at Shaftesbury was founded to provide a fitting chantry for the corporal remains of Edward the Martyr, who was reinterred there in 980. The altar is dedicated to him and what may have been some of his bones were excavated during work on the site, and will be deposited in a small martyrium here once investigations have been completed.

court and was a frequent witness to his early diplomas, but the political rivalries which had surfaced during his brother's reign were not in any sense resolved by the regicide which had occurred. Aelfhere clearly benefited from Aethelred's succession and was arguably Queen Aelfthryth's principal ally among the aristocracy. Bishop Aethelwold of Winchester was her main clerical associate in the early years. Thereafter, Aelfhere's death in 983 and that of the bishop on Lammas Day (1 August) 984 heralded a period when the queen seems to have been generally absent from court.

Aelfhere's Mercian ealdormanry passed initially to his close associate and brother-in-law Aelfric, a wealthy aristocrat with lands in the south-east Midlands who was patron of the wealthy Abbey of Peterborough and so a serious competitor to the regional influence of Athelstan Half-king's family, but he was exiled only two years later. The reasons are unknown, but one might suspect a successful coup by Aelfhere's enemies against his political heir. Ealdorman Aethelwine certainly seems to have then regained the influence at court which Edward's murder had lost him in 978 and there is not known to have been an ealdorman commissioned to govern the Mercians thereafter until the

Silver coin of King Aethelred II, minted at Canterbury. Following Aethelred's consecration in 979, the reverse side of the English coinage was remodelled to feature the Hand of Providence protruding from a heavenly cloud, flanked by alpha and omega. This change perhaps reflects the anxiety of the regime to deflect responsibility for Edward's assassination and Aethelred's consequent accession to God.

appointment of the infamous Eadric Streona in 1007. From that point the queen seems to have had effective custody of the young king's children, but she seems to have lost her wider influence within the regime, although she did attend court at least from time to time. The queen's prominence as a patroness of monastic reformers and her friendship with Bishop Aethelwold once again undermines the black and white depiction of Edward's reign and his opponents' actions by some monastic authors.

Whatever should be made of all this, Aethelred seems to have emerged from the tutelage of his mother, the Bishop of Winchester and Ealdorman Aelfhere in about 984, aged about eighteen years old. Aethelred must be absolved of personal responsibility for the context of his own accession, but several features of it continued to plague his administration. It was the moral and legal responsibility of an Englishman to pursue the culprit of any crime committed against a member of his own kin. It was, therefore, Aethelred's duty to avenge his half-brother's death. He did not, however, even once he had come to maturity, and this fact is in itself a powerful indication that his own mother was responsible. In that case, Aethelred could not avenge his half-brother without taking action against his own close kin. The moral and behavioural dilemma which this situation posed was inescapable and it had considerable potential to undermine the legitimacy of his kingship, should that run into difficulty. The Peterborough manuscript of the Anglo-Saxon Chronicle was careful not to name the queen in this context – owing in part perhaps to her prominent role during the house's foundation in 963, but its author was later in no doubt as to the moral repercussions of the crime of regicide:

No worse deed for the English race was done than this was, since they first sought out the land of Britain. Men murdered him, but God exalted him. In life he was an earthly king; after death he is now a heavenly saint. His earthly relatives would not avenge him, but his Heavenly Father has much avenged him.

This passage was obviously written after the Viking assault of Aethelred's reign, and it was quite natural that those who had experienced the new Scandinavian invasions should look back to the events with which the reign began and interpret them as the cause of God's apparent wrath against his people. The logic was inescapable.

Similar attitudes can be found elsewhere in Anglo-Saxon literature, from Bede and Alcuin onwards, and they came naturally to a community whose intellectuals saw history in terms of the working through of Divine Providence, with man's responsibility for his own destiny confined to moral issues alone. Alfred and his heirs had worked hard to convince their people that God supported their efforts against the Vikings and this had been a significant factor in their eventual success. In his 'Sermon of the Wolf to the English', Archbishop Wulfstan revived the memory of Edward's murder during the final traumas of Aethelred's reign, in 1014. If the Lord was now taking vengeance for Edward's death on the entire English people, then the Danish assault of Aethelred's reign was not merely a military issue but a moral and pastoral one in addition. The notion that the Vikings were God's agents, carrying out His punishment of a sinful people may have damaged English morale and undermined efforts to oppose them, although it is, of course, primarily retrospective comment on which we rely. The *Life of King Edward*, for example, opened with characterization of the Danes as 'God's rod of justice' by which he 'swept away . . . what had displeased Him among the people, and the kingdom'. It must be remembered in this context that the Chronicle account of Aethelred's reign post-dates his death, by which point Cnute's regime had a considerable interest in incriminating his predecessor with the crime of regicide and portraying his own activities as directed by the Lord.

It is noticeable that this interpretation of events finds little support prior to 1014 and it must be doubted whether or not Aethelred himself felt any responsibility for his brother's murder. He made a grant to the nunnery at Shaftesbury – where his brother's body was reinterred in 979 after initial burial at Wareham – in 984, and was probably involved in the translation of his remains from the churchyard into the church in 1001. He certainly shortly after granted the nuns jurisdiction over Bradford-on-Avon (Wiltshire) as a refuge for themselves and their relics in the event of Viking attack. In about 1008, the establishment of Edward's festival on 18 March was promulgated by law, but none of this demonstrates contrition on the part of the king. Rather, he may have been keen to reinforce his own regime by reference to a popular saint who was close kin to himself, rather than seek forgiveness for his half-brother's death.

By 993, Aethelred does seem to have come to regret some of his own actions but it was the internal events of the previous decade which seem to have concerned him and which he felt had compromised his kingship, rather than the nature of his accession. His expressions of remorse centred on the despoliation of several churches which he had condoned after Bishop Aethelwold's death in 984. His responsibility was in partnership with Bishop Wulfgar of Ramsbury and Ealdorman Aelfric of central Wessex – both of whom were his own appointees in the early 980s – to whom he seems to have allowed free rein with some church property they coveted. This was not, however, particularly exceptional. More

The monastery of Bradford-on-Avon, Wiltshire, with its estates, was granted to the nuns at Shaftesbury by King Aethelred in AD 1001, substantially enlarging their holdings. By a fortunate series of accidents, the chancel and nave with one flanking porch of St Lawrence's Chapel have survived intact to the present day. The core of the structure is probably eighth century with major alterations in the late Anglo-Saxon period.

savage was his ravaging of the Rochester diocese to punish its bishop, and this incident clearly inflamed relations between King Aethelred and the aging Archbishop Dunstan, but those had arguably never been cordial.

The early years of Aethelred's personal rule were, therefore, a period during which the king was less assiduous in the protection of churches and their possessions than he might have been, and more rash in his actions than he would later have wished. It was also a period when Scandinavian attacks began to impact on England, and it may be that it was these which led Aethelred to reconsider the moral position and direction of his own government in the mid-990s.

Edward was murdered in 978. The first Viking attacks occurred in 980, when fleets sacked Southampton, ravaged Thanet and raided Cheshire. At least two forces were responsible, one operating in the Irish Sea and one in the Channel. The Viking world had, therefore, woken up to the new vulnerability of England and the opportunities offered by its factional government. Its bolder souls were sufficiently encouraged to test its defences and they continued to do so in the years to come, ravaging the northern coasts of Cornwall and Devon in 981, then raiding Dorset and sacking London in 982. In 987, Watchet was raided and a local thegn named Goda killed along with others when they sought to beat off the Vikings.

The Anglo-Saxon minster church of St Mary, Reculver, Kent, which was constructed inside the Roman fortress of the same name, was an important landmark guiding shipping into the northern end of the Wantsum Channel from the seventh century onwards, although the prominent towers are twelfth century. Demolition occurred in 1805.

These fleets were mostly small and their complements did not travel far inland, but they were comparatively successful in achieving limited objectives, returning whence they had come with an update concerning England's considerable wealth and the comparative ease with which a share of it could be garnered.

In Scandinavia, a new target for sea raiding must have seemed opportune. The late tenth century saw the rise of the Saxon state in northern Germany, which had been pushing out its influence and its missionaries into the Viking world since the 930s. The Danish kings capitalized on this process to expand their own authority northwards and were the first among the Vikings to actively promote Christianity. Harald Bluetooth was depicted by the well-known runic stone at Yelling as the ruler of the Danes and Norwegians who 'made the Danes Christian' but he had arguably over-stretched his resources in the effort to enforce his own authority throughout much of Scandinavia, and his christianizing policies should be interpreted primarily as an aspect of his consolidation of royal power. One consequence of his activities was a surfeit of Viking jarls and local kings displaced from Scandinavia and eager to try their luck overseas in search of wealth with which to re-establish their fortunes at home. Another was considerable dissatisfaction with Harald's rule and his efforts to fund his numerous capital projects, even among the Danes, and he was ultimately displaced by a rebellion in favour of his own son Swein Forkbeard in 986.

Swein was, in the short term, thereafter busy imposing himself upon his father's realm of Denmark. Leadership of the Scandinavia-derived attacks on southern and eastern England fell to another notable Viking, the Norwegian Olaf Tryggvason, who headed a fleet reputed to be of ninety-three ships to England in 991, which struck first at eastern Kent then Essex, where it prevailed over Ealdorman Byrhtnoth at the celebrated Battle of Maldon. Olaf's force returned to England in 993, when Bamburgh and the Humber littoral were attacked. Swein joined him at latest in 994 (it has been argued that he was present already at Maldon in the previous year) and their combined forces attacked London and raided to such effect across the south east that the English government was reluctantly persuaded to raise a geld of £16,000 to buy them off.

Within a very few years, therefore, senior figures in the Viking world had recognized the opportunity offered them in England to circumvent the power of Saxon kings and emperors in mainland Europe and obtain substantial rewards. At the same time, they seem to have recognized that England's defences were far more formidable than those which had faced their grandfathers and great-grandfathers early in Alfred's reign. The so-called 'Second Viking Age' was characterized by a degree of military professionalism and discipline hitherto not seen in the north, a new, enhanced quality of equipment and a novel unity of purpose, which was ultimately provided by the leadership of the Danish king in person.

In England, the first Viking attacks in a generation or more are unlikely to have been seen initially as of any great consequence. The central fact of recent English history that will have been known to every Englishman in or about 990 was that the English had driven off the Vikings and accommodated on their own terms those of Scandinavian descent who had remained in England. The principal weapons by which this had been achieved were still in place: England was studded

Ealdorman Byrhtnoth confronted the Vikings across the causeway at Maldon, Essex in August 991, then withdrew to enable them to cross over and give battle. Recent investigations suggest that the causeway has survived virtually unaltered.

with defended towns or *burhs* by which a Viking assault could be held up, some of which had stone walls so were relatively impervious to attack by fire; there was an effective system of regional and national armies which could take the field against invaders, pursue them and bring them to battle; and the king deployed a fleet which could attack squadrons of raiders at sea, transport troops, close rivers and cut-off armies once they had disembarked. The basic tactics of English armies both on land and at sea had been developed by Alfred and Edward the Elder – or perhaps even earlier unbeknown to us – and seem not to have been forgotten thereafter.

In 991, however, the Vikings defeated and killed Ealdorman Byrhtnoth of Essex. He was one of the English regime's most distinguished figures and central to the East-Anglian affinity. Byrhtnoth had been an ealdorman for thirty-five years and had formerly been a close associate of Athelstan Half-king. Since the latter's retirement, he had apparently been a political ally of Athelstan's sons and ruled Essex and the south-east Midlands in their collective interest right up to his death. In the absence of much experience of warfare among England's elite at this date, Byrhtnoth was probably seen as the principal military leader of the regime and his death was a blow to Aethelred's court as well as to the East-Anglian faction. That fact could not be wholly disguised even by subsequent heroicization of his defeat in the vernacular epic poem, *The Battle of Maldon*, which is the

Mid-nineteenth century vision of late Anglo-Saxon warriors. In practice English soldiers rarely, if ever, fought on horseback, although they rode to battle, wore heavy chain mail and generally preferred the battleaxe or sword to the spear.

finest Old-English literature, as well as the most compelling piece of English propaganda, to come out of this struggle. The aftermath of the battle was the first occasion when a geld was levied to pay the Vikings to leave England, and that was a sombre outcome, the consequences of which were to come back to haunt Aethelred's regime down the years.

AETHELRED AS A MATURE KING

Byrhtnoth's death in battle in 991 also signalled the passing of the old guard within the royal government. Aethelred was himself about twenty-six by this date and surely already married, given that his wife Aelfgifu, daughter of Ealdorman Thored of the Northumbrians, is known to have borne him at least nine children by 1002. The ranks of the principal participants of the crisis years of 975–8 were thinning fast: Bishop Aethelwold was long dead; Archbishop Dunstan followed in 988 and Archbishop Oswald of York in 992. Ealdormen Aelfhere had died in 983 and his successor had been outlawed in 985. The deaths of Byrhtnoth in 991 and his ally Aethelwine – son of the Half-king – in 992 effectively completed this process. Of the three ealdormen appointed by Edward and then accommodated by the minority government of Aethelred, Edwin in the extreme south east and

Aethelmaer in central Wessex had both died in 982, leaving the regime free to appoint Aelfric to Hampshire. Only Aethelweard remained in western Wessex, and after the death of Aethelwine this distinguished man of letters and kinsman of the royal house became the premier ealdorman.

Aethelred, whose name later commentators were to pun as *Unraed* – 'unadvised' – is portrayed in a very poor light by the several Anglo-Saxon Chronicles which alone offer an historical commentary on the reign. All anticipate his failure, so depend on originals written largely in or shortly after 1016, and the general assumption is of poor judgement on his part in terms of appointments to high office, with worthy English forces made ineffective by the cowardice or treachery of the leaders whom he had appointed. He may well have pandered to the ambitions of his favourites as a minor, but that phase seems to have passed comparatively quickly, and his public repentance of certain deeds of his youth in and around 993 seems to signal his intention to adopt a more responsible, and perhaps more statesmanlike, attitude towards government. Some of the criticism which his subsequent appointments attracted is arguably unjustified.

Aethelred proved himself an effective judge of character and competence in several areas, promoting Wulfstan (probably then a monk at Ely) to the archdiocese of York in 1002, for example, and to a brilliant and effective career in the forefront of royal and clerical administration. His several choices as Archbishops of Canterbury were perhaps less distinguished than this, but Sigeric (990–4) was in origin a Glastonbury monk, who had already served as Abbot of St Augustine's and then as Bishop of Ramsbury, and he played a prominent role in government during his archiepiscopate. His advice was probably the initial stimulus for the inception of the Danegeld in 991 – an initiative which naturally attracts a certain opprobrium – but he was also involved in the agreement which led to Olaf's baptism and subsequent alliance with the English regime. Archbishop Aelfric (995–1005), a monk initially from Aethelwold's Abingdon, was clearly also a competent churchman. These two revived the ancient custom of English primates travelling to Rome for the *pallium*. Through them and their journeys to the centre of Christendom, Aethelred's regime may well have sought to regain the moral high ground by cultivating the papacy, much as Alfred had done a century before. Archbishop Aelfric showed himself a conscientious and charitable man, whose will makes it clear that he was doing all he could to alleviate the impact on his own people of the high levels of taxation and other royal demands being raised to combat the Danes. Many other clerical appointees of Aethelred were monks from the reformed monasteries, and it seems clear that the king was committed to the policies initiated by his father – at least from 993 onwards – and sought senior clergy from the ranks of the best-educated groups available to him, whose promotion might have been expected to have been pleasing to God.

It is in his selection of ealdormen and senior laymen that Aethelred has been the more heavily criticized. Certainly men like Aelfric of Hampshire and Eadric Streona of the Mercians were singled out for blame by the later chroniclers, yet Ulfkell (more normally Ulfketel) Snilling – 'the Bold' – of East Anglia fought determinedly against the Danes in 1004 and again in 1010, and eventually lost his life in support of Edmund Ironside at Ashingdon in 1016. Admittedly, Ulfkell was a *minister* and not an ealdorman, although he clearly behaved as if he was one and maintained the tradition of resolute opposition to foreigners earlier upheld in the same region by Ealdorman Byrhtnoth. Ealdorman Uhtred of Northumbria held the north for Aethelred for most of a generation, despite the Scandinavian sympathies of powerful elements within the York community. Some other ealdormen were figures who were ill-equipped for the military role that came increasingly to dominate the political agenda during Aethelred's reign. Aethelweard, ealdorman of the five south-western shires since 973, was the cultured patron of the young Aelfric – the foremost scholar of his generation – and himself translated an Anglo-Saxon Chronicle text into Latin. He was additionally a prince of the blood with connections at the highest level across much of western Europe and a representative of that family which had provided England with more queens than any other over the previous century. He was active as a diplomat and as a patron of the reform movement, but no mention occurs of this peon of English nobility as a war leader and he died, apparently of natural causes, in 998, before his province had been affected by more than local incursions by the Vikings. Aethelred inherited Aethelweard and he was far too senior a figure to discard lightly. Indeed, there is no indication that he wished to and he may have allowed his son Aethelmaer to succeed him, although opinion is now divided on this issue. The Danish onslaught eventually raised the profile of England's local leaders as generals, but they were appointed for a far wider range of duties than this and it is arguably unreasonable to denigrate them for failure in just one area of competence after a generation or so of peace.

It is not even clear that Aethelred should be held responsible for the preferment to office of the much maligned Aelfric to the ealdordom of Hampshire, since this occurred in 982 when the king was only about sixteen years old and still very much under the influence of his mother and the great men who had placed him on the throne. Aelfric was, certainly, one of those with whom he thereafter associated himself in several acts which he was later to regret. He was also the principal blamed by the chroniclers for the collapse of the campaign against the Vikings in 992 (see below), when the regime was searching without much success for a new war leader and seeking to combine several local armies into a single national force. Aethelred reacted by having his son blinded in the following year – precisely that time when he was publicly regretting his 'youthful indiscretions' – and by so doing he destroyed any ambitions that Aelfric may have entertained to pass on his office to his own heir. The ealdorman does not thereafter feature in the Chronicles as a general over the next ten years, despite becoming premier ealdorman at the death of Aethelweard in 998. Although Aethelred did not actually dismiss Aelfric from office, he does seem to have distanced himself from his failure in 992.

What, above all else, was exceptional about Aethelred's approach to war was his disinclination to lead English armies in the field. During the Viking invasions of the ninth century, every English king led their troops in battle and several lost their lives, resulting even in the collapse of dynasty and kingship. One need only think of the sanctified King Edmund of the East Angles, or the two

Northumbrian kings, Aelle and Osberht, slain by the great Danish army at the Battle of York in 867. Alfred succeeded where others had failed, and he regularly led his forces in person and accepted the risks of so doing. Certain ealdormen and the aetheling Edward also played their parts as generals, but Alfred was certainly credited by his court writers with having shouldered the principal burden. His successors did likewise, and pretty well every campaign against the Vikings over the next two generations was undertaken under the immediate and direct oversight of the king of the day.

At the start of his reign, Aethelred was clearly too young to take the field, and the initial raids were in any case too fleeting to allow the king to take effective action. By the late 980s and early 990s, however, he was old enough and opportunities to lead his army in person were becoming plentiful. Take for example the campaign of the year 992: the English fleet was concentrated at London in readiness to 'entrap the raiding army somewhere outside'. This fleet was apparently intended to await news of the enemy's arrival and disembarkation, then deploy accordingly to control its escape route and attack from the sea. In the past, such a grand strategy would have normally been under the overall direction of the king himself – and it is precisely what Harold Godwineson, for example, was to attempt in the Hastings campaign in October 1066 – but Aethelred instead gave command to Ealdorman Aelfric, Earl Thored of Northumbria (his father-in-law), Bishop Aelfstan (of either London or Rochester) and Bishop Aescwig of Dorchester. Aethelred may have been conceding leadership to superior experience, since Aelfric and Thored had twenty-three years of high office between them by this date, but even so this did not compensate for the absence of the king. Such collective leadership had perhaps some political benefits and presumably reflects the several local levies involved but looks to have been a disastrous mistake strategically and so it proved to be in this instance. Aelfric was accused by the chroniclers of betraying the plan to the enemy and then absconding on the eve of the battle, when only the ships of East Anglia and London engaged the enemy. This may well be an unfair view of his responsibility for failure, but the king himself does seem to have considered Ealdorman Aelfric to have been the primary culprit and he was perhaps the most prominent of the four commanders.

When Aethelred is noted as leading his levies in the field it is normally on expeditions against insular targets and not the main armies of the Vikings. He ravaged western Kent in 986, apparently in person, and campaigned against the British kingdom of Strathclyde and its Viking allies in 1000, then seems to have been present when his forces wasted Lindsey in 1014. Given the number and scale of Viking attacks, however, this record is paltry, and it seems clear that Aethelred only chose to take the field himself in a few instances. In the last resort, we must attempt to explain Aethelred's military inactivity during a period which cried out for royal generalship.

One solution to this conundrum is to suppose that this was a considered policy consequent upon the king's marked lack of close relatives and potential heirs of the blood royal. As far as one can judge, once his several brothers were dead in or before 978, Aethelred was the sole male representative of King Alfred's line then living and it would have been necessary to go back eight reigns, over a century and across four generations to find candidates for the succession from a collateral branch of the family such as Ealdorman Aethelweard represented. Until Aethelred produced adult children, only his life separated England from a potentially disastrous succession crisis in which no English candidate's claim was convincing, and which would necessarily have been overshadowed by a ferocious and opportunistic Viking onslaught. His first wife, Aelfgifu, obliged by producing a large number of children in rapid succession, but the date of the marriage is unknown. His son Athelstan was the oldest male of at least nine children, all perhaps born before 1002, but he need not have been adult much before about 1010, although he had by then been witnessing his father's diplomas for some years. Athelstan's will implies that he was still unmarried when he died in 1014, but he was then of an age to be owning precious weapons, so was probably in his twenties. He could even have been about thirty, but he was arguably still a child in the early to mid-990s when the pattern of Aethelred's reign became established.

Aethelred was accused of poor judgement by the chroniclers but not of cowardice. It may be that he and his advisors considered the political risks posed by the prospect of his death in battle against Viking armies outweighed the potential benefits of his presence on the battle field. It is a comparatively complex political system which can disengage the head of state from the task of leading its military forces in person. Yet late Anglo-Saxon England was becoming an increasingly sophisticated state and this separation of the roles of king and field commander certainly occurs at a later date – as, for example, when English armies in the reign of Edward the Confessor invaded both Scotland and Wales. It did, however, place considerable stress on the regime and it does seem likely that the king's presence was sorely missed. At the very end of his life, Aethelred was more often with the English forces – his presence in London with Danish mercenaries discouraged the metropolis from surrendering to Swein in 1013, he led the fleet round the south coast to the Isle of Wight then Normandy in person, and joined the army in the field in 1016 on its request, but he was by then a sick man and capable of achieving nothing.

Perhaps more important was the failure of the regime to spawn any other effective military leader. Byrhtnoth had tackled the Danes at Maldon with determination, and resolution and a modicum of luck were the bare essentials capable of generating a military reputation. Aethelred's government was, however, confronted by fearsome opponents, whom few English leaders seem to have felt confident about confronting in the field. In this respect, Maldon was perhaps a morale-sapping battle, and figures such as Ealdorman Aelfric may well have felt a lot less confident on the field of battle than when he had accepted the role of general in the comparative safety of the king's council chamber. What is more, the comparative calm of England in the preceeding generation meant that the English nobility had little in the way of active martial traditions to call upon in Aethelred's reign. The heroes of such great battles as Brunanburh were not even the fathers of this generation but their grandfathers. When Ealdorman Aelfric once more found himself obliged to lead an army against the Danes at Exeter in 1003, 'as soon as they were so close at hand that each of them looked on the other, then he pretended to vomit, and said that he was ill, and thus betrayed

Hoard of Viking spear-heads and axe-heads found, along with an anchor, at London Bridge.
Such finds may have been deposited in the river during one of the many Viking attacks on
London in the reigns of Aethelred or Edmund Ironside.

the people'. The ambitious young courtier who had secured an ealdordom in the comparative peace of 982 lost all credibility as a military leader – and any hopes for further advancement – in the fiasco of 993. By 1003 he was just a frightened old man.

In practice, the war record of Aethelred's regime in the mid to late 990s and early years of the new century was probably not as poor as the Chroniclers later implied. Most Viking attacks evinced some sort of mobilization in response, and, after the widespread ravaging by Olaf's army throughout the south east which characterized 994, no Scandinavian force over-wintered in England until 998. Several battles were fought: Rochester in 999, Dean and Pinhoe in 1001, and Ulfketel's hardfought struggle near Thetford in 1004. Most were lost, admittedly, but the Vikings rarely had uncontested control of English territory for long and most of the damage that they caused occurred within 20 miles of the coast. Given the size of the forces sailing south from Scandinavia, the problems of command and the deficiencies with regard to martial culture among the English, this is not such a bad record.

Aethelred's administration was at its best when raising and handling money. The amount of geld paid over to the Vikings was vast, yet this amounted to only a small proportion of the total revenues and expenditure of Aethelred's governments. Despite the Vikings and the disruption they caused, the administration of England's mints and the flow of bullion seem to have continued on such a scale that it was possible to export considerable quantities of silver to the Scandinavian world without dire consequences for the silver standard of English coin. This in itself was a remarkable achievement. Admittedly, the increasing demands of the government for taxes and other public dues seem to have fuelled accusations of tyranny – as the prominence given to enslavement in Archbishop Wulfstan's famous sermon would later imply – but the facts remain that Aethelred's regime proved itself extremely robust even in adversity and achieved a great deal.

Another and rather less savoury example of the administrative efficiency of Aethelred's government was the St Brice's Day (13 November) massacre of 'all the Danish men who were among the English race' in 1002, allegedly because they were plotting to kill the king. This eleventh-century precursor of the St Bartholomew's Day massacre of Huguenots seems unsavoury to modern eyes and may well have done little good, but it does demonstrate an ability to plan and execute governmental policy across the provinces. It certainly had some effect in towns such as Oxford, although it seems unlikely that it spread far into the Danelaw or caused many deaths in the countryside.

Aethelred's regime proved as able as any other when it came to diplomacy and the suborning of its opponents. The baptism of pagan Vikings had played a significant role in the formation of peace in the times of Alfred and Athelstan. Having bought off the Viking attack on London in 994, Aethelred sent Bishop Aelfheah of Winchester and his kinsman, the premier ealdorman Aethelweard, to Olaf Tryggvasson and negotiated his baptism and an agreement that he would never again attack England. At a solemn ceremony at Andover, Aethelred stood sponsor or godfather to Olaf at his baptism and gave him rich presents. With the proceeds of this transaction and his recent geld payments, Olaf returned to Norway and succeeded in making himself king there, never to return. Olaf in turn used Christianity as a vehicle to establish his supremacy in the north, although his efforts came to an end after only five years, but it is quite possible that English missionaries assisted him, so maintaining a degree of contact between Aethelred's court and his new Norwegian ally. This was a notable success which divided Aethelred's enemies and brought a temporary upturn in his fortunes, since Olaf's ambitions in Norway had repercussions for the Danish kingship which had formerly dominated the region, and tied up Swein's efforts in Scandinavia in several of the next few years.

Although his accommodation of Olaf may well have proved the more effective of the two, Aethelred's better known diplomatic initiative was his

Rochester was one of the earliest English dioceses and was a well-fortified bridgehead in the late Anglo-Saxon period. The castle and current cathedral are both Norman in date, but two earlier churches have been identified by excavation under the cathedral. Bishop Gundulf, the first Norman bishop, was appointed in 1077 and was also associated with other of King William's building works.

alliance with Normandy. The Viking fleets had on occasion crossed over from Scandinavia to the Shetlands and northern Britain, but Olaf's fleets seem generally to have used the coastal routes from Scandinavia to attack England via the short Channel crossings, and Swein certainly preferred to follow this route when he launched attacks independent of his old ally. In practice, Viking fleets used both sides of the English Channel as bases from which to launch attacks on the other. This meant that the attitudes of rulers along the continental shoreline to Viking fleets were of considerable importance to England's rulers.

Cross-Channel co-operation and alliance had played a significant part in defeating the Vikings in the ninth and early tenth centuries, but the Frankish kingdom was no longer the unified realm it had been a century before. Aethelred

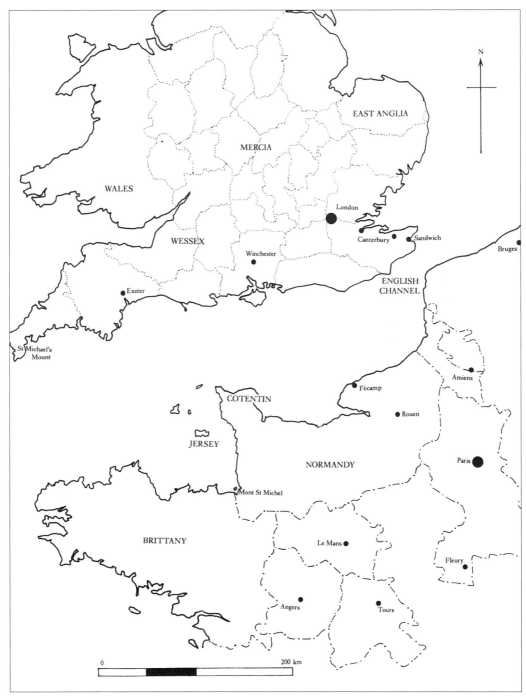

England, Normandy and adjacent French territories. This illustrates the interdependence of the two shorelines of the English Channel when threatened by Viking fleets.

sought the aid of King Robert the Pious (996–1031) – and senior figures connected with Fleury were familiar with both courts and capable of providing communication between them – but there is no evidence that the English obtained any assistance from Robert, or that he was capable of providing such even should he have chosen to. By 1000, real power lay with the rulers of individual counties and the two which controlled the bulk of the northern French and Rhineland ports were Flanders and Normandy.

In the late tenth century, England's contacts were primarily with Flanders, the Rhineland and northern Germany. The Lotharingian monasteries had been a major source of expertise and personnel during the English monastic reform and travellers passed backwards and forwards during Aethelred's reign. Earlier royal marriages contracted in the region by Alfred, Edward the Elder and Athelstan were still remembered and the social and cultural contacts formed then are known to have been retained with pride by such figures as Ealdorman Aethelweard. Merchants from the Empire were especially favoured in London under Aethelred's fourth law-code. Flemish cults were finding homes in England, and Anglo-Saxon saints had long been revered in parts of northern Germany initially converted with the help of Anglo-Saxon missionaries in the eighth century. A surprising quantity of literature concerning England and English political figures was written in the churches of Flanders during the eleventh century and several English churchmen contributed modestly to their finances. King Edgar too had been a benefactor of the Flemish church and particularly St Peter's, Ghent, to which he granted the port of Greenwich. The prosperity of this trading site is perhaps best revealed by an infamous incident in 1012, when a Danish army stationed there consumed wine enough to murder their valuable captive Archbishop Aelfheah in a drunken brawl.

These social, ecclesiastical and cultural contacts were probably formed along channels of communication based on common trading interests between London, other English east-coast ports such as Norwich, and the Rhineland. Slaves, wool, a wide range of manufactures, wine and mercenaries probably passed along this conduit each year in substantial quantities. The Viking onslaught on England which characterized Aethelred's reign does not seem to have disrupted these contacts. Indeed, it may even have increased the flow of shipping – to the benefit of suppliers of all kinds – and brought the Flemish ports opportunities to make steep profits from the sale of war booty and the treatment of the Danish wounded. Nothing is known of relations between Aethelred and Baldwin IV of Flanders (988–1035), but the latter certainly had good reason to keep the Flemish ports open to both English and Viking ships. Baldwin was to be a close ally of King Cnut, and this relationship with the Danish royal family may perhaps stem back to the previous reign, yet there are signs that England and Flanders retained contact throughout the period and there is no evidence of outright hostility between them.

It was Normandy, not Flanders, which had been settled and taken over by Norsemen, however, and there Scandinavian forces may have anticipated the warmer welcome during Aethelred's reign. Again, there is insufficient information concerning relationships between England and Normandy to reconstruct a detailed picture, but Aethelred's marriage into the ducal house can only have resulted from high-level negotiation and was apparently intended to seal an accord of some consequence to both parties. Once again, there was clearly a basis of contact between English and Norman monasticism on which to build, and Rouen was also a significant trading partner for London, and a particularly important source of wine entering England.

Papal correspondence refers to a peace agreement made in 991 between Aethelred and Duke Richard of Normandy, brokered by a papal legate, which guaranteed that neither side would shelter the other's enemies. The likeliest targets of this agreement were the several Viking fleets which had been attacking England. Archbishop Sigeric's journey to Rome to consult the papacy and obtain a *pallium* in 989 may well have eased the way and the Roman pontiff had his own motives for encouraging two Christian princes to come together to resist the heathen. The papal legate, Abbot Leo, seems to have spent Christmas 990 with Aethelred in England and he may well have proved a useful source of information on European – and particularly Frankish – affairs.

Duke Richard I of Normandy died, however, in 996, and his eldest son, Richard II (996–1026), is unlikely to have considered himself bound by his father's diplomacy. Whatever the impact of the accord of 991, therefore, it was probably in abeyance by 997, if not before.

The Peterborough manuscript of the Anglo-Saxon Chronicle noted that the Danish fleet was in Normandy in the summer of 1000. Whether the Danes were raiding there or merely refitting is unclear but they returned to the Devon coast in 1001, then established themselves once more on the Isle of Wight. That had been the site chosen by the Danish fleet as a winter base in 998, and its return was something which the English regime had to take seriously. If the Danes had Duke Richard II of Normandy as an ally, then the danger to Aethelred's realm was the more serious.

A story told by William of Jumièges three-quarters of a century later refers to a large-scale attack by the English war fleet on the Norman Cotentin at about this time, and some commentators have suggested that this was a 'cutting-out expedition' aimed at retrieving English booty from Norman ports and striking at the Viking fleet there. There must be some doubt whether this episode should be treated as historical, and even if it did occur it is undated. Perhaps the most worrying factor is the silence of English chronicles concerning such a forward policy on Aethelred's part, but it must be remembered that their accounts rest on a retrospective view of the reign, by which point Aethelred's resistance to the Danes had been shown to be ineffective and could be written out of the account.

Whether or not this attack be warranted, it was presumably the lengthy sojourn by the Danish war fleet in easy striking distance of both Normandy and southern England in 1001–2 which served to persuade Richard II of the dangers of entertaining the Danes and so enabled the two sides to move towards alliance. Aethelred was apparently by this stage a widower. If not he may have put aside his first wife Aelfgifu, and his father's bigamy, and that of his son-in-law Uhtred, should alert us to the possibility that the king might have acted in this way too.

Whatever the precise context, however, the English king now made a marital alliance with Normandy and received and married Emma (whom the English confusingly chose to call Aelfgifu), the youngest daughter of Richard I and sister of the current duke, Richard II.

This marriage was the first contracted by an English king with a foreign bride since Alfred's father married Judith, daughter of Charles the Bald, in 855. The reasoning behind it must have been very similar to that distant precedent. It brought Aethelred close kinship by marriage with the dominant figure on the Frankish side of the Narrow Seas, so had some potential to close the Channel to the Danes. This had implications for the central reaches of England's southern coastline which had taken the brunt of recent Viking attacks, and must have raised morale particularly in the West Saxon shires. It also gave Aethelred a mass of connections in the region. Emma's sister, Hawise, was married to Count Geoffrey of Britanny (died 1008) and was mother to an improbable five counts, two of whom later fought at Hastings, and from whom descended the Breton counts of Richmond. One of Emma's brothers was Robert, the Archbishop of Rouen (989–1037) and another was William, Count of Eu. Duke Richard II's daughter, Eleanor, was later to be the second wife of Baldwin IV of Flanders. It is unclear whether or not these links were of much short-term benefit to the English court but some did aid Edward the Confessor, the eldest son of Aethelred and Emma, particularly while he was in exile.

Of more immediate concern was the resolve displayed by the two parties to the treaty. If it was the assurance of Norman alliance which encouraged Aethelred to approve the St Brice's Day massacre that same autumn, then his confidence was ill-founded. A great Danish fleet struck at Exeter the following summer and sacked it before brushing aside the army of Ealdorman Aelfric and moving on to destroy Wilton and Salisbury. The Danes had managed to penetrate the Channel despite the new Norman alliance. Their targeting of Exeter may indicate their awareness of Aethelred's new amity with the Norman court, since it was a portion of Emma's dower given her by her husband and under the authority of a Norman official, one Hugh, whom the anti-Norman chronicler held to have been criminally responsible for its fall to Viking attack. If his attitude was shared by other Englishmen then Exeter's sack was as divisive as it was expensive, to the regime in general and the queen in particular.

There is little evidence on which to base an assessment of the value of the Norman treaty to King Aethelred. Normandy certainly provided a refuge for his wife and young family when England was overrun in the autumn of 1013 and the king himself retired there with parts at least of the English fleet. Yet contemporaries were well aware that only two generations separated Richard I, Emma's father, from Rollo, the pagan Viking founder of the ducal dynasty, and that the revival of Normandy's shattered churches was as recent as the 960s and '70s. Mont St Michel, for example, was restored by Duke Richard by arrangement with the Frankish king in 966. As late as the 990s, Richer, a chronicler at Rheims, was still able to refer to a Norman leader as 'duke of the pirates'. As David Douglas long ago pointed out, in the same year that he gave refuge to Aethelred II of England, Duke Richard II entertained Olaf and Lacman, the leaders of a putatively pagan Scandinavian host which had just devastated the

The defences of Exeter in about AD 1000 were based on the Roman town walls but had been substantially reinforced under late Anglo-Saxon kings. A tower today popularly ascribed to King Athelstan is in fact post-Conquest, but Anglo-Saxon masonry can still be identified along the walls nearby.

lands of his kinsman by marriage in Brittany. The Dukes of Normandy therefore plied their own route through the troubles of the age and had important and ongoing connections with both sides in the Anglo-Danish wars which they were not prepared to much amend on Aethelred's behalf.

THE UNMAKING OF AETHELRED

Aethelred's lieutenants, and in particular Ealdormen Aelfric and Eadric, were scapegoated by the chroniclers for his ultimate failure, but their responsibility can only have been partial. Another factor was undoubtedly the massing of Scandinavian forces against his regime, which was to be such a feature of the years following 1005. During this period there were often very substantial Viking forces active in Britain, which caused considerable damage, severely dented English morale and lowered the credibility of the government. Swein, who returned to England in 1013 after an absence of several years, was certainly ambitious to secure the English throne. Yet, short of overwhelming victory over England's king in person, to have any real chance of success such ambitions required the committed support of a significant phalanx within the English elite. On the whole the Danes were treated by the English as something to be suffered, occasionally resisted, but more often bought off. Swein was not acknowledged by any significant or substantial body of political opinion as a legitimate candidate for the English crown until 1013. The reasons offered for his return to England vary from vengeance for his brother's death in the St Brice's Day massacre in 1002, to anger at his own expulsion from England in the 990s, the enthusiasm of his son and followers for the enterprise and the sheer love of destruction. Indeed, all may well have been significant factors, but Swein remained to this point in the minds of the English political classes a feared outsider with little real chance of acceptance as an alternative king.

All this changed quite dramatically in 1013. Clearly, a part of the equation must be the scale of the forces which Thorkell and then Swein himself brought to bear, which offered a potent challenge to the leaders of the English provinces. Both also had considerable kudos as victorious leaders, yet Swein's challenge for the crown occurred at the point when Aethelred had hired Thorkell and his ship-men, and these two forces and their famous leaders must to an extent have balanced each other out. Swein and Aethelred were, therefore, at this point both at the head of substantial armies, made up in large part of Viking soldiery. The collapse of English resistance in 1013 cannot be explained merely as a consequence of Viking attack.

Nor was the critical deployment of his fleet and army which brought Swein to power a military campaign as such at all. The Danish king was at this point a comparative stranger to England following an absence of several years. In 1013, before August, he arrived fresh from Scandinavia at Sandwich and made his way north along the North-Sea coast past East Anglia to the Humber and thence to Gainsborough on the Trent, apparently without an animal stolen, a slave taken or a field burnt in anger. The entire process stands out as different from every other Viking campaign of the preceding twenty years.

Gainsborough – which is still a minor port characterized by small grain wharfs and storage sheds – lay between Lindsey and the Five Boroughs. It was also close to the southern reaches of Northumbria, which extended at this date south of the Humber to include southern Yorkshire. It was a place of unmitigated obscurity in the sense that it is unnamed in any surviving charter or chronicle to this date. After 1014, it slipped quietly back into the historical backwater from which it had briefly emerged. Yet in the summer of 1013, it was there that the Danish king received in rapid succession and without any recorded hostilities the surrender of the Northumbrians, Lindsey and the Five Boroughs, and all the armed men 'north of Watling Street'. Watling Street, now the A5, was part of the boundary between English and Danish territory agreed between Alfred and Guthrum a century earlier when the latter was king in East Anglia, so that region and associated parts of the south-east Midlands were probably included in 1013.

The surrenders at Gainsborough were clearly not forced – in the manner of most accommodations with the Danes of the previous decade – and Swein was not being paid off to induce him to go elsewhere, as was usual. Northumbria had not been raided by the Danes for a generation, yet its earl and principal nobility came in to offer submission to the Danish king. Nor had the north-east Midlands been badly battered by the Danes in recent years in the way that Wessex had.

Gainsborough, on the western edge of Lincolnshire, is today a minor port on the River Trent. It seems unlikely that it was a settlement of any status in 1013. Rather, the utility of the site would seem to lie in its frontier status between Lindsey and the Five Boroughs and its ease of access from Northumbria and the North Sea.

Rather, the entire process looks like a carefully co-ordinated policy which was necessarily agreed in some detail – as regards place and date, for example – by all the principals in advance. The accord with Swein included all the forces in Mercia and Northumbria not under Eadric Streona's control, and this must be significant.

The agreement reached at Gainsborough represents a major indictment by a large section of the English community outside Wessex of Aethelred's regime, to the point where they were prepared to transfer their allegiance to a Danish candidate for the throne and provide him with the necessary platform from which – at last – to achieve his ambitions. Once again, as in the 970s, the political

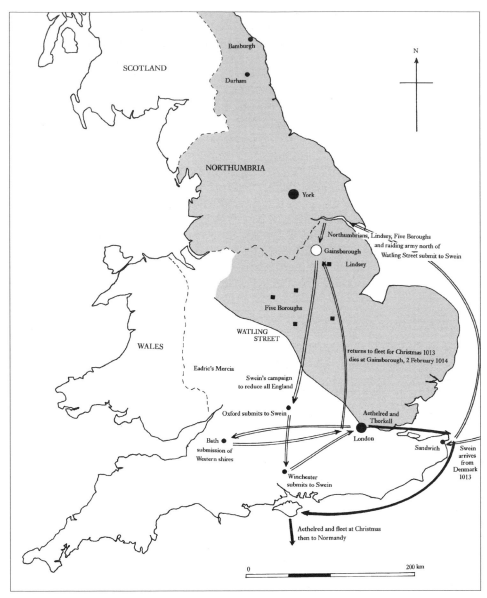

This indicates how the Gainsborough Accord was achieved in 1013 and the campaigns then launched by Swein to secure southern and western England.

community split between rival claimants to the throne, with western Mercia and an extended East Anglia opting for rival candidates. What was different was the fact that in 1013 Aethelred had been on the throne for thirty-five years and was still living, whereas the 970s had witnessed a succession crisis and the struggle between factions lining up behind two royal minors. In 1013, therefore, those who accepted Swein were actively withdrawing their obedience from a long-established monarch under whom all had previously served and who had appointed many of them – such as Earl Uhtred – to their current posts. This betrayal of their anointed king by a great phalanx of the English aristocracy was a matter of profound embarrassment to the chronicler who perhaps wrote up Thorkell's activities over the few years preceding in part as a means of shrouding his sense of embarrassment at the betrayal of the king.

Why did a significant part of the English elite abandon Aethelred and transfer their allegiance to Swein in 1013? This is a crucial question if we are to understand the collapse of the dynasty and the subsequent triumph of Danish kingship in England. Yet it is a tale which is difficult to unravel, since the evidence is, to say the least, inconclusive. An attempt must, however, be made, since this is the central issue in the collapse of English kingship in 1013–16.

THE KING AND THE ARISTOCRACY

During the latter part of the final decade of the tenth century, Aethelred had gathered around him a cross-section of the English political community which excluded the greatest families with a tradition of service and the honours of office, in a style which probably mirrored the rule of his father. At the same time, his marriage produced a clutch of sons, one of whom (and most probably the eldest) could reasonably expect to be nominated as heir and successor. The first decade of the new millennium witnessed Aethelred's departure from these policies in two areas: his Norman marriage produced male offspring, and the king seems to have proposed to secure the succession for Emma's eldest son, Edward, in defiance of his adult sons, and in defiance too of the numerous nobles who had tied their own prospects to a political future which had, until 1002, seemed entirely uncontroversial; secondly, he demoted, destroyed or otherwise marginalized several of the principal figures whom he had drawn into government over the previous decade. The brutal methods Aethelred used – or at least excused – to achieve this undermined the reputation of his regime and the trust of the aristocracy in his kingship. His growing dependence on a single favourite – Eadric Streona – further alienated the aristocracy. Aethelred's policies combined to force his own sons and many recent associates of the crown into the ranks of his critics.

It is unsurprising that deep divisions existed within the elite in the early years of the eleventh century. Such tensions were a normal part of political life and resulted from the conflicting ambitions and interests of different noble kinships as they sought to advantage themselves and their wider affinities. The management of such tensions was a normal part of royal government, and Aethelred had already by this date had considerable experience in overseeing, rewarding and containing his magnates. The most serious divisions at this time go back to the 990s and the slide into comparative obscurity of the family of Athelstan Half-king from its former position of regional dominance in the mid-tenth century. Aethelwine was the last ealdorman of his line. Aethelred denied the dynasty the further exercise of high office following his death in 992, perhaps as belated punishment for their support of his half-brother as heir to King Edgar in 975–8. Whether or not there was a punitive element, it was arguably in the king's interest to reduce the influence of the family to more manageable proportions. East Anglia was left without a formally appointed ealdorman for the remainder of the reign, despite Ulfketel's central role there, so leaving this major affinity without recognized leaders above the rank of *minister*, real influence at the royal court or a properly established system of military leadership.

Despite Aethelred's downgrading of their local leadership, men in the heartland of the Half-king's former influence proved capable of organizing themselves effectively against the Danes. Indeed, their record is better in that respect than that of any other regional group, and was probably very pointedly so. But they had to achieve what they did without much encouragement from Aethelred, and still contribute to the gelds which he raised to ransom other less doughty communities from raiders. *Olafs saga* was later to depict Aethelred and the Danes combined overcoming Ulfketel and the East Anglians at Ringmere. Although this is far from the version offered by the far nearer contemporary Anglo-Saxon Chronicle, it is quite possible that Aethelred's sympathies lay, in this encounter, with the Vikings. This implies a degree of alienation between the two sides already during the 990s and on into the first decade of the eleventh century, with the East Anglians under Ulfketel retaining the will to fight far longer than other and currently more influential rivals for power and position within the English state. Just what, if anything, Ulfketel's connection was with the Half-king's family is unclear, but he does seem to have been the heir to a well-developed affinity which was both cohesive and militarily capable. If the king was somewhat in awe of it then perhaps he had good reason.

Aethelred promoted one Leofsige, ealdorman of Essex and south-east Mercia, probably in 994, but he fell foul of the king over local issues in Oxfordshire and then on account of his murder of the king's high reeve, Aefic, early in 1002, and was driven into exile. Leofsige's place within the regional community is obscure but his family's known lands were in Huntingdonshire and Hertfordshire. Aethelred does not seem to have placed much confidence in him even from the start, and may even have intentionally undermined his authority.

Another casualty of this period was Aethelred's father-in-law, Thored, the ealdorman of Northumbria since 979. Thored's name implies an Anglo-Scandinavian origin. Since the Athelstan who was killed among the men of Cambridgeshire at the Battle of Ringmere in 1010 was probably his son, the southern Danelaw was perhaps his place of origin, although it is unclear whether or not he was part of Ealdorman Aethelwine's network of associates. He may well be identifiable as the son of that Gunnar who had ravaged Westmorland in 966, in which case he may have held family estates also in Yorkshire. The elite often had lands scattered over considerable areas, so these two personae are by no means exclusive of one another. However, Thored's last known act was the unsuccessful campaign of 992, and his successor as ealdorman, Aelfhelm, was active in Northumbria by 993. Thored was then presumably out of office and either dead or in disgraced obscurity. There may well be some connection between Aethelred's treatment of the descendants of Athelstan Half-king and that of a father-in-law he may well only have acquired as a means of pacifying Northumbria and powerful connections in the Mercian Danelaw at the outset of his reign. Whether or not this was the case, they seem to have suffered the loss of royal favour at the same time and this too strengthens the possibility that they were earlier in association, one with the other. Thored's fall may also have had implications for the influence of the queen and the prospects of her sons, so in some senses it prefaces Aethelred's marriage alliance with Normandy.

Ealdorman Aelfhelm, Thored's replacement, was Mercian in origin, from a very wealthy landed family centred on Staffordshire, and particularly Tamworth and Wolverhampton. He was the brother of that Wulfric who is often known as 'Spot', who founded Burton Abbey and whose will with its massive bequests of land stretching from Yorkshire across central England has survived. Aelfhelm's appointment therefore implies the preferment to high office of a family of considerable wealth and influence but one which was not previously prominent in the factional conflicts surrounding the throne, and he is not known to have been an associate of the house of Athelstan Half-king. Such new blood signifies Aethelred's break with the past and his intention to promote men loyal only to himself and his dynasty, and in this he appears to have succeeded.

Wulfric Spot died apparently childless in the first few years of the eleventh century, but Aelfhelm produced at least three children, two at least of whom were adult by about 995. Another brother apparently produced at least one child, a daughter Ealdgyth, who married Siferth, an influential thegn of the Five Boroughs – the north-east quarter of Mercia. Siferth and his brother Morcar were later sufficiently close associates of the king's eldest son, Athelstan, to be beneficiaries of his will. As one might expect of a great magnate who had been promoted to a major ealdormanry by the king in the 990s, Aelfhelm had a prominent place in the regime and was probably a major figure in circles close to the senior aetheling, who might be expected to succeed Aethelred at his death.

PRINCE ATHELSTAN AND THE SUCCESSION

Prince Athelstan's will is a critical document for our understanding of factional politics in the first decade or so of the eleventh century because it reveals something of the tensions between the senior aetheling and the king, and demonstrates at least some of Athelstan's associations among the aristocracy. It particularly and repeatedly stressed his right to dispose of his own property by reminding the reader that he had purchased much of it from his father or received it as gifts from named individuals. He several times reiterated his concern that King Aethelred should allow his bequests to stand, and even went so far as copying down the verbatim permission received by messenger from his father before witnesses, apparently when he was himself *in extremis*. Even then, he called

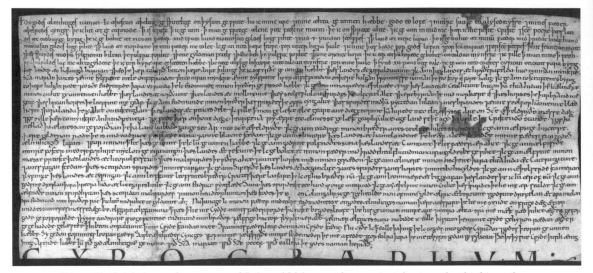

The will of Athelstan, drawn up on 25 June 1014, provides rare insights into the thinking of a core member of the royal family at the height of the dynastic crisis which characterized Aethelred's final years.

on the royal council to hold the king to his word. His anxiety is so pronounced that it seems legitimate to suppose that Athelstan believed that his will was likely to provoke King Aethelred into active opposition to its provisions. Even from beyond the grave, therefore, he sought to constrain his father and embarrass him into allowing its provisions to stand.

What was so controversial about Athelstan's will? Excluding the prince's own household, those named as beneficiaries make interesting reading – Athelstan had been contributing to the income of a certain Aethelwold's widow. Although it is a common name, this may well be the Aethelwold who witnessed Aethelred's diplomas during the period 999–1005, and whose son Aethelmaer was a prominent royal minister until about 1005 but then fell out of the limelight. These two were, therefore, among the victims of Aethelred's purge of the court in about 1005. Others named include Bishop Aelfsige of Winchester, Christchurch, Canterbury, and St Edward's shrine at Shaftesbury – that is, the burial place of Aethelred's murdered half-brother, Edward the Martyr. This last bequest might associate Athelstan with the faction who had placed his half-uncle, Edward – Aethelred's elder half-brother – on the throne in 975, and had since been to an extent excluded from power under his succesor, but Aethelred too seems to have expected some benefits from the promotion of his half-brother's cult so this provision need not have been particularly controversial.

Siferth was mentioned as a prominent associate of the prince, and he is generally identified as the senior thegn of that name in the Five Boroughs. Named too were Athelstan's brothers, Edmund and Eadwig, but of the two it was

Edmund – the nearest in age – who received by far the richer bequests. Godwine son of Wulfnoth – that Sussex 'prince' who had fallen foul of the brother of Eadric Streona in 1009 (see below) – also received an estate, as did several other figures who are not readily identifiable.

Athelstan left a competent heriot to his father but his choice of items is again illuminating. It consisted of a sword given him by Ulfketel – who may be the East-Anglian thegn who fought the Vikings so vigorously in 1004 and again in 1010 and appears as a minister in the witness lists of Athelstan's diplomas between 1002 and 1016; a coat of mail donated him by Morcar, who was probably Siferth's brother; a horse given him by Thurbrand – conceivably Thurbrand the Hold, the prominent landholder and a senior leader in Yorkshire; and a white horse which had come from Leofwine – a common name but just possibly the ealdorman of the Hwicce whose origins were also south-eastern Mercian and who was eventually to emerge from the shadows cast by Earl Eadric and assume political leadership of the western Midlands.

Taken together, these items and their carefully cited derivations just might have been intended to convey a message to King Aethelred, along the lines that he should reconcile himself with these several figures, nominate Edmund as heir and rally the English aristocracy behind a united dynasty to help him see off the Danes. Aethelred was accused of being poorly advised. Athelstan seems here at the point of death to be proffering his own advice in the hope that his father could be persuaded to adopt his agenda, to the advantage of his own friends and his close kin.

This ostensibly disconnected group of noblemen are linked primarily by the unlikely survival of Athelstan's will, but they arguably had much more than this in common. The will itself reads as a document of some political significance. What it reveals is the association of the elder sons of Aethelred by his first marriage with senior, wealthy and influential lay figures within eastern Mercia, East Anglia, perhaps Yorkshire and certainly Sussex. These are figures who had little influence inside Aethelred's regime after about 1006 but who may well have grouped themselves around Athelstan as the senior aetheling in expectation of his eventual succession. In the meantime, the king's eldest son could offer them some protection from the avaricious royal favourite, Eadric Streona, and a regime which had already demonstrated a degree of ruthlessness in ridding itself of potential opponents.

With his own death imminent, Athelstan sought to pass the mantle of succession and the leadership of his associates to his eldest surviving brother, Edmund. Not only was his sibling made his brother's executor but he received the bulk of such of his war gear as was not given to his father, and this included the so-called 'sword of King Offa'. Whether or not this was really an heirloom from the eighth century, it was obviously a famous blade and its descent surely signifies that Athelstan intended that Edmund should lead the English against the Danes. That its putative original owner was a Mercian king whose authority centred on the Trent valley – so from among the hard core of Athelstan's own associates – may also be significant. There can be no doubt that Edmund Ironside understood and accepted this message and undertook that role once his brother was dead, just

Pre-Conquest cross fragments at All Saints' Church, Bakewell, Derbyshire were excavated from the foundations in the mid-nineteenth century. This was the principal church in the Peak during the late Anglo-Saxon period and was, therefore, probably associated with both Prince Athelstan and then his brother Edmund. Part of the nave walls may be pre-Conquest.

as soon as opportunity presented itself. Indeed, the 'Ironside' epithet which rapidly attached to him might even derive from his ownership of the 'sword of King Offa', if that was indeed the blade which he bore into battle against the Danes. Edmund also received his brother's estates in East Anglia and the 'Peak valley' – presumably the valley of the River Derwent and its tributaries beneath the castle of Peveril of the Peak in Derbyshire – so the principal foci at the heart of Athelstan's eastern Mercian affinity. It is in this context that the aetheling's gift to the tomb of his murdered uncle is perhaps significant as a statement of opposition to Aethelred's policy. It might be read as a protest in favour of the right of the eldest son to the succession of his father's throne – therefore the superior right of Athelstan and then Edmund over that of Aethelred's sons by Emma. It offered too a rallying call to those whose families had supported King Edward in 975, the core of whom were East-Anglian and eastern Mercian landholders.

If Athelstan's will reveals deep dissensions between himself and his father, from what did such tensions spring? The obvious cause must be differences of opinion concerning the succession itself. In 1002, Aethelred married for the second time. The name of his eldest son by his new Norman wife appeared as a witness to royal charters in 1005, so this was probably the year of his birth. He was considered old enough to act as an envoy from Normandy to the English in 1014 and his prominence in that capacity has often been taken as a sign that he was by then Aethelred's preferred heir. From 1013 onwards, both Edward and his younger full brother Alfred appear as witnesses, implying that they were on occasion present at court.

Just as Aethelred, the son of a second marriage, had ultimately come to the throne with his father's nomination and despite the prior claim of his elder half-brother, so too may Aethelred have intended that his second family supplant his first, and Emma at least was surely tendering that advice from 1002 onwards. Indeed, it may even have been written into the marriage contract drawn up before Emma arrived in England, but if such existed it does not survive. Unlike Queen Aelfgifu, Emma is likely to have gone through some sort of coronation ceremony, and that could have given her sons some advantage, and also raised expectations on their behalf regarding the succession. If Aethelred viewed the Norman alliance as a significant part of his efforts to exclude the Vikings, he may have had little option but to reserve the crown to Emma's sons.

There is some admittedly non-contemporary evidence that this was indeed Aethelred's intention, and several distinguished historians have already argued along these lines. The *Life of King Edward*, written in or shortly after 1066, claimed that: 'When the royal wife [Emma] of old King Aethelred was pregnant in her womb, all the men of the country took an oath that if a man child should come forth as the fruit of her labour, they would await in him their lord and king who would rule over the whole race of the English.' This is, of course, a text the author of which had good reasons to argue that Edward was preordained to the crown from birth – or even earlier – but the incident referred to may well have occurred. There is, however, no direct comment on this matter from any nearer contemporary, even if circumstantial evidence does tend to support this late testimony.

If there was a serious move afoot in the year of his birth to establish Emma's eldest son as heir to the throne, then the aetheling Athelstan and his brothers had every reason to oppose this aspect at least of Aethelred's policies, and those who had associated themselves too closely with the princes had good reason to fear for their own political futures should Athelstan fail. Given the contents of Athelstan's will, these seem to have included an important Sussex noble family (the Godwine named was the future earl), perhaps an influential Yorkshire thegn, two prominent noblemen from the Five Boroughs and various other eastern Mercian and East-Anglian figures, such as Aelfric at Barton, which may be Barton-upon-Humber in Lindsey. It may also have connected the ealdorman of the Hwicce in south-west Mercia with the prince, but as a benefactor rather than a beneficiary. This does, of course, assume that the identifications suggested above are correct, but several are at least probable and two or three are virtually certain.

There is further evidence of significant changes within the English regime which broadly coincided with Edward's birth, as well as the notorious famine of the year 1005. In 1005–6, a major change occurred in the witnessing of

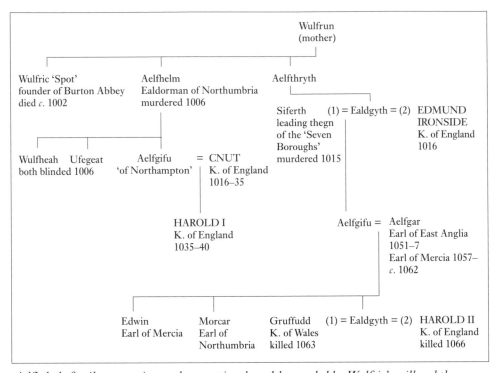

Aelfhelm's family connections – the exceptional wealth revealed by Wulfric's will and the ease with which members of his close kin forged marriage alliances with kings and senior earls underline their political significance in the first half of the eleventh century.

Aethelred's diplomas. Several figures, such as Aethelwold and his son Aethelmaer, disappeared, and only the elder of these two is likely to have died. At the same time, the numerous brothers of Eadric Streona ('the greedy') began to dominate the court. In 1006 King Aethelred deprived one Wulfgeat 'of all his territory'. This was another of his close henchmen of the 990s and the first few years of the new century, whose attestation of royal writs began in or before 986. During the 990s he seems to have been a close associate of Wulfric and Wulfheah, the sons of Ealdorman Aelfhelm, so it is no coincidence that his fall coincided with Aethelred having the ealdorman of Northumbria killed and the same Wulfheah and a second of Aelfhelm's sons blinded. Aelfhelm was connected by marriage to Siferth (who had married his niece) and his brother Morcar, the two thegns of the Five Boroughs mentioned in Athelstan's will. He is not known to have committed any wrong against the king and was apparently arraigned for no crime but rather murdered by Eadric Streona at the king's behest and – unlike Wulfgeat's exile – without due judicial process. One possible motive in the twelve months following Emma's successful delivery of a baby boy might be his closeness to the aetheling Athelstan, but the available evidence only demonstrates his association with those linked to Athelstan several years later. Yet the prominence of his family in the 1013–16 crises certainly suggests that his was a central role within a powerful affinity, which Aethelred had suddenly and quite dramatically ceased to trust and decided to marginalize. Aelfhelm's murder may, therefore, have served notice that Aethelred was serious about his support for the succession of the children of his second marriage, but other factors could, of course, also have been involved – and several have been suggested.

The regime was still eager to prove itself effective against the Vikings and Wessex was under attack in this same year. In the late summer of 1006, therefore, Aethelred called out the forces of all Wessex and Mercia to oppose the Danish raiding-army's ravaging of Berkshire and Hampshire. His armies were, however, defeated at the Kennet – and this was another morale-sapping defeat – but the government had at least showed energy and resolve in addressing the issue. What was worse was that the Danes were left to carry off their booty to well-prepared winter quarters on the Isle of Wight, where English forces were powerless to touch them.

THE CHRISTMAS COUNCIL, 1006

Aethelred took council with that group who had now become his principal henchmen – Eadric and his kinsmen – when he held court in the heartland of their power in distant Shropshire the following Christmas. Apart from the proscriptions earlier that year, it is this solemn midwinter crown-wearing staged in an unprecedented location and presumably with Eadric as host to the royal household that really marks the beginning of Aethelred's plunge into the factional politics in which his regime finally perished. The succession is very likely to have been high on Aethelred's agenda at this meeting, and he presumably already had the unconditional support of Eadric and his kin in this respect. His own prospects for advancement arguably dominated the thinking of Eadric himself, but the king and his councillors also took counsel for the future defence of England against the Danes who were still entrenched beyond the prospect of English attack on the Isle of Wight. The collective wisdom was that the Danes should be bought off and an agreement was made to that effect. In 1007 £30,000 pounds was paid over, which seems to have staved off further attack until late summer 1009. The regime then used the lull in hostilities to build up the English fleet – the Peterborough Chronicle for 1008 recorded that the king ordered that one warship should be supplied from every 310 hides and a helmet and mailcoat from 8 hides. This signifies that a prodigious new effort was to be made to build an effective deterrent which could make winter quarters such as that which Swein had established on the Isle of Wight untenable in future years, and the decision was presumably taken at the Shropshire court that Christmas.

An English fleet did already exist and the obligation to provide seamen was certainly imposed on some at least of England's estates – as in the list of such commitments owed by the Essex estates of St Paul's, London, in the last few years of the tenth century. When Archbishop Aelfric of Canterbury died in 1005, he left King Aethelred 'his best ship and the sailing tackle with it, and sixty helmets and sixty coats of mail' and a further vessel to each of the shires of Kent and Wiltshire. The obligation to provide ships may have been imposed by Edgar – whose fleet was clearly formidable – but it may have existed even earlier; Alfred certainly constructed and deployed a fleet, although we do not know how this was built or organized. What Aethelred was now about, therefore, was not entirely new but it represented a national effort on a different scale to pre-existing provision, designed to produce naval forces superior to those deployed by the Danes and capable of protecting England. Had he succeeded in this ambition, Aethelred could have posed as the saviour of his country and the consequent kudos would in turn have freed him to pursue whatever internal policies he chose as regards his choice of councillors and the succession itself.

At the same Christmas council, Aethelred presumably agreed to promote Eadric Streona – his reward no doubt for doing the dirty deed *vis-à-vis* the king's previously well-regarded servants, Ealdorman Aelfhelm and his sons, whom he had murdered during the previous year. Eadric was actually appointed to the long vacant ealdormanry of the Mercians in 1007. His was to be no localized office – rather, the chroniclers imply that his authority extended across all the Mercians, even as far as the edges of East Anglia where no ealdorman was now officially in office, and over Lindsey and the Five Boroughs, where the core estates of Siferth and Morcar lay. Eadric was nicknamed 'the Greedy', and so perhaps he was, but this Shropshire nobleman was raised up by Aethelred from comparative obscurity to become the premier ealdorman in England to do his own bidding. The period during which he exercised an ever-increasing influence in royal councils began with the birth of Prince Edward to Aethelred's second marriage. It began too with pre-emptive strikes against men who had previously been among the king's most trusted associates. Their joint responsibility for these acts tied Aethelred and Eadric to one another, but these acts alienated many of the king's former supporters from both ealdorman and king. Thereafter, Aethelred invested ever more power and influence in Eadric. In 1012 he became the premier ealdorman, despite his comparatively recent appointment, and he received the notable distinction of marriage to one of Aethelred's daughters. It is quite possible that this was already part of the agenda at the same Shropshire Christmas council meeting, but the marriage is undated.

The man whom Aethelred promoted as the next ealdorman (or earl, since the terms now become interchangeable) of Yorkshire was Uhtred of Bamburgh, who was already ealdorman of Northumbria beyond Yorkshire in succession to his father, Waltheof, and the close associate of the newly established see of Durham and its bishop, whose daughter he had married. Uhtred's defeat of a Scottish invasion at Durham in 1006 was presumably what brought him to the king's attention and the regime must have welcomed an English leader who had established a reputation in war against a foreign attacker. Aethelred had, however, little option but to appoint a figure with northern connections and resources, but one from outside Yorkshire's Anglo-Scandinavian community – where the powerful Thurbrand may already have been linked with the aetheling Athelstan. The promotion of a nobleman from Lindsey or surrounds might also have seemed inappropriate, given Athelstan and Aelfhelm's powerful connections in that

Bamburgh Castle stands on a rocky headland in Northumberland overlooking the North Sea. It was a significant royal site from the sixth century onwards. Following the fall of York to the Vikings, Bamburgh became the stronghold of English rulers of northern Northumbria, who may well have descended from Northumbrian kings. Until the reign of Cnut, England's rulers often recognized them as hereditary ealdormen or earls and several, such as Uhtred, also ruled Yorkshire on behalf of the king.

region. As a military leader unsullied by association with those whom Aethelred now wished to exclude from power, Uhtred uniquely fitted the bill and Aethelred invested heavily in his new lieutenant, giving him an ealdormanry of unprecedented size extending from the Humber to the Scottish border. Uhtred did what he could to establish himself in Yorkshire, marrying the daughter of a wealthy figure at York. It has often been suggested that it was this that brought him into conflict with Thurbrand the Hold, but tensions between the two may have originated also from their very different attitudes towards Ealdorman Aelfhelm in 1006. Uhtred clearly tied his own career to that of Aethelred for the moment at least and seems to have held down the north for him until 1013. At some stage he too married one of Aethelred's daughters, and by that process he also became brother-in-law to Athelstan Aetheling, but it may be more significant that he became son-in-law to Aethelred and brother-in-law to Eadric, and so was tied in to the faction in control of the court. This new appointee to the great northern earldom may well have participated in Aethelred's Shropshire council in 1006.

From 1007, therefore, both Mercia and Northumbria were under single ealdormen, both of whom were new appointees of Aethelred's and both of whom at some stage married his daughters. Both these regional communities contained prominent figures who had reason to oppose both the new ealdormen and the current trend of that royal policy which had brought them to prominence. Since the birth of an heir from Aethelred's second marriage, the succession had once again become a divisive issue which had the potential to alienate Aethelred's existing sons. It was arguably his sensitivity to opposition on the question of the succession which led Aethelred to invest so heavily in Eadric and Uhtred. Yet those who felt themselves threatened by either of these ambitious figures and their efforts to monopolize royal influence naturally gathered around the senior aetheling and he seems to have developed a significant power base among the aristocracy, particularly in the east Midlands.

AETHELRED'S GRAND FLEET

Aethelred's great fleet-building initiative proved highly successful. A prodigious effort made at enormous expense on a national level brought into existence a very large ship force, staffed by well-armed soldiers and ready for the campaigning season of 1009. The results clearly impressed later commentators: 'there were more of them [ships] than there had ever been before in England in the days of any king. And they brought them all together to Sandwich, and should lie there and guard this country against every foreign raiding-army.' The royal navy at anchor on the Stour estuary must have been an impressive sight, which gave all concerned real hope that England had at last been delivered from Viking attack.

In overall command of the fleet was the king himself, accompanied by his close advisors and friends, Eadric and his brothers. The few weeks when they could pose as the commanders of the largest fleet in northern waters represented a brief moment of unalloyed triumph for Eadric and his associates, and they used the opportunity to turn against another of their internal rivals. Aelfhelm and his sons had been liquidated in 1006, but other noble English families retained strong links to Prince Athelstan and arguably opposed the king's policy on the succession. What is more, such men were rich and Eadric's kin might expect to be rewarded for the destruction of the king's enemies within by the grant of some at least of the forfeited estates. They took this opportunity, therefore, to move against the family of Prince Athelstan's only documented associate with substantial estates on the south-east coast. Ealdorman Eadric's brother, Beorhtric, accused 'Prince' Wulfnoth, Godwine's father, to the king. Wulfnoth was clearly a man of considerable local influence. He could not expect unbiased justice from King Aethelred and may have feared the fate already suffered by Ealdorman Aelfhelm. He was not, however, entirely without followers of his own and detached twenty ships from the king's grand fleet. These vessels may well have been the contribution to this mobilization from his own estates – a possibility which emphasizes his prominence in Sussex – and they were probably more competently manned by men from the Sussex coastal havens than many of Aethelred's vessels. Wulfnoth and his squadron was able to get away from the royal fleet at Sandwich and they then ravaged the southern coast – exclusive perhaps of his own Sussex territories and those of his friends. He was pursued by Beorhtric with eighty ships, who 'thought that he would make a great reputation for himself in that he would get Wulfnoth dead or alive', but his vessels were cast ashore by a high wind. Chances are that Beorhtric led the men of his own home shire and his family's estates in the chase, in which case these are likely to have been among the least-experienced men with the fleet – given that Shropshire is landlocked. The greater seacraft of Wulfnoth and his crews enabled them to turn on the pursuit when that got into difficulties, despite the adverse conditions, and fire their ships.

Nothing more is known of this South-Saxon nobleman, but he was presumably thereafter *persona non grata* with Eadric and Aethelred, and may well have departed from England into exile. His son Godwine, the beneficiary of the will of the aetheling Athelstan, was deep in Cnut's councils by 1018, suggesting that he had joined the Danish candidate for the throne promptly during the final succession crisis of 1016, if not before.

When the news of Beorhtric's fiasco reached the remainder of the fleet at Sandwich, morale plummeted. At least 100 ships had been lost to no purpose, in pursuit of factional interests, and the high command was exposed as incompetent even to sail vessels in pursuit of much smaller squadrons which showed no intention of fighting. What could be expected from a fleet of half-trained men led by inexperienced politicians should they confront the Danes *en masse* could be imagined only too easily, and the initiative lost all credibility. The king withdrew and he was followed by Eadric and the other councillors, and the crews took their vessels back to London.

The entire episode underlined the contrasting strengths and weaknesses of Aethelred's government. It was capable of the enormous feats of organization and management needed to bring a fleet such as this into existence, to arm and armour its soldiery and presumably also to supply them with provisions for the campaigning season – or at least command that others should provide for them. The mobilization of the fleet was itself an impressive achievement, and it seems, while at Sandwich, to have had some deterrent effect. However, Aethelred's government was pursuing policies in other areas which were unpopular and dangerously factional, and the king had placed his trust in a small clique of courtiers to the exclusion of other lay nobles. It was a political necessity to retain command of the fleet within that clique despite its apparent lack of military – and particularly naval – experience or expertise. Furthermore, it proved too tempting a proposition to exploit this great military command to pursue factional interests. Many ships built by inland communities were presumably crewed by amateur sailors. Beorhtric's incompetence contrasts with the ability of Wulfnoth and his sailors to exploit adverse weather conditions to their own advantage, and many among the shipmen at Sandwich must have recognized that the fleet would have stood a better chance under the leadership of such men.

Faction, therefore, undermined Aethelred's undoubted achievement in bringing his great fleet into existence. The prospect of security from

Scandinavian attack which it had briefly offered in 1009 proved an illusion, laid bare by an inexperienced high command more intent on factional politics than England's defence against the Vikings. For the future, Aethelred would have to proceed without the kudos which might have attached to himself and his friends had his naval forces indeed served to shield England from the Danes. The cost to both government and country of attacking another of the noble families who had ranged themselves with Athelstan Aetheling was to prove extremely high.

Thorkell's great raiding army arrived in August and overran much of south-east England over the next few months. Although the chroniclers do not expressly record the fact, the timing suggests that the Danish commander had viewed Aethelred's naval forces at Sandwich with considerable respect and delayed his appearance until the English ships had withdrawn. The forces with which he then struck at England were considered unusually large, and had presumably been built up in the knowledge of Aethelred's own massive preparations and in expectation of a trial of strength. Thorkell had only narrowly avoided being confronted by impressive English defences and he set about undermining the ability of Aethelred's regime to organize anything comparable for the future, with unprecedented ferocity. His aim was the extraction of booty and geld and he pursued these objective with ruthless efficiency.

Thorkell's policy seems to have been to exploit the dissolution of Aethelred's forces by attacking and overwhelming the English defences severally in one locality after another, in circumstances where the numerical advantage was his. He began in east Kent – in the immediate hinterland of Sandwich itself – then struck at the Isle of Wight, Sussex, Hampshire and Berkshire. Aethelred called out forces against him and is even reported on one occasion to have successfully interposed his own army between the Danes and their ships but no battle occurred. The chroniclers blamed Eadric, and it may well be that he and his brothers had reason to fear that engaging with the Danes was too great a risk lest defeat should undermine their hold on the regime. From Eadric's perspective, political tensions within England always seem to have taken precedence over the Danish threat in his own assessment of what the government should and should not attempt.

Thorkell therefore escaped from this potentially dangerous encounter and in November retreated to winter quarters on the Thames estuary, where the Danes supplied themselves from Essex, Kent and their environs, and whence they launched several unsuccessful winter attacks on London. In late winter they marched through the Chilterns into Oxfordshire, burnt Oxford and ravaged the Thames valley before returning to their ships in Kent, via crossings of the Thames at Staines to avoid an English army gathering against them at London.

After Easter 1010 the Danes raided East Anglia, where the men of Cambridgeshire – the very core of what had been Ealdorman Aethelwine's affinity – took the field against them apparently under Ulfketel's leadership, but lost a heavily contested field and suffered significant casualties. Among the dead was one Athelstan, whom the chronicler described as 'the king's son-in-law', but who was probably related to him through his first wife, Ealdorman Thored's

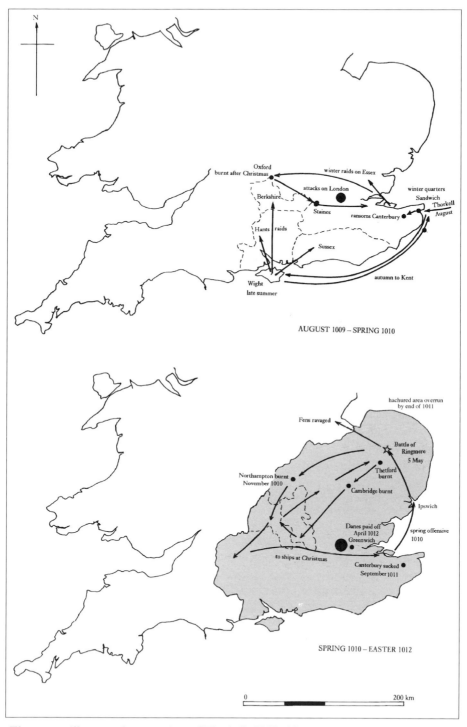

These maps illustrate the campaigns of Thorkell, 1009–11.

daughter; Oswy, the son-in-law of that Ealdorman Byrhtnoth who had been slain at Maldon, and his son; Eadwig, described as Aefic's brother, and this Aefic is arguably the royal high-reeve killed by Ealdorman Leofsige of Essex in 1002; lastly Wulfric, described as Leofwine's son. This Wulfric cannot be identified with any precision but it may be that he was the son of that Leofwine the Red who received land by grant from Godwine in Kent in 1013–18, and perhaps even the owner of the seal bearing the name Wulfric from this era found at Sittingbourne. It is, however, a common name, and neither of these individuals need be apposite.

The death-roll was clearly a distinguished one, and it looks very much as though the Danes had been withstood by the soldiery of a powerful faction. Among them were several figures with connections to the crown earlier in the reign but currently without much influence with the king, and their determination to stand up to the Danes could be interpreted as a serious challenge to Eadric and his faction, who now dominated the court but had shown little ability to protect the land. There are several possible links between this group and the sons of Aethelred's first marriage, and the candidacy of Prince Athelstan for the succession is likely to have benefited from their resolution. The effect was far less than it might have been had they been victorious, however, in which case Aethelred would arguably have come under considerable pressure to dismiss his current courtiers – displacing Eadric and his clique from their near monopoly of royal favour and restoring the succession to Athelstan.

With the Battle of Ringmere won and lost, East Anglia lay at the mercy of the Danes and they ravaged widely, burning Thetford and Cambridge and wasting even the fenlands before moving on to Oxfordshire once more, then Bedford and Tempsford. The affinity which had withstood them may have gained something by its defiance but it lost senior figures and failed to achieve the victory which might have returned it to power and influence. Danish success left the court under the influence of Eadric Streona and Aethelred's policies regarding the succession unchanged.

Thorkell's campaigns of 1009–10 exposed the inability of Aethelred's regime to protect England, but the chroniclers emphasized not just the efficiency of the Danish operations but more particularly the reluctance of Aethelred's main forces to confront the Vikings: '. . . when they [the enemy] were in the east, then the army was kept in the west: and when they were in the south, then our army was in the north'. This is not a charge of incompetence so much as criticism of a regime which was pursuing objectives which differed from those of the chroniclers, who believed that English armies should have sought out and defeated Scandinavian ones. Aethelred and Eadric are represented as raising armies and yet consistently avoiding battle, and this appears to be a deliberate tactic which may even imply that they believed that a frontal assault on the Danes was not in their own best interests.

In the end, of course, the failure to provide an effective field army doomed the English defences and the entire system of regional defence broke down: 'there was no head man who wanted to gather an army, but each fled as best as he could; nor even in the end would one shire help another'. By the end of 1010, the Danish

St Martin's at Canterbury is the most substantial survivor of the town's churches from the pre-Conquest period. In popular literature this font is often associated with the baptism of King Aethelberht. In fact, it is an interesting amalgam of Anglo-Saxon and Norman styles and is, unusually, made up of at least twenty different pieces of stone.

force was able to march and ravage pretty much at will, but Aethelred's behaviour seems to have been conditioned by other factors than the simple matter of Danish attacks.

In 1011, Aethelred and his councillors asked the raiding army for peace in return for tax and provisions. The author of the Peterborough manuscript of the chronicle castigated the king and his advisors not for their choice of policy but its timing, which was considered unreasonably late. Had Aethelred followed this course before, much damage might have been pre-empted, but the Danes nonetheless took Canterbury by treachery. The man held responsible was one Aelfmaer, whom this author remarked that Archbishop Aelfheah had earlier saved, but it is unclear whether he should be identified with the Abbot Aelfmaer of St Augustine's – whom alone of their numerous valuable ecclesiastical captives the Vikings quickly freed, apparently without ransom. If so, this treachery was the act of a senior cleric. The details are, of course, beyond reconstruction, but it should be remembered that other men had already been driven into exile – and perhaps even into the arms of the Danes – by Eadric and his friends, and there is an outside chance that this figure was connected in some way with, perhaps, Prince Wulfnoth, or other figures openly hostile to the governing clique. Prince Athelstan was himself to include a Canterbury church among the beneficiaries of his will.

The new geld was raised over the winter 1011–12 and a full meeting of the royal council at London occurred before and during Easter, which then paid £8,000 to the Danish army encamped at Greenwich. Archbishop Aelfheah had not permitted his tenants to ransom his person and he was now slain by drunken Viking soldiers during the course of what seems to have been a ceremonial feast, organized perhaps to mark the success of their campaigning and to divide the spoils. Whatever the precise context, the archbishop was certainly killed and the bulk of the great host split up and dispersed thereafter, while Thorkell himself with a substantial force reputed to have consisted of forty-five ships took service with King Aethelred.

At this point, Aethelred and Eadric must have felt that they had weathered the storm of Danish attacks, and that the tactics they had used – of raising forces but avoiding battle, then paying the Vikings to disperse – had been the correct ones. Their domestic critics had tried a more direct approach at Ringmere but had been defeated. The withdrawal of most of the Danes left the existing regime in control and its policies intact, and Thorkell's entry to Aethelred's service with a sizeable fleet offered the best chance for freedom from external attack since the failure of the great armada in 1009. Furthermore, it freed the regime from its previous dependence on a broad spread of English political and military support and provided a powerful weapon which could be used as easily against domestic opponents as external enemies. The ending of the Danish war therefore left the English government in a stronger position *vis-à-vis* its own aristocracy than at any stage previously – since that is Aethelred sanctioned the murder of one of his most senior lieutenants in 1006 and placed his faith in Eadric Streona. It must be significant that it was in 1012 that Eadric at last displaced the longer serving ealdormen, Aelfric and Leofwine, to top the lists of signatures to Aethelred's diplomas. As Simon Keynes remarked, Eadric effected a considerable coup thereby, but this should be seen only as the culmination of a longer political process pursued jointly by the king and his favourite ealdorman ever since 1006. What now enabled the king and his favourite to push this far was the backing of their own Danish army under the leadership of the most famous commander of the day. Once more Aethelred was in control of events and his domestic opponents had good reason to fear a relapse into tyranny backed up by Viking warriors.

ATHELSTAN'S DEATH AND THE GAINSBOROUGH ACCORD

When precisely Prince Athelstan died is of critical importance to the reconstruction of the politics of these years. Mention of Bishop Aelfsige in his will provides a *terminus post quem* of 1012–13, and the event must have already occurred before the deaths of Siferth and Morcar and Edmund Ironside's promotion of himself as a candidate for the succession, all of which occurred in the summer of 1015. The date can, however, be established with an unusual degree of precision from Athelstan's receipt of a message from his father 'on Friday after midsummer's massday' (24 June, the feast of St John the Baptist), which requires that the will was written in 1014, when that Friday fell on 25 June, because that was the obit kept at both Christchurch, Canterbury and Winchester and Athelstan cannot have died before receipt of his father's message. By that reasoning, Athelstan died on the very day that he received his father's permission to leave his estates and possessions as he saw fit, and also, of course, on the day that the final paragraphs of his will were written.

The prince attested his last surviving royal diploma in 1013, which is a royal grant of land at Twywell (in Northamptonshire), to a certain Northman. Since that grant was also witnessed by Earl Uhtred, it necessarily occurred before his submission to King Swein at Gainsborough in the late summer of the same year. Prince Athelstan does not attest any document produced after Aethelred's return from exile in Normandy in the spring of 1014, and in particular a grant to Sherborne Abbey which was witnessed by Edmund, Eadwig, Edward and Alfred. Unfortunately that cannot be more tightly dated, but it may well be that it post-dates 25 June. None of the aethelings witnessed a diploma of the same year to Ealdorman Leofwine of the Hwicce, so Athelstan's omission need not be significant.

That Athelstan died in June 1014 is, therefore, virtually certain. What is noteworthy, however, is his insistence on leaving bequests to senior members of the aristocracy of the Five Boroughs and Lindsey who were necessarily prominent among the English faction who supported Swein at Gainsborough in the summer of 1013. Siferth and Morcar were still supporting the Danish army even after Easter 1014 and their territories were ravaged by the king and his English forces during the same summer in which Athelstan died. That Prince Athelstan should at this point have bequeathed them items from his estate is a potent indication of very different agendas being pursued by the prince and his father.

Prince Athelstan had, therefore, retained strong links with various regionally powerful kindreds whom Aethelred elected to exclude from central government from 1006 onwards. In particular, he was associated with the family and associates of the murdered Aelfhelm in the north-east Midlands and the associates of the Half-king's family in East Anglia and the south-east Midlands, and thus ranged himself in opposition to Eadric Streona and his ambitions in eastern Mercia and East Anglia. Behind Eadric stood Aethelred and his ambitions concerning the succession. The uneasy balance of power between these two groups tilted towards the court when Aethelred hired Thorkell the Tall and forty-five ship crews in the early summer of 1012. The king's critics already had experience of Thorkell's army in battle and were faced by the possibility that Eadric and Aethelred might now use their Danish forces against their internal enemies for their own profit. The fates of Ealdorman Aelfhelm and his kin and then Prince Wulfnoth provided Eadric's enemies with plentiful reason to fear both for their lives and their lands.

Northman's grant of Twywell in 1013 (discussed above) was also the first surviving diploma to have been witnessed by both Aethelred's sons by Queen Emma, following periods in 1008–9 and 1011–12 when Edward's name does not appear on several charters witnessed by his elder half-brethren. With the court back in confident mood in the summer of 1012, Eadric acknowledged as premier earl and the regime backed by Thorkell and his soldiers, both Edward and his brother were brought to court and Aethelred was in a position to pursue his own policies regarding the succession.

It was the alliance of Aethelred, Eadric 'the Greedy' and Thorkell which had the capacity to throw Prince Athelstan and his associates into the arms of Swein and his Danish forces – and that is what seems to have occurred. The Anglo-Danish accommodation which might be termed the Gainsborough Accord took place after midsummer, but before August, in 1013. The smoothness of the entire operation requires that it was very carefully planned and fully orchestrated, and the preparations presumably occurred over the previous twelve months. Swein was apparently in Denmark, so the necessary discussions occurred over very long lines of communication, and the need to await Danish mobilization meant that nothing could be openly achieved before 1013. The result was the abandonment of Aethelred by a substantial coterie of the English elite, who were capable of speaking for entire regional communities, as soon as Swein and his fleet arrived on the English coast at Sandwich.

The critical question which is beyond resolution must be just whom was this alliance of Danes and English regions planning to place on the throne? In Athelstan, the English leaders had the obvious candidate to set up against Aethelred, Eadric and Thorkell but for some reason his claims were ignored and they threw their weight instead behind Swein and a dynastic revolution. Perhaps Athelstan's fatal illness had already begun in 1013, providing Swein with an opportunity to seize the kingship. Perhaps the prince had second thoughts concerning open rebellion against his father, leaving his supporters hopelessly compromised and ready to support Swein. We cannot know, but it is reasonable to say that the Gainsborough Accord was struck between a group of regional rulers of whom the prince had previously been the unofficial leader and a Danish war-lord who had no other claim but military might to the English throne.

The accord was sealed by a marriage alliance. Ealdorman Aelfhelm's only known daughter was Aelfgifu of Northampton and she became Cnut's first wife, so Swein's daughter-in-law. Although the inception of their relationship is undated, it arguably occurred in 1013–14 when Cnut was stationed with his father's fleet in the Mercian Danelaw. Indeed, his youth would seem to exclude a date much earlier than this. Aelfgifu brought him considerable influence in central and eastern Mercia, and a claim to the leadership of a powerful affinity which had been alienated from Aethelred for almost a decade, as well as the duty to pursue a blood feud against Eadric Streona.

The Gainsborough Accord worked well for both parties in the short term. Athelstan's associates now recognized Swein as king and gave him their full support, provisioned his forces and found horses to mount his ship men. In return, Swein protected them and their lands from Eadric and Thorkell and threw the court back on to the defensive. Swein, on the other hand, was enabled to treat the east of Mercia as a secure base from which to conquer England. He crossed Watling Street and forced Eadric's Oxfordshire to submit, then passed over the Thames and reduced Winchester and central Wessex. His forces were then badly affected by losses due to drowning when they tried to cross the Thames and Aethelred and Thorkell held London against him, but the Danish king disentangled his army and retired to Bath, where Aethelmaer – the son of Ealdorman Aethelweard of western Wessex – submitted to him, apparently without any hostile act on the part of the Danes. It seems probable that Aethelmaer was as disillusioned with Aethelred and Eadric as some of those joining Swein at Gainsborough, and it may be significant that his family owed their earlier promotion to Edward the Martyr, not Aethelred, who had latterly perhaps marginalized them and denied Aethelmaer himself the status of ealdorman. Both he and the king's uncle, Ordulf, retired from active politics into their own monasteries – Aethelmaer into Eynsham – in about 1005, a date which coincides with the emergence of Eadric to prominence. That Aethelmaer was still considered an appropriate figure to lead the West-Saxon submission some eight years later emphasizes his continuing political weight and it seems likely that his retirement from affairs of state had not been entirely voluntary. His kinship with the royal house now brought Swein's party the acquiescence of a very senior figure, and must have helped to legitimize his attempt on the crown. Aethelmaer could presumably have fought the Danes. That he chose not to says much about the isolation of Aethelred's court by this date, and the unpopularity of the policies which the king had sanctioned.

No mention occurs of Eadric, who was presumably with the king and Thorkell at London, but every other senior layman and region had submitted by the end of the campaigning season and the Londoners felt obliged to follow suit. Emma and her children were conveyed by Bishop Aelfhun of London to Normandy, and Aethelred eventually followed them there.

Perhaps the biggest conundrum lies in the location and attitude of Athelstan and his brothers in this crisis. There is no record of their leaving England but it is far from clear that they would have been content to allow Swein to take over their patrimony unfought.

SWEIN'S DEATH AND THE REVIVAL OF AETHELRED'S REGIME

By Christmas 1013, therefore, all England had accepted Swein as king and an improbable dynastic revolution had taken place. The leaderships of East Anglia, eastern Mercia and Northumbria had submitted their own accord at Gainsborough in July. The remainder had then been forced to acquiesce with more or less violence, or at least a show of force, and had given hostages, but not a single battle had occurred. Eadric Streona's opponents in eastern Mercia and East Anglia could congratulate themselves on having responded effectively to Aethelred's hiring of a Danish army by doing the same, although they had discovered that alliance with the Dane involved more than they had perhaps bargained for. Swein had then fulfilled his side of the bargain by effectively destroying the influence of Eadric and driving Aethelred overseas. The relationship had probably already been cemented by Cnut's marriage to Aelfgifu of Northampton, the daughter of the murdered Ealdorman Aelfhelm and cousin by marriage to Morcar and Siferth, so they could expect to prosper under the Danish kingship which they had helped to bring about. Edmund Ironside and his brothers excepted, those who were to be the beneficiaries of Prince Athelstan's will had reason to congratulate themselves for their political adeptness as they feasted over Christmas in 1013, with a dynastic revolution of extraordinary suddenness successfully negotiated.

All this was, however, undermined by Swein's death, apparently at or near Gainsborough, where he had retired to spend the winter with his fleet on the Trent. The Danish king died on 2 February 1014. This was a severe, and probably also an unexpected, blow which lost his supporters the initiative and their fragile cohesion, and threw the entire issue of tenure of the crown, and of course the succession, back into the melting pot. Those who were not too deeply committed to the Danes began to swing back towards Aethelred, whom significant groups had of course only abandoned in 1013 under pressure from Swein's forces, and who had probably been the focus of many guilty consciences over the winter months. The Danish succession was itself unclear, since Swein had left two sons and there was no certainty that the one who was present – Cnut – would be able even to establish himself as an effective leader, despite the acclamation of Swein's troops. He had no significant military reputation, so his capabilities as a general were untried.

Amid the confusion brought about by Swein's death, many reconsidered their hasty repudiation of Aethelred during 1013. The legitimacy of his kingship could not be doubted and Swein's sudden death can only have reinforced perceptions of his candidacy as something which was illegitimate. What is more, Aethelred still seems to have had the support of Thorkell and some sort of fleet, so his military resources were far from inconsequential. Aethelred was, therefore, brought back from Normandy by the collective will of the bulk of the English political classes. He was required to mend his ways and 'govern more justly than he did before'. This feeling was surely aimed at the sort of atrocities and injustices which Eadric had carried out on his behalf in 1006, but there were few sanctions available to them should the old king resume his unpopular practices and restore Eadric to his side to assist him. Edward, the eldest son of Aethelred and Emma, travelled to England with the old king's messengers, and his prominent role is likely to have been interpreted by all sides as confirmation that he was Aethelred's own nominee as heir to the throne. The king promised that he would 'be a gracious lord to them, and would improve each of the things which they all hated, and each of those things that were done or declared against him should be forgiven, on condition that they all resolutely and without treachery turned to him'. Their final concord also declared 'every Danish king outlawed from England for ever', and this underlines just how severe a shock widespread English support for Swein's candidacy in 1013 had dealt the royal court.

While all the rest of England rushed back to make their peace with Aethelred's camp, the leaders of Lindsey and the Danish fleet backed Swein's son Cnut and promised to take the field with him. Some of the more prominent of Prince Athelstan's associates therefore recognized the danger posed to themselves by the revival of Aethelred's regime and preferred to stand by the untried and youthful successor of Swein than trust the king who had destroyed Aelfhelm. They agreed to supply Cnut with horses – as they had his father – and to join him in a raid on Aethelred's England after Easter. There is no reason to think that Athelstan was present there, since he died in Wessex, but his interests were clearly once more at issue. Cnut was, therefore, being expected to provide the same sort of military protection to a specific regional community as had his father in the previous year, but they were too leisurely in their preparations and lost the initiative to superior English forces led by the king himself, which advanced on the region. Cnut was forced to depart by sea, bearing with him the hostages whom so many English nobles had given his father the previous year, and he avenged himself on them and their kin by mutilating them before putting them ashore at Sandwich. The Danish fleet left Lindsey to be overwhelmed by English forces, among whom several prominent figures, including the king himself, had cause to seek vengeance on the hard core of Swein's supporters.

That Siferth and Morcar were the principal leaders of Lindsey in 1014 seems certain from consideration of their fate at the great assembly at Oxford in 1015, concerning which they were described as 'the foremost thegns in the Seven Boroughs' – Eadric organized their deaths – and the description of these as 'dishonourable' implies that he did it with undue savagery, then denied them decent burial; the king seized their property and ordered Siferth's widow, who was Ealdorman Aelfhelm's niece, to be secured and placed in a West-Saxon monastery. The principal events occurred at Oxford, the scene of much Danish damage in 1013 and thus a place where English attitudes towards those siding with Swein is likely to have been particularly inflamed. It was also, of course, a town dominated by Eadric.

Eadric and Aethelred therefore took advantage of their adversaries' political embarrassment when Swein died to move against them, and they did this with their customary ferocity and lack of judicial process despite Aethelred's promises to the English nobility concerning good government. In 1014, Siferth and Morcar went the way of Aelfhelm in 1006, having contrived to avoid precisely this fate by swinging their political support behind Swein in 1013. The backing of Athelstan's associates for the Danish king at that stage looks to have been a panic measure brought about by their sudden exposure to the inimicable power of the same Eadric and King Aethelred. Before this the prince's favour had protected them from the fate of Aelfhelm and his sons.

There is a circularity, therefore, to the entire conflict, which implies that the ostensibly unpatriotic behaviour of certain sections of the English elite was largely a consequence of Aethelred's willingness to sanction brutal and extra-legal means by which to rid himself of those whom he considered opponents of his own policies. Wulfnoth's treatment in 1009 was a case in point. A central issue appears to have been the succession to Aethelred's crown, and the primary conflict seems to have been within the English royal dynasty itself, with King Aethelred heading a government which was intent on placing his eldest son by Emma on the throne as his heir. That those who feared Eadric's greed should seek the protection of Prince Athelstan was entirely natural at a time when Aethelred had lost credibility as an impartial judge in any matter relating to his favourite ealdorman. Thorkell's employment by the court in 1012 necessitated that those who feared the king's anger likewise seek Danish protection and opened the door to recognition of Swein as king.

EDMUND AETHELING AND EALDORMAN EADRIC

In many respects it was Athelstan's brothers who lost most in the conflicts of 1013–14. Whereas Athelstan seems to have used his own will to attempt to wrest the support of his various friends back from the Danes to the advantage of Prince Edmund, the men of Lindsey panicked and supported Cnut. The ravaging of Lindsey and the murders of Siferth and Morcar in 1015 reduced the effectiveness of that affinity and made Edmund's task the more difficult, but he took up his brother's legacy with a forthrightness which Athelstan is never known to have shown and sought long and hard to regain the leadership of his brother's affinity from his Danish rival.

In 1015, Edmund seized Siferth's widow from her incarceration in the monastery of Malmesbury – and he did so expressly against the King's will – then travelled north in late August or early September and secured the property and lands of both Siferth and Morcar, and the leadership of the men of the Five Boroughs. By so doing, Edmund claimed for himself the focal role within that affinity which Aelfhelm, then Athelstan and then Siferth and Morcar had led and he presumably purposed to take over their retinues and associations and use this as a base from which to pursue his own ambition to be the next king of the English. He necessarily did so in defiance of Ealdorman Eadric as well as his father. He also did so in defiance of Cnut, who had already married a prominent noblewoman from within this political grouping – Aelfgifu, Aelfhelm's daughter – and so sought to tie it into his father's and then his own ambitions to be king of the English. Edmund's prompt action effectively destroyed any hopes which Cnut may have entertained of immediately resuming the support of a powerful affinity in England upon his return but it also constituted rebellion against his own father, Aethelred, and this makes it the more likely that his brother Athelstan had been deeply implicated in the negotiations leading up to the Gainsborough Accord of 1013.

Edmund probably considered that King Aethelred was at this point on his deathbed, and his commands of no real account. The Chronicle reports that he lay sick at Cosham (now a suburb of Portsmouth) in the summer of 1015, while Edmund was securing Lindsey. Cnut returned to Sandwich. It was from there that his father had sailed for Gainsborough in 1013, but Cnut presumably learnt of recent events there and instead sailed the familiar coastal waters westwards to the mouth of the Frome in Dorset, and raided that shire, Wiltshire and Somerset. Without the committed support of a powerful affinity within England for his candidacy for the throne, the Danish leader was once more merely an outsider ravaging part of England, whom the English treated as a Viking.

With thoughts of opposing Cnut, both Edmund and Eadric Streona raised armies but failed to find a solution to their differences. The Chronicle placed the responsibility for this impasse on Eadric, who it claimed 'wished to betray the aetheling', but it must be recalled that this account is likely to have originated at Ramsey, a house which was East Anglian to its roots and as hostile to Eadric as it had previously been to Ealdorman Aelfhere. Edmund was in active revolt against his own father and Eadric could as well be interpreted as a loyal minister of the king. Eadric, however, seems at this point to have despaired of his lord's recovery, and of Prince Edward's prospects as heir, and he can have had few illusions concerning his own future prospects in the event of Edmund's succession – he took forty of the king's ships and submitted to Cnut rather than await the prospect of Edmund succeeding as king. It is not surprising that the West Saxons followed the example of Aethelred's principal ealdorman and minister, whose behaviour effectively proclaimed Cnut as Aethelred's preferred heir at this juncture.

In 1015, therefore, a new train of events led another prominent English faction leader to throw in his lot with the Danes rather than risk losing everything in the event of the succession of a man whose path to the throne he had hitherto been instrumental in blocking at the behest of the king. Again, it was irreconcilable divisions within the royal family which provided a Danish candidate with an opportunity to secure the English throne for himself. From Cnut's viewpoint, it mattered little whether he had the support of Eadric's opponents or Eadric himself, since either was capable of providing him with a substantial base within England and a degree of legitimacy. One should remember in this context that Eadric was married to one of Aethelred's daughters and was the old king's most trusted lieutenant. Furthermore, the forty ships with which he joined Cnut – which were arguably crewed by his own men – were probably sufficient to tilt the balance of military advantage, and certainly sufficient to ensure that Eadric found a warm welcome. Cnut was himself credited with the complements of 160 vessels, so this addition amounted to a quarter of his own force.

The stage, therefore, seemed set at this point for a straight fight between the two principal faction-leaders inside the English royal family. Eadric, previously Aethelred's principal courtier and son-in-law, had thrown his weight behind Cnut, while Aethelred's eldest surviving son, Edmund, was promoting himself as his father's heir. The necessity of fighting for the throne squeezed out the claims of Prince Edward, despite his father's preference. The West Saxons had submitted to Cnut, in part perhaps from confusion at the stance adopted by Eadric. Edmund had resurrected the affinity which had previously supported his elder brother, and had successfully prised that group away from Swein and Cnut, to whom they had looked for military protection in the previous year. Edmund could also pose as the legitimate heir, the eldest surviving son of the only king that anyone in 1015 was likely to remember and a *bona fide* member of the house of Cerdic, and that must have given him the advantage. Neither side had a leader with a significant military reputation, at least so long as Thorkell remained on the sidelines in Aethelred's pay and loyal only to his pay-master.

Aethelred did not, however, die in the late summer of 1015 but seemed to recover. The issue of the succession lost, therefore, something of the urgency which had characterized it while Aethelred lay on his sickbed, and both sides found themselves having to accommodate the prospect of a new period of unpredictable duration with Aethelred still at the helm. Having already committed himself to the Danish camp, Eadric seems to have had little option but to march with Cnut in the winter of 1015–16, when he invaded Mercia, and their combined forces ravaged Warwickshire, of which, as ealdorman, Eadric himself had formerly been the protector. Edmund raised a force, apparently intending to pose as England's protector and evict the Danes, but his authority was undermined by his father's unexpected recovery. His soldiers demanded the king's presence and that of the London garrison. Edmund's actions in contradiction of his father's orders in 1014, and Eadric's presence on the opposing side, arguably made the English thegnage suspicious that the aetheling was leading them in defiance of the king, and respect for his office – if not for his person – clearly remained very high. Nothing was achieved, therefore, and Edmund was forced to abandon the enterprise and went north to join Uhtred of Northumbria.

Earl Uhtred had his own viewpoint on these events, which was probably both fundamentally northern and self-serving. He had joined in the Gainsborough Accord and submitted to Swein in 1013 but is unlikely to have been the originator of this plan, which served the interests of leading Yorkshiremen such as Thurbrand at least as well. It did, however, enable him to challenge Eadric's greater influence at court, and there are some signs that he was jealous of the premier ealdorman who had been promoted above himself in 1012. Uhtred was of far more distinguished lineage than Eadric and he too was son-in-law to Aethelred. The earl was also probably wily enough to calculate that Swein would succeed in 1013, in which case his interests would be best served by joining the winning side at an early stage. If that was his view, he was proved correct, but not for long. When the Danish king died in the following February, Uhtred joined the many who returned to their allegiance to Aethelred, presumably again sensible of the likely outcome and relying on his kinship by marriage and prompt reactions to forestall any unpleasant consequences of his earlier treachery. His actions in 1013 had, however, surely lost him Aethelred's confidence, and the old king's sickness can only have encouraged him to look to his own future prospects. Several factors are likely to have encouraged Uhtred to now support Edmund as the next king: firstly, they were brothers-in-law by virtue of his marriage to Ethelred's daughter, Aelfgifu; secondly, his abandonment of Cnut in February 1014 meant that he was unlikely to retain his northern office, or indeed his life, should the Danish candidate succeed to the throne; thirdly, his own support for Edmund had some potential to neutralize the influence of such figures as Thurbrand the Hold and the survivors of Aelfhelm's affinity, whose association with Edmund's brother Athelstan had perhaps previously sustained his position in Yorkshire where he was a potential rival to Uhtred; fourthly, Eadric's involvement with Cnut at this point provided a legitimate opportunity to attack him. Uhtred, therefore, seems at this stage to have concluded that his interests were better served by supporting the emerging heir rather than either the declining king or that king's erstwhile chief minister. The earl threw his forces into the balance behind Edmund, therefore, but their army did not march south to confront Cnut, but instead travelled only as far as the heartland of Eadric's power in the north-west Midlands and they ravaged that region during the remainder of the winter of 1015–16. This campaign arguably reflects their shared hatred of Eadric Streona and seems to have been intended to destroy his regional power base.

Cnut's response was to strike at the lands of those who had joined his father in 1013 but who had now apparently regrouped around Edmund Ironside: he 'turned himself then out through Buckinghamshire into Bedfordshire, and from there to Huntingdonshire, along the fen to Stamford, and then into Lincolnshire, from there to Nottinghamshire, and so to Northumbria towards York'. This rapid progress in strength drew Uhtred back to the north but with insufficient forces he could do no more than submit and give hostages, and Cnut now took his revenge for the earl's abandonment of his cause in the spring of 1014 by allowing Thurbrand to murder Uhtred while under his own protection. Eadric, too, arguably welcomed his death and one version of the Chronicle claims that it occurred at his suggestion, but Cnut would have needed to have been improbably obtuse not to have come to this conclusion himself.

Edmund seems to have remained in the north-west Midlands to this point, but he had to retreat when Cnut turned back to the west of Mercia, having secured Yorkshire and the eastern strip of the Midlands. Edmund fell back on London and his ailing father, but Aethelred died there on St George's Day, 23 April 1016. It may well have been the imminence of his father's death that drew Edmund there, and he obviously had much to gain from oversight of his father's councillors as they considered the question of the succession and Aethelred's views. His presence, the fact of Danish invasion and Eadric's defection to Cnut all militated against the elevation of a minor to the English throne, and Edmund at last succeeded with the approval of his father's councillors, the London garrison and perhaps even Queen Emma, although there are later stories of her willingness to betray her stepsons in pursuit of an advantageous settlement for herself from Cnut.

At last, the war issue was focusing on a straight fight between a Danish and an English candidate for the throne. Cnut could claim that his father had been acknowledged as king before him by the vast majority of the English political classes, and legitimize his own claim thereby. The greater legitimacy was, however, obviously that of Edmund's claim. His descent from Cerdic via his grandfather King Edgar and father Aethelred was direct, and his father's own witan had recognized his kingship, although whether or not Aethelred finally nominated his eldest surviving son is unclear. Both had support within England, but Edmund could now appeal to the loyalty of the core constituency of any English king of the age – the West Saxons, and that is precisely what he did. The new king left London to stand siege and rode west into the heartland of his ancestors' realm. Cnut saw his danger and dispatched ships to Dorset which arrived quickly enough to hinder Edmund's mobilization, but they were defeated at Penselwood (near Gillingham) and then Sherston (near Marlborough) and Edmund succeeded in raising an army sufficient to temporarily relieve London, until part of his forces were lost by drowning in Essex. He did, however, eventually free London and the Danes took refuge in what look like prepared positions, back in eastern Kent, where Thorkell's great army had overwintered in 1009–10.

Up to this point, Eadric Streona had worked with Cnut for Edmund's downfall but he seems now to have despaired of Danish success. Should Cnut be finally expelled from England – as surely now looked likely – Eadric also risked being forced into exile. He and his west-Mercian followers therefore negotiated their

London's city walls in the eleventh century were based on Roman originals and were of a size which made this the most important single defensive site in the kingdom. Roman and Anglo-Saxon work can still be identified beneath the later medieval walls, which form the bulk of what is now above ground.

own settlement with Edmund at Aylesford as he advanced on the Danes. Cnut's response was to raid towards Mercia, presumably to avenge himself on the disloyal ealdorman, but he was overtaken by the full English army at Ashingdon in Essex, and the decisive battle of the campaign occurred there. English defeat is blamed by the chroniclers on Eadric, who supposedly started the flight of the English army and well he might – Aethelred's closest associate had nothing to gain from the victory of either party, since both leaders now had good reason to avenge themselves upon him. Only the deaths of both Cnut and Edmund had the power to free him, and in that circumstance he could reasonably hope to broker the succession of a more grateful and less inimical king in place of either – and perhaps even the Prince Edward whose candidacy his royal master had long favoured. Although it would be foolhardy to place too much reliance in the fact, the later *Olafs saga* placed the responsibility for killing Edmund squarely with Eadric.

The death-roll at Ashingdon included the Bishop of Dorchester and Abbot of Ramsey – the monastery which was probably responsible thereafter for the original of the several extant Chronicles and which of course points the finger at Eadric. They also included Ealdormen Aelfric of Hampshire, the longest serving

Ashingdon, in Essex, sits on a low ridge between the marshes of the River Roach (to the south) and the River Crouch. It was here that Cnut decisively defeated the pursuing English forces of Edmund Ironside on 16 October 1016.

of Aethelred's ealdormen; Godwine, apparently Edmund's lieutenant in Lindsey; the doughty Ulfketel of East Anglia and Aethelweard, son of Ealdorman Aethelwine and grandson of Athelstan Half-king of the East Angles. This short list confirms that it was the East Anglians and eastern Mercians who made up the most resolute part of Edmund's forces. It was these – his own long-term rivals for power within Mercia – whom Eadric betrayed at Ashingdon, as much as Edmund himself. The affinity of the dead Prince Athelstan had finally regrouped around Edmund, therefore, but the passage of this affiliation through time had witnessed considerable casualties. Edmund was in no position to maintain his protection of their lands and influence thereafter since he seems to have been gravely wounded in the same battle. Certainly his behaviour changed dramatically once Ashingdon was fought and lost, withdrawing to Gloucestershire and the heartland of Eadric's ealdormanry. The Ealdorman and Edmund's councillors brokered a peace between the two kings on the Severn near Deerhurst which preserved Edmund's rule of Wessex but conceded all Mercia and the north to Cnut – and of course sustained Eadric's own influence as a power broker on their borders powerful enough to influence any future struggle between them.

Edmund perhaps hoped to be able to resume the war and drive out the Danes from all England once he had recovered from his wounds but instead he died on 30 November 1016. He was buried at Glastonbury, the first reformed monastery in England, where King Edgar also lay – and Athelstan Half-king, of course, whose political heir as a faction leader he had sought to become. His death was one too many in too short a period of time and tenure of the English throne by the West-Saxon line died with Edmund. It was very much an accident that it was ever revived.

FACTION AND KINGSHIP

There are several features of this period that can usefully be stressed in conclusion, since they tended to recur through time and influence events during successive reigns. One was the breakdown of England into four regional communities – Northumbria, East Anglia with the eastern Midlands, western Mercia and Wessex. Each had its own elite which was, to an extent at least, independent of the others, and coalesced around powerful patrons and protectors. Each had its own regional government. Early in the tenth century, English kings had attempted to break down these divisions and unify England into a tighter and more hierarchically organized kingship. King Edgar, however, was prepared to recognize a degree of separateness in their secular elites, but attempted to utilize monastic reformation and royal patronage within the church as a vehicle for effective control beyond the Thames, alongside the power to appoint the ealdormen. It was this model of a king presiding over powerful regional magnates with an interest in royal patronage that was to characterize the remainder of the Anglo-Saxon period.

Northumbria was a political headache from the viewpoint of the English crown, but it was comparatively clearly defined and successive kings worked out ways of keeping it at least quiescent. With Wessex most kept a close personal relationship. Problems of definition only regularly bedevilled the Midlands, where western areas which had seen little Danish penetration confronted eastern areas which had. Until 975, a single family, that of Athelstan Half-king, had dominated all central England and much too of the south but King Eadwig had then deprived the family of control of western and central Mercia in the process of reducing their influence to manageable proportions. Thereafter, the dominant families in west and east vied, and on occasion fought, for control. Edgar had given qualified support to the ambitions of Athelstan's family but pursued a balanced policy which recognized the interests of several powerful groups. The struggle between that same family and their enemies at his death, however, led to, or at least contextualized, the murder of his eldest son. Yet that does appear to have been a revolution organized and carried out primarily from within the royal dynasty itself.

Once Aethelred II had achieved his majority, he seems to have generally supported western and/or northern Mercian leaders and downgraded the leadership of the East Angles below the rank of ealdorman. Eadric of western Mercia eventually became his most trusted advisor, his son-in-law and premier ealdorman. In consequence, the disadvantaged East Angles and eastern Mercians rallied around Aethelred's eldest son, Athelstan, presumably in expectation of a regime more favourable to themselves once he succeeded, so faction penetrated deep into the royal family itself.

Aethelred's Norman marriage in 1002 threatened Athelstan's succession. Once that relationship had produced a male child, the rivalry of western Mercian and East-Anglian elites for regional power naturally found a further outlet in dissension over the king's inheritance. This issue was, however, complicated by Danish attacks and King Swein's own ambitions concerning the English throne. There is some evidence that a party among the East Saxons had already supported Swein as early as the 990s, but it was alarm concerning Aethelred's employment of Thorkell and a Danish army in 1012 that threw the substantial East-Anglian and eastern Mercian faction – so Eadric's enemies – into alliance with another Danish leader, for fear of Eadric himself and the partiality of his royal master. A string of political assassinations, mutilations and other autocratic acts perpetrated by Aethelred and Eadric justified such fears.

The principal power brokers clearly pursued their own interests before those of any particular dynast in the confused fighting and shifts of power in 1013–16. That things had reached this point was, however, in large part the responsibility of Aethelred himself. It was, after all, the king who had sanctioned the use of assassination and mutilation against such of his own lieutenants whom he no longer trusted, so undermining the confidence of many others in his regime; it was also the king, by his attitude to the succession, who alienated his own eldest sons; furthermore, his dependence on a small clique of noblemen and willingness to support their ambitions antagonized many of his more important subjects. There is a fine line between strong royal government and open tyranny, but Aethelred does seem to have strayed across the divide on several occasions. The matter was exacerbated, of course, by the pressures resulting from Danish raids and the cost of response. In such circumstances, local disputes translated themselves on to the stage of national politics. One can detect a feud between Eadric and the family and friends of the murdered Ealdorman Aelfhelm; a contest for power in Yorkshire between Uhtred and Thurbrand, and another developing between Eadric and Uhtred – the less successful of Aethelred's two distinguished sons-in-law. The pursuit of these feuds and the developing history of relations between such figures and the principal claimants to the throne led some of them into careers which became extremely volatile, switching backwards and forwards between rival candidates as immediate circumstances and the behaviour of their competitors demanded. The paths followed by some were to be interpreted by near contemporaries as betrayal of the national interest and treacherous inconstancy, but such were not exclusive to those who were singled out for blame by chroniclers, whose viewpoints were retrospective and consistently eastern Mercian and East Anglian. In fact, there is a fundamental consistency in the behaviour of every senior figure whose career we can follow through these years, primarily to be found in their attitudes to each other, and it is these interactions which go a long way to determining which candidate for the throne they were supporting at any one time.

There was, however, a downside to the volatility displayed by many of the principals during the period 1013–16, since the claimants to the throne valued loyalty above much else. By 1016, even some of those great men who had given them considerable support were distrusted by both Edmund and Cnut, and Eadric was particularly vulnerable to a conclusion of hostilities and the clear victory of either party.

Ultimately, the House of Cerdic did not lose the crown of the English to overwhelming Danish assault, although that was clearly a factor. Rather, it fell as much as anything from within. Viking attacks coincided with the lengthy reign of a king who proved incapable of presiding over regional rivalries with the necessary degree of circumspection to avoid driving one party to take desperate measures designed ultimately to unseat himself and overthrow his nominee as successor. His apparent insistence that his adult sons should stand aside from the succession in favour of his young family by Emma divided the royal dynasty, and his eldest sons naturally found partisans within the provincial rivalries of the day. It was Swein of Denmark who benefited in the short term. In the last resort, Edmund's efforts to restore the dynasty – and of course to secure the throne for himself – were seriously compromised by his father's policies, and he died in the attempt, allegedly owing to the inimical intervention of his father's principal lieutenant on the field of battle at Ashingdon.

When central England divided between those who acceded to the Gainsborough Accord and those who did not, it was along Watling Street that the fissure opened. A century earlier, Watling Street had been a boundary between English and Danish territory. Aethelred still legislated separately for his English and his Danish subjects, as the Wantage Code demonstrates, and Watling Street may well have been the boundary between these two law codes. In a sense, therefore, the struggle for political dominance between western and eastern Mercia did reflect wider cultural and societal issues, which derived from unresolved and perhaps unresolvable matters to do with the so-called 'Reconquest' of Edward the Elder and his sister Aethelfaed at the beginning of the tenth century. But that is to look backwards. It is our business instead to look forward, and follow the fortunes of England under Danish rule, and of Cerdic's descendants in adversity.

The messages which emanated from Aethelred's reign to that of his son Edward were powerful ones of real significance to the succession crisis of 1066: firstly, Aethelred's own views on the succession seem to have been overridden by the pressure of events and by the opinions of powerful men around him; secondly, civil conflicts allowed in an outside candidate for the throne, whose reign benefited few even of those who initially supported his candidacy – and an abhorrence of warfare between Englishmen was to be a recurring theme of 1042–66, probably for this reason; thirdly, Aethelred's own half-brother and predecessor had been murdered and set aside in favour of a younger sibling, and such precedents offered important messages to the hard men gathering around the succession in 1066, when they necessarily reduced Edgar Aetheling's prospects of an undisputed accession; fourthly, Aethelred's regime seems to have banked heavily on achieving the succession of a son who was far from being the eldest aetheling and whose candidacy was opposed by many of the political community. It seems likely that Edward also committed himself at a comparatively early stage of his career to the candidacy of a figure whom the remainder of the elite were unwilling to accept – Duke William, of course. Fifthly, Aethelred's reign terminated in a long, drawn-out succession crisis which resulted in a dynastic revolution, and the separation of the native dynasty from power in England. Collectively, the circumstances in which Aethelred's reign ended did much to undermine the hitherto immutable bonds securing the kingship of the English to Cerdic's line, and encouraged powerful figures at home and abroad to imagine that they could exert sufficient pressure to divert the throne away from the royal house, to themselves, perhaps, or to their own advantage. These were important precedents, about which the generation of Harold Godwineson seem to have thought deeply.

First, however, Alfred's descendants had to survive a period of Danish kingship from which they long seemed unlikely to recover the English throne, and we must consider the nature of power and the organization of the kingdom – and their plight – under Cnut and his sons, kings of the English between 1016 and 1042.

TWO

Power and Legitimacy: Danish Kingship and its Opponents

Cnut was one of at least three children born to King Swein's highly political marriage to a Polish princess, perhaps named Sigrid, who seems earlier to have been married in Sweden. The inception of the relationship occurred in about 995. These royal children were Cnut himself, his brother Harald and a sister, Estrith. They had in addition a much older half-sister, a daughter of Swein named Gytha, who married the Norwegian, Erik Hakonsson, before 998.

That Cnut should finally emerge from the complex governmental crisis of 1013–16 as the king of all the English was unpredictable right up to the death of Edmund Ironside on St Andrew's Day (30 November) 1016, for all the oft-vaunted power of the Danish fleet. His triumph arguably owed more to an unusually high death rate – with Athelstan, Aethelred and Edmund dying in rapid succession – than any intrinsic potency of his own campaign. Prior to the death of Swein, King of Denmark, early in 1014, Cnut was merely one of two potential heirs to his father's position, and it seems likely that his brother, Harald, was the senior of the two and the more likely to inherit. This interpretation is certainly consistent with Swein's naming of his two sons, the elder of whom was the more likely to have been given his father's name. It is also consistent with his having left Harald in Denmark while he, with Cnut, sought power in England. Despite his formidable record as a military leader and his considerable political achievements, Swein's position in 1013–14 was far from stable in the majority of the realms where he exercised influence, and nowhere less so than in England.

Aethelred's efforts to destabilize Swein's power in Scandinavia by promoting Olaf Tryggvasson as king of the Norwegians had been effectively neutralized in 999, when the Danish king defeated and killed his opponent. Thereafter, Swein successfully re-established his father's superior kingship of Norway, ruling through Erik and Swein, Earl Hakon's sons, as his jarls. Thereafter, Swein was freer to turn his attention to England. Despite his acceptance there by the English in 1013, however, his supremacy remained a very personal one and his rule an agglomeration of unequal relationships, rather than deeply entrenched. None can have been particularly surprised, therefore, when the various parts of his 'empire' fell apart at his death. Most of the English failed to transfer their several acts of submission to Cnut and instead recalled Aethelred and restored the native dynasty; his son Harald secured his native Denmark, but both the Norwegians and the Swedes rejected Danish rule. Swein's death released, therefore, a conflicting mêlée of political aspirations and ambitions within his own family and throughout the Scandinavian world which threatened to demolish his initial supremacy for good.

Cnut was with the Danish fleet at Gainsborough when his father died, and had probably already by this date married Aelfgifu of Northampton, so had sought to identify himself with that faction in English political life which had been the anchor for his father's candidacy for the throne. The ship men elected him as successor to Swein, presumably intending that he inherit both his new-found kingdom of England and his Danish-centric Scandinavian supremacy. He had some dies cut ready to mint coins proclaiming himself king of the Danes before departing from Lindsey, but events in Scandinavia did not await his return, by which time his brother Harald was comfortably established as king in Denmark itself.

Aethelred, returning to power in England, seems to have encouraged the ambitions of one of Thorkell's more prominent associates, another Olaf, to make himself king of the Norwegians, so Swein's death was perceived by his enemies in England as an opportunity to revive the forward policy towards Scandinavia which they had earlier used with some success in the 990s. Olaf Haraldsson – St Olaf – eventually amassed a considerable reputation within Scandinavia and Sighvalt the Scald and Ottar the Black later recalled his playing an heroic part in Viking attacks on London, the Battle of Ringmere (1010) and the capture of Canterbury (1011). According to Ottar, Aethelred owed his return to power in 1014 to Olaf, with Thorkell the Tall barely mentioned at all, but this was presumably a matter of poetic licence. Olaf is likely to have received a significant share of the gelds raised to pay Thorkell's soldiery and may well have been subsidized still further by Aethelred for the purposes of destabilizing the Danish royal family in the north. He and his friends had wrested control of Norway from the jarls by 1016 and were busily harnessing anti-Danish feelings among his countrymen and utilizing Christianizing policies on behalf of his own kingship. Olaf Tryggvasson, Aethelred's previous ally, seems to have been his role model, and it is likely that the broad thrust of his approach had been agreed in advance with Aethelred's regime. Certainly, it is important to recognize that Swein's enemies had good cause to co-operate in their efforts to counter the influence of his heirs. These included Swein's underking of Sweden, another Olaf (Skotkonung), who refused to transfer his allegiance from Swein to his sons, and henceforth pursued an independent political path.

The *Encomium Emmae*, which was written soon after his death, describes Cnut returning to Denmark upon being ousted from England and asking his brother for a share of the kingdom and assistance to conquer England. All he could offer

The Encomium *of Queen Emma, wife successively of Aethelred II and Cnut. She is shown here seated in royal state to receive a work which was written in her praise, watched by her sons Harthacnut and Edward (the Confessor).*

in return was the dubious prospect of a share in England should they succeed in this hazardous enterprise. It is hardly surprising that Harald refused, preferring to hold Denmark himself and leave his brother to secure what he could in England. By late 1014, therefore, Cnut was nothing more than the commander of a substantial Viking fleet, and there may well have been some doubt as to whether he could even maintain that in existence. Despite his illustrious forebears, he had little military experience and few resources, and he was barely, if at all, out of his teens.

It was, therefore, as a fleet commander and little more that Cnut returned to England in the summer of 1015. Edmund Ironside's initiative had deprived him of any surviving sympathy among the associates of his English wife and shifted the survivors of the English magnates who had joined Swein at Gainsborough to his own side. Cnut was, therefore, without any significant body of noble support in England, and could do nothing except go Viking to raid the English countryside and supply his troops with provisions and the opportunity for profit. He began to ravage western Wessex, just as so many Viking squadrons had done before him. As a candidate for the succession, his prospects at this point must have looked bleak, despite Aethelred's apparently terminal illness, and any comparison with the status conceded to Swein in 1013 merely serves to underline the weakness of his position.

The situation changed dramatically, however, soon after Cnut's arrival, owing to the submission of Aethelred's principal ealdorman and councillor, Eadric Streona, and it was his support and then that of the West Saxons (which Eadric presumably mediated) which suddenly made the Danish candidacy once more appear respectable. Eadric did not, of course, have any intrinsic interest in the claims of the Danish kings. He joined Cnut for entirely negative reasons in a last-ditch effort to retain power and influence in the face of the apparently imminent death of Aethelred himself. This was, therefore, an alliance of convenience brought about by mutual hostility towards Prince Edmund, and a poor basis for long-term co-operation. Furthermore, it seems most unlikely that the aristocracy of the south-west provinces had submitted to him with any enthusiasm, particularly since they had been among the last to recognize Swein in 1013. Cnut's primary English supporters in 1015 provided, therefore, support which was characterized by its conditional qualities and temporary nature.

Aethelred's survival of a severe illness in 1015 had some potential to strengthen Cnut's position. The presence of Ealdorman Eadric, Aethelred's favourite, in Cnut's host may well have enabled him to pose as heir to an English king who was clearly hostile to the policies and ambitions of his eldest surviving son. Indeed, it is far from clear that Aethelred was prepared to back Edmund's candidacy against Cnut, and the antagonisms of king and aetheling disabled the English war effort and enabled Cnut to take the initiative in Mercia and Northumbria. When Aethelred died, Edmund was acclaimed king in London, but Cnut had returned to his ships, probably at Southampton, and John of Worcester ('Florence') later asserted that he too was acclaimed by another assembly of English nobles and clerics, on the assumption perhaps that Aethelred had nominated him as heir. Had his seige of London succeeded in the spring of 1016, then Cnut would have been in a position to secure the succession at an early date.

Once Aethelred was dead, however, Edmund's candidacy clarified with the support of the royal council, and it was at this point that his war leadership proved capable of rallying the English effectively against the invader. England's leaders disposed of very considerable military resources at this date – superior certainly to the Danish army. Once divisions within the royal family had been resolved, Edmund Ironside raised army after army and Cnut came under considerable military pressure. His political advances were also annulled. It was the old king whose partiality for Eadric gave him the status to confer a degree of legitimacy on Cnut's aspirations. With him dead, Eadric's role was reduced to that of a renegade ealdorman, and his widespread unpopularity outside his core west-Mercian territories came into play against Cnut. Aethelred's policies regarding the descent of the crown had been the principal impediment to the succession of Edmund Ironside. Once he was dead, the West Saxons detached themselves from Eadric and swung their support behind a royal house which they perceived as peculiarly their own. By the eve of the Battle of Ashingdon, 18 October 1016, Cnut had lost the support of all significant sections of the English elite and was nothing more than a Viking war-lord facing the prospect of imminent defeat at the hands of superior forces closing in upon him under resolute leadership.

As already discussed above, it may well be that Eadric contrived to ensure that Cnut was not decisively defeated at Ashingdon – as the chroniclers claimed – so as to enhance his own prospects of survival, and he must have known that he could expect little in the way of a future from Edmund once the Danes had been expelled. Cnut's accession thereafter occurred in two stages. The first resulted from an accommodation engineered by Eadric and then hammered out between himself and King Edmund on an island in the Severn near Deerhurst shortly after Ashingdon, at which the two leaders 'affirmed their friendship, both with pledge and with oath, and set the payment for the raiding-army', and divided England between themselves, Edmund taking Wessex and Cnut, Mercia. This reflected the about-turn in their fortunes which occurred at Ashingdon, not so much as a consequence of Edmund's defeat in battle but more because he thereafter seems to have been seriously incapacitated. He died only weeks after peace was arranged.

The accord of Ola's Island therefore established the initial foundations of Cnut's kingship by conceding him the role and title of king in part of England, but that was always likely to be a temporary expedient by the West-Saxon king to carry him over a period of weakness while he convalesced. Although it gave Cnut the east-Midland affinity which he and Edmund had so hotly contested via their several marriages, it still placed him in charge of the periphery of England and left the political core to Edmund. In a sense, therefore, Edmund retained the upper hand for himself, and might well have been considered the senior king. The issue was finely balanced, and the real winner of the Ola's Island accord was Eadric Streona, who could reasonably expect to retain his pre-eminence in western Mercia and a position of power sufficient to play one of the kings off against the other at need.

It was undoubtedly Edmund's death – almost certainly from wounds received at Ashingdon – on 30 November that cleared the path for Cnut to become sole king of the English. In so doing, he could, and clearly did, direct the eyes of the English back to the precedent set in 959, when King Eadwig of the West Saxons died and was succeeded by Edgar, king of the Mercians, but those two were brothers while Cnut and Edmund were entirely unrelated and – for all their oaths – enemies divided by very different histories, nationalities and personal ambitions. By appealing to the laws of the good King Edgar, Cnut was, however, consciously reminding the English political classes of the achievements of a previous king of the Mercians who preceded the reputedly tyrannical Aethelred as king of all the English, and whose reign was viewed in retrospect as a 'golden

St Mary's, Deerhurst, in the Vale of Gloucester, is one of the best-preserved pre-Conquest monastic churches in England. Edward the Confessor granted the bulk of its property to Westminster and the remainder (including the church) to his physician, after which it became an alien priory. The fabric preserves successive alterations and enlargements of an original pre-Viking core.

age'. Such rhetoric was probably important in the new king's drive to reconcile his new subjects to his kingship. Edmund Ironside was arguably engaged in the same style of propaganda in 1016 – he named his sons Edward, after his murdered uncle, and Edmund after his grandfather, noticeably omitting all reference to his own father, Aethelred.

Cnut certainly brought military pressure to bear on the issue but his accession was ultimately a matter of political accommodation between himself and the English, and this seems to have taken some time to be accepted by all parties. The Winchester manuscript of the Chronicle had Cnut 'chosen' as king in 1017, while the Peterborough text reads: 'King Cnut succeeded to the whole kingdom of the English race', but both give an impression of clarity and certitude which was arguably lacking at the time. John of Worcester may have been interpreting little more source material than this when he sought to explain Cnut's accession by suggesting that the English magnates sought his favour by informing him dishonestly that Edmund had himself wished Cnut to succeed him so that he could act as guardian to his sons, yet it is not entirely clear how implausible this story is. It certainly opens up the central issue of relations between Cnut, the English political classes and Aethelred's surviving family.

From 1017 onwards Cnut was behaving as king. His initial management structure for England differed little from that of King Edgar before him. In 1017 he was said to have divided England into its four principal constituent parts, retaining Wessex for himself and setting Thorkell as earl over the East Angles and Erik over the Northumbrians while leaving Eadric Streona in power in Mercia. Erik was Hakon's son and his own (half) brother-in-law, who had joined himself to Cnut in 1014–15 and was his most loyal senior supporter. Otherwise Cnut was merely recognizing the realities of power, since both Thorkell and Eadric still arguably retained significant military forces under their own control in the winter of 1016–17. His most resolute opponents at Ashingdon had been the East Angles and eastern Mercians, so it was perhaps inevitable that a powerful Viking leader with earlier experience of Aethelred's court should be given responsibility for this district. In general, this settlement reveals the comparative weakness of the young king and his efforts to satisfy the ambitions of the surviving power brokers and involve them in his own regime.

Cnut also married Emma, the dowager queen, in the summer of 1017. It has often been assumed that this marriage involved an alliance between Cnut and the ducal court in Normandy, but Emma probably remained in England following her husband's death in 1016, when she was certainly trapped by the Danish investment of London. A long and detailed account of negotiations between Emma and the Danish army was included in the near-contemporary chronicle of Thietmar of Merseburg, according to whom the queen proved ready to give up the aethelings (her step-sons) and all London's vast military equipment, and pay a great ransom, in return for her life and those of her companions. However, this account is notoriously faulty as regards names in particular, referring to Prince Athelstan, for example, instead of Eadwig, and Dunstan instead of Archbishop Aelfheah. This looks like a much elaborated account told from a rather boastful Viking perspective and perhaps reaching Thietmar at fourth or fifth hand. The

King Cnut and Queen Emma present an altar cross to New Minster, Winchester. Cnut made every effort to portray himself as a Christian king and a generous patron of the church.

Danish host was, for example, reputed to be 340 ships strong, each holding 80 men, so the total investing force numbered some 27,200, yet it was reputed in the Chronicle to be a mere 160 ships when Cnut opened his campaign and he had certainly suffered heavy losses by this date.

Even so, some sort of negotiations may well have occurred, and a marriage between Cnut and Emma had some potential to legitimize Cnut's kingship at Edmund's expense in the late spring of 1016. However, the queen did not surrender London to the Danes nor marry Cnut at this stage. To do either would have placed her in an extremely vulnerable position and threatened her continuing occupation of her rich dower lands, should Edmund win. Instead, she probably retired to her estates and walled towns – Exeter was after all presumably still hers – following Edmund's ejection of Danish forces from Wessex and relief of the city. Assuming her dower lands were concentrated in Wessex, it was only after Edmund had died that she became vulnerable to renewed pressure from Cnut, and was unable to resist when he 'ordered the widow of the former king Aethelred, Richard's daughter, to be fetched to him as wife'.

This marriage was, therefore, primarily undertaken by Cnut as a means of legitimizing his kingship. His willingness to take as wife a dowager who was old enough to be his own mother – she had after all been married in 1002 and bore her first child in 1005 – emphasizes the insecurity of the Danish regime in its first year. This was, of course, a comparatively commonplace mechanism by which to reinforce dubious title to land and office during the period, and Cnut may well have anticipated that his position *vis-à-vis* Aethelred's courtiers and clergy would be strengthened by association with a queen who had exercised considerable influence at the centre of English politics for a decade and a half. Furthermore, the marriage brought Cnut authority over her extensive dower lands and influence over her numerous connections. A political marriage, therefore, but this seems to have proved a very successful one, and Emma threw her weight behind Cnut and their son Harthacnut.

One circumstance of this marriage merits attention, since Cnut was, of course, already married to Aelfgifu of Northampton, who bore him two sons whom he recognized and named after his father, Swein, and grandfather, Harald. Aelfgifu was still very much alive in 1017 and remained at the centre of the regime thereafter, eventually representing Cnut and her son Harald in Norway. The king was, therefore, in some sense a bigamist. However, his marriage to Aelfgifu was probably one established without Christian rites, and this type of marriage 'by Danish custom' seems to have been acceptable even alongside Christian marriage in the eleventh century. Harold Godwineson, for example, was reputed to have enjoyed a similar relationship with Edith Swan-neck a generation later. Furthermore, previous English kings such as Edgar himself had produced and recognized children by different women who were alive concurrently, so Cnut's behaviour had well-known precedents within the English royal family.

Cnut's marriage to Emma was, therefore, one facet of his efforts to reconcile the English to himself as king during the first year of his reign, when he was very much feeling his way and attempting to build bridges towards the English elite which might create confidence between them. In fact, the final settlement of the

Silver penny of Cnut. In general, the design mirrors that of Aethelred's coinage. The details are, however, significant – the helmeted figure of the king portrays a warlike image, while the sceptre emphasizes his regality.

succession crisis did not occur until 1018, when at a great assembly at Oxford, 'Danes and English were agreed'. Precisely what was meant by this enigmatic statement by the author of the Peterborough manuscript of the Chronicle is only in part elucidated by the Worcester manuscript, which recorded that both sides accepted Edgar's laws. The choice of Edgar has implications, of course: all sides were agreeing to place the bitter conflicts of Aethelred's reign behind them and seek legitimacy in the golden age reputedly presided over by his father; Cnut was additionally promising to reign justly, in contrast to perceptions of Aethelred as an unjust king whose methods had been tyrannical. Edgar was in many ways an appropriate role-model for Cnut: his youth when he succeeded and his initial tenure of the Mercian crown were obvious similarities, while his reputation as a patron of the church and as a powerful protector of the English will have been features which both the king and such figures as Archbishop Wulfstan will have seen some merit in promoting in support of Cnut's kingship.

In the same year Cnut raised a great geld, variously assessed as £82,500 or £83,000, of which London was expected to contribute not much short of one-seventh, and this enabled him to pay off all but forty ships' crews. To this point, therefore, Cnut had retained the fleet with which he had attacked England in the summer of 1015, so had effectively stayed on a war-footing, and ready to suppress resistance to his kingship within England.

It may also have been as late as 1018 when Cnut's regime introduced its first coinage. Aethelred's coins – the 'last small cross' type – therefore continued to circulate despite his death in April 1016 for at least one year and perhaps as long as two. The great geld of that year certainly focused the attention of the government on coinage, and the very large numbers of coins necessary would have made recoining at this point unusually lucrative, but the delay from 1015 – when it was arguably intended to renew the dies – to 1017–18 once again reflects the political insecurity and confusion of the period between Aethelred's incapacitating illness at Cosham and the great assembly at Oxford presided over by Cnut, which brought peace under Danish rule. Indeed, the very choice of

Oxford for Cnut's meeting recalls Aethelred's 'great assembly' at the same town in 1015, where Eadric 'betrayed Siferth and Morcar . . . lured them into his chamber, and in there they were killed dishonourably'. Eadric had already been killed in 1017, and Cnut and his advisors surely chose Oxford as a means of advertising the qualitative differences between his regime and that of Aethelred, with whose victims the Danish king was aligned by his first marriage.

Therefore, 1018 appears to be the end of the first, and the most insecure, period of Cnut's reign, during which the succession issue dominated all others. Only with that period passed was Cnut comparatively secure on the English throne, and only then did he leave England to pay an extended visit to Denmark over the winter of 1019–20, where his brother Harald seems to have died in or about 1018–19. Cnut became thereafter king of Denmark, but he did so with the English kingship already his. Unlike his father who was king of Denmark for two decades before securing the kingship of the English, Cnut made England the principal seat of his power and it was always to be his primary concern and the kingdom in which he spent the bulk of his time.

Opposition to Cnut: The Conspiracies of 1017 and 1020

All parties to the initial agreement between Cnut and the English early in 1017 must have recognized what a revolutionary event the dispossession of the Cerdicings represented, but there was no candidate available from within that lineage with the stature, military experience and proven qualities of leadership to offer a serious challenge to Cnut and his Danish forces in the sudden event of Edmund's untimely death. Cnut was recognized by the English elite before any alternative could be organized, so for the future resistance to him could be accounted treasonous. There was, however, considerable sympathy for the native dynasty even after the general submission to Cnut in 1017, and it was the very real possibility that such sympathy would break out into active and full-scale rebellion in favour of a candidate from Alfred's lineage which prolonged the succession crisis at least until 1018.

In the winter of 1016–17, there were five aethelings living who were descended from Aethelred. Only one, Eadwig, was by this date anything like mature, having been born probably late in the 990s to Aethelred's first wife Aelfgifu. His name first appears on a witness list in 997. Given that the name of his half-brother, Edward, appeared in what seems to have been the year of his birth (1005), one might be justified in arguing that Eadwig was born in that year, in which case he was probably about nineteen when his brother died in November 1016.

During his father's reign, Eadwig's attestations of royal documents were far less regular than those of his elder brothers, Athelstan (until 1014), Edmund, and Eadred (until 1012). From 1009 to 1012, his name only occurs on a single surviving diploma (in 1011), and it may be significant that Prince Edward's only occurs on the same document. It seems likely, therefore, that he was not always at his father's court. He did attest in 1013–14, but not in 1015.

Although the successive deaths of his brothers after 1010 gradually improved Eadwig's prospects of eventually attaining the throne, this can never have looked

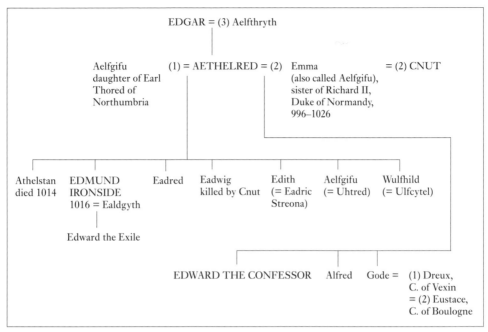

Aethelred's family and potential heirs – Aethelred fathered two families by different queens but in the male line only a single grandson, Edward the Exile, survived to manhood.

likely even during his father's last regnal year: his elder brother, Edmund, had married in the summer of 1015 and his bride, Siferth's widow, was perhaps already pregnant, and known so to be, before Aethelred died in April 1016; furthermore, Aethelred may still have intended to pass over his elder family in favour of his eldest son by Emma. In these circumstances, even Edmund experienced considerable difficulty in constructing a political platform from which to launch his own challenge for the succession during 1015–16. In the circumstances of the Danish war, the hostility of Eadric and the king's own preferences concerning the succession, there was clearly no room for another aetheling from Aethelred's first marriage to be pursuing ambitions which could be construed as rivalling those of Prince Edmund.

Nor is Eadwig likely to have been able to have accrued much in the way of resources or supporters by the winter of 1016. As a junior aetheling whose half-brothers had long been preferred to himself, he is unlikely to have been granted much in the way of estates by his father. Nor did he receive any additions from his eldest brother's will, which merely provided him with a sword, while Edmund was left the bulk of such of his substantial estates as were not conferred on the church in which he proposed to be buried at Winchester. The property available to the brothers was arguably too important to their aspirations to succeed their father to be willed away from the eldest.

Edmund is also unlikely to have given much thought to his brother's position in the hectic climate of 1016, when he was consumed with the need to establish himself as king and drive out the Danes. Additionally, the succession was further complicated by the birth of at least one son to his own bride within the year. Eadwig arguably played the part of a loyal brother, and Thietmar's Chronicle may imply that he fought by Edmund's side, but the new king's youth and energy must have seemed sufficient in themselves to re-establish the dynasty without worrying overly about his younger full brother.

Thereafter, the rapidity with which his regime collapsed – between 18 October and 30 November 1016 – left Eadwig little opportunity to prepare his own candidacy and rally support. Even so, it is worth remarking that Cnut is not recorded as having been acknowledged as king by the West Saxons until 1017, and it was not necessarily even in the opening weeks of the new year. There occurred, therefore, a short but significant interregnum in December 1016 which may even have stretched some way into the new year, before the West Saxons accepted Cnut. Without contemporary comment on the matter it is impossible to reconstruct what was going on, but it seems at least likely that Edmund's councillors and the leaders of the West Saxons were considering Eadwig's candidacy as his brother's successor and only agreed upon the more discrete course of accommodation with Cnut and his substantial army after some delay. Edmund's funeral at Glastonbury was perhaps a crucial event in any such discussions.

Prince Eadwig was, however, by age and birth, the only credible alternative to Cnut available within the English royal house. His movements following the West-Saxon submission to Cnut are unrecorded. Cnut is often supposed to have sent him into exile outside England as soon as he was able. However, it seems more likely that he concurred in the general submission to Cnut – much as Edgar Aetheling later did to William in 1066 – and remained at liberty in England, and more particularly in western Wessex. The Worcester and Peterborough manuscripts of the Chronicle contain some information concerning him in, at latest, midsummer 1017: 'King Cnut put to flight the aetheling Eadwig, and Eadwig , "the ceorl's king".' The former, at least, must refer to Aethelred's son. If the sequence offered in this annal is to be believed, the events to which it so enigmatically referred occurred before August. If not – and 'Florence' places Eadric's death at Christmas – then these several events should be treated separately. Whichever, Eadwig was in England sometime in 1017, and, what is more, he was then in arms against Cnut.

In both versions of the Chronicle, this brief comment follows notice of a series of killings, all of which seem to have been sanctioned by the king, and all of which included very senior figures among the English magnates. The first was, of course, Eadric Streona, but they included also Northman, son of Ealdorman Leofwine; Aethelweard, son of Aethelmaer the Fat, and Beorhtric, son of Aelfeah in Devonshire. Later writers suggested that numerous others were also slain, but failed to name them. These killings have generally been interpreted as Cnut's clearing the decks of potential enemies in a brief purge at the outset of his reign, but there is something very incongruous about this view inasmuch as it makes a nonsense of his appointments to govern England's provinces earlier in the same year, when Eadric was clearly considered necessary to the regime. Additionally, Cnut was busy at this very time attempting to distinguish his own style of government from that of Aethelred, and such killings were precisely what he did not need as he attempted to put forward a cleaner image. Ealdorman Leofwine and his family, at least, retained considerable influence under Cnut and it seems most unlikely that his treatment of Northman and the others in 1017 could have been seen by either party as unjustified. Rather, the segregation of the individual from his family as the object of royal vengeance suggests that a very serious and specific issue accounted for these several deaths.

Interpretation is much simplified if the highly compressed Chronicle account of the year's events is divided into three essentially separate items: first come the king's recognition by the English magnates as king of all England, and the organization of its several provinces under his own appointees, a necessary part of that same event, which arguably occurred early in the year; second, divided from the first by the phrase, 'In this year also', come the several killings of English nobles, including one of those same appointees, and Cnut's successful action against Eadwig; third, introduced by 'And then . . .', comes notice of Cnut's forceful wooing of, and marriage to, Emma. Only the last is even approximately dated, 'before 1 August'. This might provide an end date for the whole sequence, but they are not otherwise connected in this terse narrative, although there is likely to have been at least a degree of causal linkage.

On this basis, Cnut's killing of several prominent English nobles should be interpreted as part and parcel of his dealings with the aetheling Eadwig. The names of his victims suggest that Cnut believed that a group of magnates with considerable influence in western Mercia and western Wessex, were conspiring against him, and his subsequent confrontation with the aetheling surely confirms that his suspicions were well grounded. The killings may well, therefore, have been a pre-emptive strike by Cnut against the ringleaders of a plot to supplant him only months after the submission of the West Saxons, in favour of Aethelred's eldest surviving son.

Something of relevance can be said concerning some of the principals involved. At the centre, of course, was Eadwig himself, for whom the collapse of Edmund's kingship represented both a dynastic catastrophe and an opportunity to press his own candidacy for the throne. That had clearly not carried the day in midwinter, in that short time between Edmund's death and the submission of the West Saxons to Cnut, but a determined and well-supported rising might well have been considered to have had considerable potential to overthrow a Danish kingship which the English had accepted only very recently, reluctantly, largely by default, and under considerable military pressure. At this date, Edmund Ironside's victories in 1016 still held out hope that Cnut could be resisted with some success. Cnut's appointments to the most senior secular offices earlier in the same year established Scandinavians in three of the four top posts, and this is unlikely to have endeared the regime to nobles who had wielded power and influence under both Aethelred and Edmund.

The best known of the ringleaders was Eadric Streona and his motives are also perhaps the easiest to guess at. Eadric's entire career had been built upon loyalty to Aethelred and his career was seriously threatened by his patron's decline and death. Having swung his own support behind Cnut out of fear of Edmund in 1015, Eadric had then abandoned the Danish host at Aylesford in 1016 when his cause seemed lost. Despite his alleged responsibility for the English defeat at Ashingdon, therefore, he had already given Cnut good cause to doubt his loyalty and commitment. Eadric was too powerful to either ignore or move against without just cause in the early months of 1017, and this may well explain his re-appointment to the governance of a substantial province at the beginning of the year. However, Cnut's sanction in 1016 of the killing of ealdorman Uhtred, who was Eadric's counterpart in many ways, provided a significant precedent which arguably gave the Mercian leader cause to fear that Cnut would dispense with his services, and his person, as soon as he was sufficiently well established to do so. Until then, he was a minority of one English senior ealdorman at a court where all the other top secular offices were held by Vikings, and Cnut had arguably already begun to limit his power even in western Mercia by establishing men such as Hrani to minor earldoms in the core of his earldom. Hrani was to be associated with that same *Magonsaete* – basically Herefordshire – where Eadric was alleged to have recruited his own forces in 1016. This is unlikely to have been a comfortable position for Aethelred's premier lieutenant.

In contrast, the prospect of exercising power within the regime of a newly established, grateful and still youthful son of King Aethelred may have seemed preferable. Eadwig was also his brother-in-law, a relationship which might well be worked to advantage, particularly given the recent losses among Aethelred's kin. All these factors may well have encouraged Eadric to conspire with the West Saxons – a group with whom he apparently carried much influence – to place Eadwig on the throne.

Eadric was apprehended and killed at London. The Canterbury manuscript of the Chronicle adds the judgement that it was done 'very justly'. This may, of course, be later comment generated by the general unpopularity of Eadric among the chroniclers, but it could equally reflect the author's perception of him in 1017 as guilty of conspiracy against the king. His death was elaborated by the *Encomium Emmae*, which gave Earl Erik responsibility for actually beheading him, and John ('Florence') of Worcester later remarked that his body was flung over the city wall and left unburied. His end was, therefore, as dishonourable as those of many of his own victims in earlier years.

Northman was the son of that Leofwine who served Aethelred as ealdorman of the Hwicce in south-western Mercia from 994 through to the end of the reign. Leofwine was one of the most regular witnesses of Aethelred's charters, so apparently in frequent attendance on the king and a member of his inner circle. Given his area of responsibility, he was necessarily an associate of Eadric Streona and may well have been responsible directly to him rather than the king, and this may help explain his son's behaviour in 1017. Additionally, both Leofwine and his adult sons probably felt considerable loyalty to their patron, Aethelred, and his family, as well as entertaining the expectation that their own careers would be better served by the succession of his son than of Cnut. The family had an additional grievance against the Danish king – Leofwine's grandson, Aethelwine, had been among the hostages given to Swein Forkbeard in 1013, and he was then reputed to have had his hands cut off by the Danes, presumably as part of Cnut's more general mutilation of these hostages when he was forced out of Lindsey in 1014. It may well be that this was Northman's own son, in which case his prominence as a conspirator is the easier explained.

In the aftermath of the 1017 crisis and Northman's death, Cnut seems to have successfully reconciled the family to himself. Leofwine retained his ealdormanry and his surviving sons were given office as sheriffs – Leofric in Worcester and Edwin at Hereford. 'Florence' remarked that Leofric was made *dux* in place of Northman, but this comment arguably compresses the chronology beyond all recognition since Leofric is not known to have become earl until the last years of Cnut's reign. Leofwine probably died in or soon after 1023, when he last witnessed a royal charter, and his office eventually passed to Leofric, suggesting that Cnut was by then entirely satisfied of the family's loyalty to himself. Aethelred's long-serving ealdorman did therefore eventually retain his position of power and influence under Cnut, but this may well have seemed improbable in the early summer of 1017 and he always seems to have had to share it with Scandinavian earls operating in the same vicinity. Northman, at least, then opted to support the native dynasty. His reasons were arguably several but he paid for it with his own life.

Aethelmaer the Fat is generally, but not invariably, identified as the distinguished leader of the south-west shires of Wessex. Only if that is the case can we make any useful comment on the involvement of his son in the 1017 conspiracy. In defence of this association, it is at least plausible that Aethelmaer should have named his eldest son Aethelweard after his famous father, the premier ealdorman, author of a Latin chronicle and patron of the new learning. It was Aethelmaer who founded the monastery of Eynsham, appointed the great homilist Aelfric to be its first abbot and then retired there, apparently in about 1005. By so doing, he escaped from the factional politics of Aethelred's later years, and this may well have been in part at least his intention. He did, however, come out of retirement to lead the surrender of the West Saxons to Swein in 1013 and remained active as ealdorman in 1014, but then disappears from the witness lists, so presumably died, leaving the ealdormanry vacant at the very end of Aethelred's reign. If this vacancy coincided with Cnut's attack on Dorset and neighbouring shires in 1015 – and this does look like a classic case of Viking opportunism – then the consequent void in regional power structures may well have encouraged the West Saxons to submit to Cnut later that summer, once Eadric had done the same.

There was already, therefore, a link between Eadric and the West Saxons, in their common submission to Cnut in 1015. Aethelmaer's son is likely to have harboured ambitions to follow in the family tradition as ealdorman, and Cnut's retention of Wessex for himself at the beginning of 1017 was an impediment to his own promotion. Additionally, Aethelweard came of a line which was notoriously proud of its derivation from the West-Saxon royal family in the late ninth century, and were probably the most prominent kinsmen of the line represented by Aethelred and his sons. Cnut's actions, pride in his own royal lineage, loyalty to the native kings and an estimation of his own self-interest are all likely to have suggested to Aethelweard that his ambitions were unlikely to be realized under Danish kingship, and would be better served by promoting Eadwig Aetheling to the throne.

The West Saxons had also given Swein hostages in 1013 and it seems almost certain that ealdorman Aethelmaer would have been expected to contribute a kinsman of his own, so there may well have been bad blood between Aethelweard and Cnut on account of the latter's hasty vengeance on his father's captives.

Aethelmaer also had a son-in-law called Aethelweard, who held lands in Oxfordshire and the south west. An Aethelweard did become ealdorman in western Wessex and it is likely that it was this individual, but it is unclear when this occurred. His first appearance on witness lists occurs in 1018, so it is quite likely that his appointment post-dated the 1017 conspiracy, in which case it may be that once again – as seems possible in the case of Leofwine's family – Cnut decided to disarm opposition by dispersing offices and regional power more widely among the pre-existing aristocracy and thereby seducing his critics. This Aethelweard was probably not in origin a West Saxon, and it is just possible that he should be identified with the brother of Eadric Streona of that name, in which case the last point made is perhaps of greater consequence, and Cnut's victims begin to look more and more like a group of individuals representing several closely allied noble families.

Beorhtric's father, Aelfheah, could conceivably have been one of the *ministri* of that name who witnessed an unusually well-attested royal diploma in 1009, but neither name is uncommon and that document had no local connections, conveying as it did land in Derbyshire. We can only, therefore, assume that Beorhtric represented a local landowning family in Devonshire, but it is quite likely that they were connected with Aethelweard's family, which had exercised patronage and power in the area over three generations. Cnut's ealdorman of that name was reputed to be the founder of Buckfast Abbey in Devon, and persuaded Cnut to renew the privileges of St Mary's at Exeter in 1018, so there is at least circumstantial evidence for their association.

What we seem to have from the chroniclers, therefore, is a highly abbreviated account of the suppression of an uprising against Cnut and in favour of Eadwig. It occurred in 1017, after the submission of the West Saxons to Cnut and his appointment of men to head England's several provinces but before he sent for Emma, 'before 1 August'. Implicated were several very senior figures among the English aristocracy, at least two of whom – Aethelweard and Eadric – could boast close kinship with the native royal house. Cnut appears to have obtained intelligence of this rebellion before his opponents could mobilize, and he had four prominent leaders killed. This may well have undermined the entire operation and the king seems to have had little difficulty in dealing with Eadwig, whom he 'put to flight'.

Cnut's decision to marry Emma came very quickly after his suppression of this loyalist rising and may well have been in part at least conditioned by that event. Emma could provide one route at least by which to accommodate English sympathy for the native dynasty to the new regime and build bridges between Cnut himself and families with close connections to Aethelred's. As already suggested, Cnut also seems to have sought to share power with the English aristocracy to a greater extent after 1017 and so integrate them into his regime and reduce the risk of their supporting his rivals.

The appointment of Ealdorman Aethelweard, however, turned out less well from Cnut's perspective than did his patronage of Leofwine's family – when the king returned from Denmark in the spring of 1020 he held a second great assembly at Cirencester, following that is the one he had staged at Oxford in 1018. Cnut had been absent from England for some months, during which Earl Thorkell had been left in charge, and had been busy organizing the governance of Denmark. Ealdorman Aethelweard was apparently accused to the king at Cirencester, and one manuscript of the Chronicle associates him in this respect with Eadwig, 'king of the ceorls'. Both were outlawed and Aethelweard disappears at this point from history, yet Cnut does seem to have made one more effort to swing this influential family over to his own side. The king is not known to have made any attempt to obstruct the election of Aethelmaer's son, Aethelnoth, to the vacant see of Canterbury in 1020, and relations between king and primate thereafter seem to have been cordial enough, although it is of course quite possible that his initial election was viewed by the monks there as a statement of solidarity with the old English aristocracy and against the *nouveau* Danish administration.

It may well be that the ealdorman of the south-western shires had taken the opportunity offered by Cnut's temporary absence from England to conspire with Eadwig to overthrow the Danish kingship in England. Cnut's return, long enough before Easter to then organize a great assembly to coincide with the festival, may even smack of a certain amount of haste on his part. Once again, he successfully pre-empted an uprising on behalf of the native dynasty, and on this occasion it seems to have been an entirely West-Saxon affair.

Eadwig himself apparently survived the collapse of his efforts in 1017, but may well have been forced to flee abroad. Cnut's marriage established a form of kinship between them, however tenuous such might appear, but this did not ultimately save him. Although the Danish king had good reason to avoid the opprobrium which would presumably attach to him should he have Eadwig killed, that was probably what occurred – the aetheling's end is obscure. If the Eadwig who was outlawed at the Cirencester assembly in 1020 was a supporter (as is implicit in the 1017 Chronicle entry), then he was possibly then still alive. This 'king of the ceorls' was perhaps a popular leader fomenting opposition to Cnut and using the prince's name as an alias. Eadwig was eventually buried at Tavistock in Devon, in the heartland of his support, and the Chronicle is probably correct in assigning ultimate responsibility for his death to Cnut. A praise poem by Sighvat the Scald concerning Cnut refers to him having either killed or driven away all Aethelred's sons without exception, and Eadwig seems to fit either category. It may be that he made one last, unrecorded and abortive effort to regain his brother's throne, probably by attempting once more to raise the south-western province. If so, he failed and paid for his pertinacity with his life.

Although Eadwig's career, and in particular the two conspiracies on his behalf in 1017 and 1020, are barely recorded in the Chronicles, it does seem that there was a serious attempt on the part of a significant section of the English nobility to overturn Cnut's kingship in the first few years of the reign. The magnates concerned included members of the old aristocracy as well as the new. They were prepared to take substantial risks in pursuit of their objectives and several prominent figures paid the ultimate penalty for their audacity. Cnut seems on both occasions to have been saved from outright rebellion by the excellence of his intelligence – which itself suggests that the English aristocracy were far from united in their opinions. The first conspiracy was suppressed by means of a few selected killings and what was probably a minor campaign in the field; the second was resolved by outlawry. It seems likely that there was a third thereafter, and that this led to the death of the aetheling himself. Supposing he returned to England while still outlawed, he could then be killed with relative impunity and with little opprobrium attaching to the king. Eadwig's death brought the danger to Cnut's regime from English insurrection to an end, and with it any real prospect of an early revival of the English royal house.

EADWIG'S SURVIVING KIN

Eadwig is not known to have married or produced children, and it seems very likely that he did neither. Only two other of Aethelred's sons had survived to 1016, and these were Edward and Alfred, born to Queen Emma. Edward was probably born in 1005 (see above) and Alfred's name does not occur on royal diplomas until 1013, implying that he was delivered little earlier than this. Both had been removed to safety in Normandy by late 1013 but Edward at least, and probably both, were back in England in 1014–15. How they and their advisors reacted to Edmund's succession is unclear, although later Scandinavian writers portrayed Edward as fighting alongside his half-brother in 1016. Given his tender age, however, this may well have been a fictional improvement on reality. Whether or not, they were arguably in London with the queen their mother early in 1016 and then dispatched back to Normandy on her authority, either when London was relieved by English forces or perhaps when Edmund died.

In Normandy, they and their sister were given shelter by their maternal uncle, Duke Richard II, but their relative youth precluded any extravagant gestures of support on behalf of Edward, supposing that is that their uncle had any desire for such adventures. This has a bearing on speculation concerning an Anglo-Norman alliance in the summer of 1017, which has so often been postulated on the basis of Cnut's marriage to Emma. However, this marriage is more likely to have been mooted when Emma was in England than Normandy, in which case the ducal family were not really involved. Emma therefore probably married Cnut as dowager queen rather than as a Norman princess.

The English aethelings were consistently portrayed by Norman writers as wronged princes worthy of considerable esteem, and Edward's sister, Godgifu, was procured a marriage of the highest status available to the ducal court, to Drogo, Count of the Vexin. This was a political match and Drogo was a

Gisors Castle was the principal stronghold of the Vexin, a small but strategically significant county north of the Seine which Norman dukes and kings of France each attempted to dominate.

significant figure and in control of a county of considerable strategic value to the Normans, midway between themselves and Paris and on the north side of the Seine, so Godgifu's hand in marriage was being treated as a valuable asset.

When Edward and Alfred grew to maturity later in Cnut's reign, there is some evidence that Duke Robert (1027–35) provided them with sufficient resources to attempt to oust Cnut from England and restore Edward to his father's throne. Both the aethelings were attesting ducal charters dating from the period 1031–4, and Duke Robert's charter to the Abbey of Fécamp was witnessed by 'King Edward'. A charter of Edward as 'king of the English' conferred St Michael's Mount and several English estates in the south west on Mont St Michel at a similar date and, although this is often rejected as an obvious forgery, it just might reflect Edward's political aspirations and his recognition as king at the Norman court. William of Jumièges noted an expedition launched against England by Robert I on Edward's behalf from Fécamp which was then blown off course to Jersey and returned to the mainland at Mont St Michel. That fleet was allegedly commanded by one Rabel, whose name also occurs on the Fécamp charter.

*The ancient church of Fécamp was
destroyed by the Vikings in 842 but
rebuilt and re-endowed, supposedly
initially by William Longsword. William
promoted several of its inmates to high
office in England. It is today L'Abbatiale
de la Sainte-Trinite. Fécamp was an
important royal port during the eleventh
century.*

There is, therefore, just enough evidence to postulate a serious effort by the
Norman court in the early 1030s to restore Edward to his inheritance. William of
Jumièges also wrote that Cnut offered half his kingdom to the two aethelings in
1035, when he was gravely ill, but that nothing came of it. If so, this may well
have been a subtle piece of diplomacy aimed at deterring foreign intervention
during the succession of Cnut's own heirs, yet it may equally reflect the state of
the king's own conscience, having deprived Aethelred's sons of their rightful
inheritance.

To return to 1016–20, however, it is clear that Aethelred's sons by Emma were
too young to offer any effective resistance to Cnut, with or without Norman
assistance. Furthermore, Edward's candidacy, once his father was dead and his
mother's influence marginalized, was overshadowed by that of his half-brother,
Eadwig, who was some eight or so years his senior, present in England for
significantly longer and far more capable of rallying support to his cause. Although
their sojourn in Normandy kept Edward and Alfred safe, it precluded their
becoming a centre for disaffection inside England, since there was no great pool of
political refugees congregated there around them. Cnut's growing confidence
regarding Aethelred's second family is perhaps visible in his grant of an estate in
the vicinity of Rye and Winchelsea in Sussex to the Norman ducal Abbey of

Fécamp in 1017, and it was certainly by then warranted, since his marriage to Emma occurred in the midsummer, making him technically at least their stepfather.

Just when Edward began to emerge as a serious contender for the throne in Norman eyes is unclear. It has been suggested that Cnut's presence on the Isle of Wight in 1022 could have been connected with the Norman threat, but that is more likely to have been part of measures taken against Earl Thorkell, whom the king had exiled in the previous November. Thorkell may have then wintered in northern France rather than risking the North Sea in midwinter – but if so the fact is unrecorded. Edward was at this date only seventeen. Even so, the earlier and comparatively lengthy association of Thorkell with Aethelred and Emma between 1013 and 1016 could have predisposed the exiled earl to have at least considered throwing his support behind his old patron's favourite son – or perhaps one should argue that the possibility is likely to have occurred to Cnut. If so, Thorkell thought better of it, returning instead to Denmark where he seems to have so destabilized Cnut's regime that the king felt obliged to return there in 1022 to restore his own position, and to reconcile Thorkell to himself in 1023. If that was something which Cnut had in mind, then he perhaps considered that the possibility of an alliance between Thorkell and Duke Richard in support of Edward's candidacy for the English crown was something best countered by diverting Thorkell back to his own side.

Thorkell's exile was probably the only fleeting opportunity for Edward to promote his own candidacy prior to Duke Robert's more active support a decade later. In the intervening years, Cnut had plenty of time to establish himself in England and accommodate the English aristocracy and clerisy to his own regime. In this respect the lack of any other serious contender during the 1020s was arguably crucial. When Edward did reappear with a fleet off the English coast, in 1036 following Cnut's death, he was treated as an outsider and driven off. By then twenty years had passed since a Danish king had seized the throne and displaced Aethelred's sons and a very different group of men held power, all of whom owed their prominence to Cnut himself.

The remaining two aethelings in 1016 were Edmund Ironside's sons by his marriage to Siferth's widow in the summer of 1015, who cannot have been more than babes in arms when their father died in November 1016. They were either twins or born in very rapid succession, with the second probably delivered after their father's death. The infants, Edward and Edmund, were removed from England, presumably in reaction to Cnut's takeover. Although some versions of events suggest that it was Cnut himself who was responsible, they seem to have escaped from his inimical intentions to parts of Scandinavia where local leaders were reasserting their independence of Swein's sons. Connections between the aethelings and Sweden once again reminds us that the enemies of Swein's successors had much to gain from mutual co-operation, and Aethelred's involvement in St Olaf's ambitions in Norway may well supply the crucial link between these two theatres in 1016. Thence they were eventually dispatched to Kiev and finally to the court of Karoslav in Hungary, arriving there by the 1040s. At some stage Edmund died or was killed, but Edward made a prestigious marriage to Agatha, a member of one of the several families which had provided candidates to the imperial throne, and they had three children.

Throughout Cnut's reign, however, Edward the Exile was too young to be a serious contender for his father's throne. By the time he had reached maturity, he was resident in distant Hungary and had lost almost all prospect of regular contact with England. He had no obvious prospects of return to his father's kingdom short of the sort of diplomatic efforts which eventually led him and his family to make the journey in 1056–7, and these were initiated in England, not Hungary. He could not, therefore, himself take responsibility for asserting a meaningful claim to the English throne, despite his royal lineage, although his naming of his son after King Edgar certainly implies that he retained ambitions in that direction.

Cnut's kingship of England was threatened, therefore, only by Eadwig Aetheling, and only in the first part of his reign. Serious movements in his favour were pre-empted by prompt action in 1017 and 1020. Ultimately – and arguably not that much later – Eadwig was killed. Thereafter, there was to be little serious threat to Cnut's tenure of the English crown from the native royal house.

ASSEMBLY, GOVERNANCE AND POWER

English government depended to a very large extent on face-to-face contact, and assemblies of one kind or another were a regular and normal part of life. The courts of the shire and hundred were a case in point, to which, for example, the law code known as VIII Aethelred, in 1014, made specific reference. Such were not, however, meetings on a national level. Although the royal council probably met quite frequently, this was a comparatively small group, comprising perhaps no more than between ten and thirty individuals at any one time, and capable of all meeting together inside a large hall. More representative meetings above the level of the individual shire or ealdormanry were less common.

The coronation of a new king was one obvious example of such broader meetings, but Cnut is not known to have been crowned and it is possible that he experienced some initial difficulty in persuading the bishops to consecrate him. The first few years of Cnut's reign did, however, witness an unusual series of great ceremonial occasions which involved much larger groups congregating from a wide area. The precedent was perhaps the Oxford assembly of 1015, staged by Aethelred and Eadric, and it must be significant that the first certain assembly of Cnut's reign, in 1018, also occurred there. There may, however, have been earlier meetings on a considerable scale, associated with the several submissions to Cnut. These assemblies were great occasions and clearly well attended by the political classes. Their purpose was presumably in very general terms to reduce tensions between a Danish king at the head of a Scandinavian army and the English leadership, to normalize political processes and channels of communication in the aftermath of a dynastic revolution and to affirm Cnut's kingship. Many present on both sides necessarily felt vengeful for the dead and wounded among their own kin, lords and followers – and instances are known from the more prominent individuals on either side – but the new regime needed personal animosities to be set aside and peace reinforced. Some English leaders clearly felt uncommitted to Cnut as king, and would have preferred to restore Aethelred's dynasty. The great assemblies are unique to the first six years of the reign, and were not apparently thereafter considered necessary. The probability is that they ceased to occur as soon as Eadwig Aetheling was dead.

Although it seems likely that the initial year or two of a new kingship did generally witness an upturn in meetings of this sort, the exceptional circumstances of Cnut's kingship, its usurping characteristics and questionable legitimacy perhaps encouraged the regime to stage more such assemblies than normal and over a longer period of time.

The only subject known to have been dealt with at the Oxford assembly in 1020 was law, and the reference to this in the Worcester manuscript of the Chronicle should probably be linked to Archbishop Wulfstan's being commissioned to produce a new code of law for Cnut, to be based on those previously promulgated by Edgar and also – largely by Wulfstan himself of course – by Aethelred. Both Cnut's surviving codes reflect Wulfstan's style and there are several indicators which suggest that he was personally responsible for them, in which case his death in May 1023 implies that most of Cnut's law-making belongs to the first few years of the reign. He surely was present at Oxford and was then empowered by general agreement concerning the appropriateness of Edgar's law code to carry the matter forward. I Cnut is, in fact based both on II and III Edgar and VI Aethelred, with additions which closely resemble Wulfstan's homilies.

Cnut's general proclamation to his subjects in 1020 – sent from Denmark to Thorkell and the council in England – exhibits the same preoccupation with just kingship and law enforcement in its very first declaration (clause two): 'And I declare to you that I will be a gracious lord, and will not fail to support the rights of the church and just secular law.' Cnut goes on to stress his alertness to papal and ecclesiastical instruction and his concern for England's security from further Viking attack, then reverts to the theme of good and just government by his agents, under '. . . the law of Edgar to which all have given their adherence under oath at Oxford'.

There is, of course, a significant rhetorical purpose to such correspondence, which is arguably more to do with the appearance of just and Christian government as a source of potential legitimacy than the reality, but it does reflect the concern of Cnut's regime in this early period of comparative insecurity to project a virtuous image. His injunction to Thorkell therein has an important political context:

> If anyone . . . is so presumptuous as to defy the law of God and my royal authority or secular law, and will not make amends or desist from so doing, . . . then I pray and likewise enjoin upon Earl Thorkell to bring the evil-doer to justice if he can.
> If he cannot, it is my will that he should make use of both his own resources and mine for the purpose of driving him out of the country or crushing him, if he remains in the country, whether he be of high or low station.

Cnut returned to England before Easter and then staged his second great assembly at Cirencester, whereat he put into practice his own injunction by

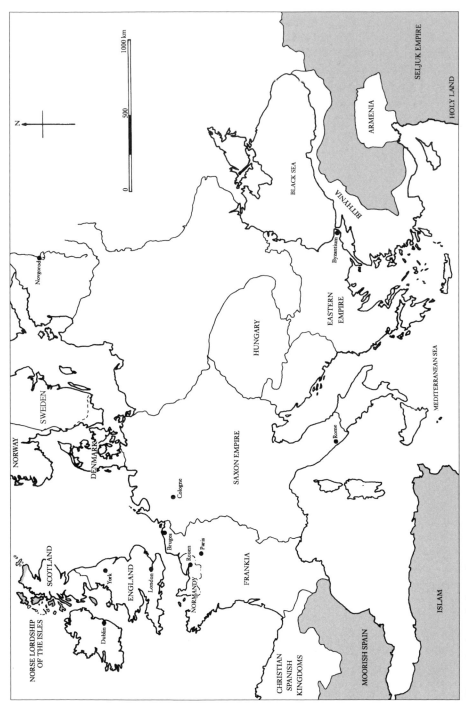

Europe in the mid-eleventh century.

outlawing Ealdorman Aethelweard – and one must sympathize with Thorkell's presumed inability to discipline men of such status, despite all the urging of the king's proclamation, in his master's absence.

Following the great assembly at Cirencester, Cnut returned to Ashingdon, where he had defeated Edmund in October 1016, to attend the consecration of a new minster on the site of the battle. This probably occurred on the anniversary itself. Parallels with the foundation of Battle Abbey forty years later are irresistible, and the solemn ceremony was well attended. The king was accompanied by Earl Thorkell, who had probably then been his companion in arms and was now his principal lieutenant and the premier earl, Archbishop Wulfstan, the leading ideologist, lawyer and 'prime minister' of the last three regimes, and other bishops, abbots and monks unspecified. It was, in other words, a comparatively full turn out by the regime and its clerics, so a meeting to rival in importance the Cirencester assembly itself but now with the emphasis on the king as patron of the church. That assembly had confirmed Cnut's kingship by outlawing his lay critics; the Ashingdon ceremony was also arguably intended to affirm the king's position, but this time by reminding all concerned of his great victory, yet at the same time establishing a minster where masses could be offered for the souls of the dead in both armies. To that extent, Ashingdon represented a major effort at reconciliation between Danes and English under Cnut's leadership, and the partnership of Cnut and Wulfstan personified that intent. The by now elderly and highly distinguished Archbishop of York had served two kings before Cnut and his close association with the Danish regime was an important source of legitimacy during these early years.

A similar ceremony took place in 1023. Archbishop Lyfing of Canterbury died in 1020 and the opportunity was taken to underline the legitimacy of the consecration of the first primate to be established under Danish rule by a detailed and exceptionally reverential notice in the Chronicles of his reception in Rome by Benedict VIII. When Archbishop Aethelnoth returned from there, he presided over the translation of the body of St Aelfheah from St Paul's at London back to Canterbury and his own Christ Church. Aelfheah had been slain by members of Thorkell's Viking army when Aethelred was king. Now under a Danish king, his body was to be restored to Canterbury and the entire episode brought to an honourable and dignified close with the establishment of the relics of a major new saint in the senior archdiocesan church. The regime turned out in force for the first stage of the ceremonial journey and Cnut reaped substantial benefits from it. Indeed, this is one of the longest continuous narratives of a single event in the entirety of the Worcester manuscript of the Chronicle, owing perhaps to Wulfstan's involvement in the planning – although his death earlier in the year ('Florence' gives 28 May) prevented him from attending.

The king, the archbishop, his bishops, the earls, and many others accompanied the relics by ship from London to Southwark on 8 June, where they were entrusted to the archbishop and his companions. From there the clergy conveyed them to Rochester where the entourage was joined by Emma and her son by Cnut, the child Harthacnut, and then on to Canterbury on 11 June and a new home on the north side of the altar of Christ Church. The participation of the entirety of the regime at the outset offset the original responsibility of the Danes for Aelfheah's martyrdom in April 1012, and the involvement of Emma and her son provided a much needed link between the legitimacy of Aethelred's government when the deed occurred, and Cnut's when the relics were translated. Harthacnut's presence, as heir to both, gave the regime the appearance of permanence. Once again, therefore, the Danish king was making intelligent use of a ceremonial opportunity: he associated himself with a recent martyr in much the same way that Aethelred and his sons had linked themselves with St Edward, and arguably expected similar benefits from it; his protection provided the context for the translation of these important relics and he associated his entire regime with the process; Emma's special role was then exploited. The long-serving queen had probably witnessed the deposition of the archbishop's corpse at London. Now she participated in the latter stages of the translation, where it may have been felt undiplomatic for either Cnut or Earl Thorkell – who had recently returned from Denmark with the king – to appear. Reconciliation between Englishman and Dane was, therefore, the crucial theme once again, with an English saint expected to legitimize Danish kingship. These ceremonies played an important part in reinforcing Cnut's kingship in England, during the years when that still remained very questionable.

CNUT'S APPOINTEES

As already recognized, it was an essential part of Cnut's new and youthful kingship of the English in the early months of 1017 to appoint those whom he wished to act as his lieutenants in the several provinces. While retaining Wessex under his own control, he placed Thorkell in East Anglia, confirmed his previous appointment, at the beginning of 1016, of Erik in Northumbria, and reinstated Eadric to Mercia. Within a few months, however, Eadric – the only Englishman among them – had been killed, apparently on a charge of treason, and Cnut was forced to rethink his governmental strategy.

Of his principal early appointees, only Erik looks to have been a long-time and trusted supporter. He was the son of Earl Hakon in Norway and had shared in the governance of that region under King Swein and received his eldest daughter's hand in marriage, then joined Cnut at the start of his campaign in England, probably in 1015. When Earl Uhtred was killed near York, Erik was the loyal lieutenant and experienced politician and general whom Cnut left in the north to rule it on his behalf. If he was the *dux* who beheaded Eadric at London in 1017, then he was not always in Northumbria, and his comparatively regular attestation of royal charters between 1018 and 1023 confirms the impression that he was frequently at court, in which case he served as an important link between York and the south.

It is unclear how much of the north he actually controlled, since Uhtred's brother Eadulf Cudel was recognized as earl of the far north in later Durham histories and the house of Bamburgh were defeated by the Scots at the Battle of Carham in about 1018 unaided by Erik. In consequence, it seems likely that Uhtred's murder brought Northumberland and Durham out into a long-sustained rebellion against Cnut's regime, which was only finally put down by a mixture of force and accommodation by Earl Siward on the eve of Edward's succession in 1042. Even so, Earl Erik governed one of England's most volatile provinces for the first six years of Cnut's reign with a loyalty which could not be doubted, and he probably ruled with the assistance of men such as that Thurbrand the Hold who had slain Uhtred. He disappears from history in 1023 after briefly becoming premier earl during Thorkell's exile and, given that he had been militarily active since the 990s, is likely to have then died. His career was sufficiently distinguished to be recalled in skaldic verse in Scandinavia.

The other senior Viking to whom Cnut deputed power and influence in 1017 was Earl Thorkell, who was also renowned in Viking story telling and a veteran of the great battles fought in and around Norway in the late tenth century. Following his ravaging of southern England with an 'immense raiding army' in 1009–11 (described above), Thorkell and forty-five ships took service with Aethelred, and arguably helped defend London from Swein in 1013. His ships, based on Greenwich, are likely to have been an important part of the fleet with which Aethelred sailed to the Isle of Wight and then on to Normandy later that year and Thorkell probably participated in his patron's return to England in 1014. Just how long he remained in the service of Aethelred and his family is unknown. It is possible that he served in Edmund's armies in 1016; it is equally possible that he joined Cnut at some stage in 1015 – when his fellow-courtier and associate, Eadric Streona, abandoned the sick king. The most attractive solution, perhaps, is that Thorkell was among those at Southampton who allegedly acclaimed Cnut when Aethelred died, but the fact is that we do not know. One Scandinavian source claimed that he was present at Ashingdon on Cnut's side and there killed Ulfcytel, the leader of the East Angles, then married Ulfketel's widow, Aethelred's daughter Wulfhild, but John ('Florence') of Worcester named his wife as Edith, who has been provisionally identified with another of Aethelred's daughters and the widow of Eadric following his execution in 1017. That Thorkell married one of Aethelred's daughters is not improbable given his high status in England from 1017 onwards, and three of them were certainly widowed in 1016–17, any of whom would arguably have brought him significant estates and enhanced his position.

Whenever he joined Cnut, therefore, his support was necessarily very recent when he was appointed Earl of East Anglia early in 1017, and he had certainly been Swein's enemy in the recent past. Cnut's decision to appoint him and, indeed, to treat him consistently in 1018–19 as his premier earl, is therefore an interesting one. It may be that he believed that Thorkell's reputation as a warrior was such that his presence within the regime was warranted almost irrespective of his recent track record, and his fame and fortune arguably necessitated he be given seniority over the other earls. There may, however, have been other considerations. Despite his prominence as a fleet commander, Thorkell never appears to have had ambitions to the English crown for himself – as some scholars have recently suggested – and his career reveals a history of faithful service, even in adversity, which suggests that Thorkell the Tall was a man whom others could trust. Furthermore, his comparatively lengthy commitment to Aethelred arguably

The prominent west tower of St Mary the Virgin at Sompting, Sussex will have been well known to Earl Godwine, who held nearby Worthing. In 1066 this considerable manor was held by a certain Leofwine from King Edward and it is possible that this unusually well-endowed thegn was in fact Godwine's son, the earl of that name.

Cnut when accompanying him on an expedition to Denmark to counter rebellion there, which could be a reference to the king's visit to his homeland in 1022–3. Whether or not that was the occasion, he obtained in consequence of his distinguished service the hand in marriage of Gytha, sister of Earls Eilifr and Ulfr, the husband of Cnut's only full sister, Estrith. Although this was not marriage to Cnut's sister, as the *Vita* alleged, his bride certainly was a member of Cnut's extended family, and this arguably occurred before her brothers' fall from grace – if that indeed occurred – in 1025. This was, therefore, a prestigious match, which had considerable potential to tie Godwine to Cnut. The *Vita* also claimed that Cnut made Godwine '*dux* and *baiulus* ['earl and lieutenant'] of almost all the kingdom', and this may well indicate the expansion of his responsibilities to encompass the whole of Wessex – so to include even the western shires previously managed by Aethelwold – and the role of regent of the kingdom when the king was absent. From 1023 onwards, Godwine was accorded the status of premier earl and he retained that position throughout the remainder of the reign.

Godwine and Aethelweard therefore represent very different political phenomena in the early years of the reign. Aethelweard's instincts were to restore Aethelred's line to the throne and he was eventually outlawed in consequence. In contrast, Godwine's experience of Aethelred's regime made him something quite exceptional – an English aristocrat who was totally committed to Cnut's kingship and who was prepared to build his own political career on support for the Danish kingship from the very beginning. Cnut's success provided a vehicle for Godwine's meteoric rise to become his most trusted English lay associate, and he rapidly became a powerful figure, second only to the king throughout England below the Thames.

Other senior figures held power during at least part of these years. As has already been noted, Ealdorman Leofwine witnessed royal charters between 1019 and 1023 and exercised power in Worcestershire and perhaps elsewhere. Earl Erik's son, Hakon, witnessed in the period 1019–26, and exercised similar power in the same area. An Earl Sihtric seems to have been appointed in Hertfordshire in the mid- to late 1020s, and a variety of other figures make occasional appearances, probably largely as visitors to the court from other parts of the Scandinavian world.

The successive departure from office of Eadric, Aethelweard, Leofwine, Thorkell and Erik and Eilifr in the period 1017–24 does not, however, seem to have led to the promotion of a comparable number of new appointees. The position is, admittedly, rendered somewhat obscure by the almost total absence of surviving charters from the period 1027–31, but the pattern which then emerges is a rather different one. Just two earls dominate the witness lists in the last years of the reign, Godwine of the West Saxons and Leofric of the Mercians, with occasional appearances by Siward, Earl of the Northumbrians and the obscure figure of Earl Aelfwine, who was probably in fact merely a prominent thegn.

Of these figures, Godwine – the king's kinsman by marriage and close friend – was the earl whose authority ran with that of the crown most closely and he clearly occupied a special position and was accorded exceptional status. Godwine's pre-eminence was not unlike that of Eadric under Aethelred. Both

Eadric and Godwine were chosen for this role and raised up from noble families of only local significance by the king of the day, then married into the dynasty, and this distinction separates these two figures from such as Thorkell and perhaps even Erik, both of whom were figures of considerable status quite independent of Cnut. Godwine arguably held quite exceptional power during the late 1020s, when there is no evidence of earls appointed to Northumbria or even much of central England, but this must be in part a consequence of the poverty of our sources in a period for which the annalistic literature is exceptionally meagre and charters virtually non-existent. Even so, Cnut's frequent absences in Scandinavia and at Rome (in 1027), arguably required that England be left in the charge of a royal council which looked to a single executive chairman, and Godwine is by far the likeliest candidate for that role.

Cnut's appointees to senior positions in the English church display a very different pattern. From the very beginning of the reign and consistently thereafter, the Danish king sanctioned and himself selected English candidates for almost every vacancy. This was arguably in part, at least, because he had no option, since very few Danish candidates were available. Even so, this feature of his reign has very real significance. While Scandinavian appointees took up a substantial proportion of royal patronage in the area of lay appointments early in the reign, there was never any real threat to the other major career path open to the English aristocracy – within the clerisy. This fact had considerable potential to reconcile a substantial number of senior English figures to Cnut's kingship at a comparatively early stage, and it may be significant that none of the 1017 killings or 1020 outlawries included churchmen. Emma's experience as a patron of the church was probably a considerable asset to the regime from 1017 onwards, and Wulfstan certainly seems to have accommodated Cnut's kingship by 1018. The bishops and principal monasteries were very wealthy, with control collectively of lands equivalent in value to the crown itself, so their political weight was considerable. There is an enormous contrast between Cnut's patronage of English clergy and King William's subsequent replacement of an entire generation of English churchmen by continentals. Under Cnut, opportunities for Englishmen to find profitable employment in the church actually increased – with the more adventurous finding positions in Scandinavia – while under William they all but dried up.

That is not, of course, to suggest that relations between the king's officers and English churches were always entirely amicable. One issue was undoubtedly the king's marital practices, which men such as Wulfstan cannot have condoned. Other churches had their disagreements with the king, and both Ely and Ramsey may be cases in point. Cnut permitted the replacement of canons by monks at St Edmund's, Bury, and this pleased some but had the potential to displease others. At Canterbury, his *burh*-reeve and the archbishop harboured various animosities, but such were not uncommon in late Anglo-Saxon England. In general terms, Cnut learnt quickly and adopted the role of Christian king very publicly. As a church patron, it is difficult to distinguish him from his immediate predecessors.

Several of the king's Scandinavian associates similarly distinguished themselves – the staller, Tovi the Proud, for example, founding the great minster of Holy

Cross at Waltham, Essex, to accommodate the great 'black rood' which had been discovered on one of his Somerset estates, along with a smaller cross, a gospel-book and a bell. Yet Cnut's English contemporaries must have been well aware of the newness of the Christianity of the Danish royal house and the paganism and only very superficial Christianity of many of his followers.

In 1025, Cnut lost the Battle of the Holy River, in southern Sweden, and for several years his entire position in the north was under threat. The chroniclers claimed that it was with significant English forces that he then campaigned in Norway in 1028 and evicted Olaf, who returned but was ultimately defeated and killed in 1030. Thereafter, Cnut was unchallenged in Denmark, but the unfortunate death by drowning of Earl Hakon robbed him of the obvious figure to manage Norway on his behalf. The king dispatched Aelfgifu and her elder son Swein there, but the arrangement proved unpopular and eventually enabled Olaf's son, Magnus, to regain power in the north. Even so, Cnut appeared to have everything under control in 1031 when he returned to England. He immediately marched north and procured the submission of Malcolm of Scotland, who had been campaigning in Northumbria, and seems to have taken measures to stabilize the northern frontier and suppress the separatist ambitions of the house of Bamburgh. It seems likely that the appointment of Siward to the rule of all Northumbria was an immediate consequence, but he seems to have had to spend considerable time and energy making his rule effective.

Leofric's emergence as the dominant figure in all central England is another feature of this period. Leofric was the son of Ealdorman Leofwine and witnessed a surviving charter as earl for the first time in 1032. He had presumably by this date had plenty of opportunity to prove his loyalty and recover his family's place in the king's favour after Northman's death in 1017, and it is quite possible that he had served with distinction in Cnut's English forces in Scandinavia. Our sources are simply much less interested in Leofric than in Godwine, whose daughter was eventually to marry Edward the Confessor. Whatever his route to power, by 1035 Leofric had risen to a dominance of Mercia the equal of that exercised by Eadric Streona from a comparable base in the West Midlands. Leofric's regional supremacy brought to an end a period of several generations during which different factions contended for power in Mercia and East Anglia and confirmed the victory of west-Mercian magnates over East-Anglian and north-east and east-Mercian families. The last figure from within the latter group known to have been influential at Cnut's court was Aelfgifu, and she passed most of the closing years of the reign in distant Norway.

By 1035, the combination of Leofric's influence and affinity and those of Siward in the far north was sufficient to counterbalance that of Godwine at the centre. Yet none of these three had been in power for very long – and only Godwine for over a decade. What is more, none sprang from a family with strong associations stretching back over generations across very much of the vast region in which they now ruled beneath the king – Godwine's family interests are unlikely to have much transcended the boundary of Sussex a generation earlier and Siward the Fat is not known to have had any association with his earldom

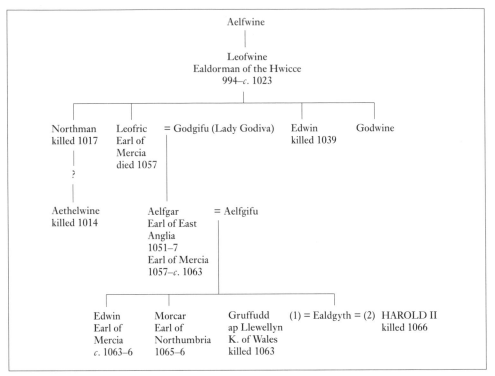

The family and descendants of Ealdorman Leofwine of the Hwicce.

even five years previously. Only Leofric had any claim to long-lived connections with a regional aristocracy, and that only in one corner of his much enlarged territory. Both Leofric and Siward made strategic marital alliances with influential aristocratic families in other parts of their territories – Leofric with Godgifu (Lady Godiva), whose kin were probably part of the nobility in Lindsey, and Siward with the house of Bamburgh – but each could only use this tactic once.

In important respects, therefore, these grand earls occupied positions which were comparatively fragile, and each depended heavily on the goodwill of the king of the day. Few of their estates were family lands, and only the continuing support of the crown could ensure that each retained what he already had, maintained his position at the head of a swollen affinity and obtained opportunities to further reinforce that position. The death of their patron while still a comparatively young man was, therefore, a matter of very real concern to all three of the senior earls, and posed serious dangers to each.

Cnut died at Shaftesbury – where the nuns still guarded the shrine of England's most recent, royal saint, Edward the Martyr – on 12 November 1035. The body was taken to Winchester and buried in the Old Minster, one assumes with fitting pomp and solemnity. In this, his last great ceremonial appearance,

Cnut was buried in the Old Minster at Winchester, but it is unclear what happened to his remains when that was demolished in 1093–4 to make way for the nave of the present cathedral. Several mortuary chests still preserved contain assorted bones which are reputed to belong to various royals. The largest skull of those seen here has the words 'Edmundus Rex 1765' inscribed on it in pencil, although neither king of this name is known to have been buried here.

Siward presided over the least English of the major earldoms in the mid-eleventh century. This view across the River Eden at Deepgill in Mallerstang to take in Shoregill Fell and Ling Hill reveals a landscape which was largely named by speakers of Old Scandinavian and – to a lesser extent – Old Welsh.

Cnut emphasized the legitimacy of his own kingship for the last time. Assuming that this was his choice of resting place – as seems very probable – he opted for the royal sepulchre of greatest antiquity within Wessex, where kings stretching back to Egberht and Cynewulf via Alfred, his young son, Edmund, and his successor, Edward the Elder were interred. More recently, King Eadred had been buried there. By this choice, Cnut lay claim to membership of the English royal line and sought once more to reconcile his kingship with those that had gone before. If that was still then necessary almost two decades after he had come to power, the succession crisis which followed offers no indication, and it was his heirs, not those of Aethelred or Edmund, who were to dominate the subsequent contest for his crown.

THREE

Crisis, Mishap and Opportunity: English Kingship 1035–65

THE SUCCESSION: CNUT'S SONS

Cnut died on 12 November 1035, several years before his fortieth birthday. He had by then produced three sons by two marriages: the less 'official' but earlier marriage to Aelfgifu had born him Swein and Harold, whose paternity was contested by some contemporaries; the second to Emma who was his 'official' queen produced just Harthacnut, who was almost certainly the youngest of the three. Harthacnut cannot have been born before 1018 and was described as a child in 1023, so was still in his teens in 1035, when even Harold can have been no more than twenty years old.

Cnut seems to have died of natural causes. The wording of his grant to the monks of Sherborne in 1035 suggests that he anticipated his death so he presumably had some time to arrange his effects and nominate heirs to his several kingdoms. Whatever dispositions he may then have made are, however, unrecorded. Even so, there are indications that he intended to leave positions of considerable influence to more than one of his sons. Aelfgifu and Swein had been established in Norway in 1030, and this may imply that the king had it in mind to leave this realm to his eldest son, perhaps to rule under Harthacnut's overall suzerainty much as Hakon had once done under his own. Similarly, Harthacnut had been in Denmark for several years in 1035 and was its titular king, issuing his own coins even while his father was still alive. He had, therefore, already been established as superior in status to his half-brothers and as heir to the stem kingship of the dynasty. This left Harold in England, and it is possible that Cnut had entertained the notion of his occupying a Thorkell-like position there after he had gone, ruling on Harthacnut's behalf and in his frequent absences in war-torn Scandinavia. He had not, however, granted him a great earldom on which to base such status. It does seem very likely that Cnut intended that Harthacnut should succeed himself as king, and the support of Earl Godwine – Cnut's closest political ally – for his candidacy in England certainly suggests that he was his father's nominated heir to his island kingdom.

Matters did not, however, progress as Cnut seems to have intended. Just prior to his death, the Norwegians evicted Swein and elevated Magnus, the son of St Olaf, to the throne. Swein retired to Denmark and promptly died there and the resurgent Norwegians attacked the Danes, so engaging Harthacnut in the defence of his dynasty's primary kingdom at precisely the time when he needed the freedom to absent himself so as to secure the throne of England – the largest, richest and most populous realm hitherto ruled by his father.

In England, a meeting of the royal council took place soon after Cnut's death at Oxford – which by this stage was perhaps becoming the preferred site for such major political gatherings. The Peterborough manuscript of the Chronicle describes a confrontation there between Earl Leofric, backed by thegns from north of the Thames and the fleet at London, and Earl Godwine, with the West Saxons and presumably the queen behind him. Knowledge of current events in Scandinavia meant that both parties could anticipate that the interregnum before Harthacnut's arrival would be a long one and the immediate issue was control of royal patronage and executive power in the interim. Earl Godwine was necessarily a candidate for the regency pending Harthacnut's arrival, and Queen Emma – Harthacnut's closest kin – was another. The two were clearly close allies and jointly operating on Harthacnut's behalf, and, one must presume, to his instructions when such were available.

The prospect of Godwine's dominance – either as regent himself or as the power behind the dowager queen – posed considerable dangers, however, to the very recently established Earl of the Mercians, who was his natural rival for power. He countered the influence of the West-Saxon earl by aligning himself with Harold's candidacy for the regency, and a share also in his father's kingship. Harold's maternal background tied him into the east of Mercia, and he probably had connections with influential families in and around Lindsey, where Leofric had married and was seeking to augment his own authority. His influence may well have been greatest in Northamptonshire where his mother's principal seat lay, but his grandfather had presumably had a broad spread of estates in the northern and eastern Midlands where Harold might expect to find support. The alliance of earl and aetheling arguably had considerable advantages for both parties at the regional as well as the national level, and held out the prospect of easier access to royal patronage for the aristocracy of the Midlands over and against the south. The ship men perhaps preferred an internal candidate as king to a Danish ruler who already had his own fleet, with whom they might have to share the bounty of England's king. Harthacnut's arrival might even raise the prospect of their dispersal as the force less intimately connected with his royal person, much as Cnut had previously paid off much of his fleet early in his own reign. Harold himself clearly had ambitions on the English throne from the beginning.

The immediate result of the Oxford meeting was a compromise. Emma was to hold Winchester – where the king's treasure lay – and to have command of Cnut's housecarls; with these resources and Godwine's assistance she would act as regent in Wessex. At the same time, Harold asserted his right not just to the regency but to full kingship north of the Thames, and Leofric's support must be what enabled him to secure this. A new coinage was issued – the 'jewel cross' type – which was unique to the period of joint kingship.

This settlement has important resonances of previous attempts to resolve disputes over kingship, and particularly of the Ola's Island Accord of 1016 which similarly divided England between kings of Wessex and Mercia. In the event, it proved no more permanent. Harold established himself as king of the Mercians and within the same year sent his own men to Winchester to obtain a share of his father's treasure. Neither Emma nor Godwine felt capable of effective resistance to the legitimate demands of a king whom most believed to be Cnut's son – despite the several authors who cast doubt on his claim on their behalf. With no sign that Harthacnut could even set out from Denmark in the foreseeable future, his half-brother's candidacy acquired a momentum which threatened to become unstoppable.

In 1036, Emma seems to have despaired of Harthacnut's arrival and concocted a plan to bring one or more of her sons by Aethelred back to England, presumably with the intention of having him crowned in Wessex as a counterweight to Harold's kingship in Mercia. Admittedly, the *Encomium Emmae* later claimed that Emma's invitation was a fiendishly clever fabrication by Harold, but this looks very much like a later attempt on behalf of the queen to deny responsibility for an initiative which went horribly wrong.

Cnut's two stepsons were still at this date in Normandy but dramatic changes had occurred at the ducal court there. Duke Robert the Magnificent had attained power in 1027 but the early years of his rule were characterized by internal warfare. From about 1030 onwards, however, he was in effective control of his own territory, and as has already been mentioned he had the means to interfere outside. The possibility that he recognized Prince Edward as King of the English at this time and even provided him with a fleet to attempt to regain his father's kingdom has already been discussed. Robert departed, however, for Jerusalem as a pilgrim late in 1034, but died in Bithynia while returning in July 1035, leaving his duchy to his young bastard son, William. Edward was not, therefore, well placed to press his own candidacy for the English throne when Cnut died some four months later, since he had neither the committed support in England of a militarily significant faction nor the assistance of an adult duke.

Emma's invitation redressed the first of these issues by offering her sons the prospect of a welcome at Winchester, where Cnut's housecarls still presumably provided the core of a standing army which the queen might have been able to mobilize on their behalf. Edward seems to have sailed with a small fleet direct to Southampton, but there found no support for his candidacy so cautiously withdrew rather than pushing inland and placing himself and his companions in jeopardy. His brother travelled by a different route, crossing to the south east from Boulogne and attempting to reach Winchester thence overland, but he was captured by Earl Godwine, who brought an end to the entire enterprise with considerable brutality. As the Abingdon manuscript of the Chronicle records:

But then Godwine stopped him, and set him in captivity, and drove off his companions, and some were variously killed; some of them were sold for money, some cruelly destroyed, some of them were fettered, some of them were blinded, some maimed, some scalped.

Godwine had clearly not been consulted by Emma before she chose to recall her sons from Normandy and he had no reason whatsoever to support her initiative. His own family had been victims of Aethelred's courtier friends in 1009, when the king had apparently seized the entirety of his patrimony. Godwine had been an associate of Prince Athelstan after that – the rival of Edward for the succession – but his death and then Edmund's robbed him of any chance of regaining his father's lands from the native dynasty. He had since rebuilt his family's fortunes and risen to heights undreamt of by his father by dint of commitment to the Danish kingship, but at the expense of numerous families which could be expected to seek the return of lands and honours should Aethelred's sons return to power. Godwine, therefore, had very strong reasons to fear for his own position should Aethelred's half-Norman sons regain kingship in Wessex. It was his responsibility to protect Southampton against hostile fleets and to apprehend unauthorized parties of travellers in his earldom and he undertook both tasks with a will.

Emma's realignment also destroyed any last chance of holding the south for Harthacnut, since it was she who was technically the regent. Godwine was left with no option but to make the best deal he could with King Harold. Anger at his own exposed position *vis-à-vis* Harold and Leofric and at being forced to abandon Cnut's intended heir may have made his treatment of Alfred and his companions the more savage, but his custody of the aetheling did at least provide him with bargaining power. Alfred was eventually blinded at Ely and died there in the care of the monks, perhaps on 5 February 1037. That location lay well outside the ambit of the West-Saxon earl and suggests that Godwine was not responsible for this ultimate atrocity, which seems to have overtaken the aetheling after he had been surrendered to Harold. From the latter's viewpoint, the capture of a rival for the throne who was associated with his enemy, the dowager queen, who had hitherto been safe in Normandy and who had few if any sympathizers in Mercia provided a convenient opportunity to eliminate him.

With Emma's initiative in ruins and Godwine forced to throw his weight behind Harold's candidacy, the way was open for Cnut's elder son to assume the kingship of all England. In 1037 Emma was driven out and took refuge at Bruges under the protection of Count Baldwin V of Flanders, where she seems to have had some contact with Edward but otherwise reverted to her earlier support for Harthacnut. In England, Harold's regime established itself and produced a new design of coin, the fleur-de-lis style, thus distinguishing itself from the period of joint kingship of 1035–7.

Little is known of Harold's kingship. There are no surviving charters from his reign and the chroniclers record little of political import, concentrating instead on the deaths of senior churchmen and 'the great gale' of 1039. Only the deaths of Leofric's brother, Edwin, and several other prominent figures in battle against

Silver penny of Harthacnut. This coin is of the 'Arm-and-Sceptre' type, dating to 1040–2. Its similarity to Cnut's coinage and emphasis on the sceptre perhaps underlines Harthacnut's need to establish himself as king following five years of what he and his partisans considered usurpation by his half-brother.

the Welsh in 1039 receives attention. This battle near Welshpool signalled the beginning of the career of Gruffudd ap Llywelyn as king of Gwynedd, in which role he was to affect English politics during the reign of Edward the Confessor, but his energies were devoted to wars inside Wales over the next decade.

Harold died on 17 March 1040, perhaps at Oxford, and was, unusually, buried north of the Thames, at Westminster. In the same year Harthacnut had at last secured peace with Magnus of Norway and was in the process of leading a fleet variously described as of sixty or sixty-two ships southwards to press his own candidacy in England, so Harold's death averted a real prospect of war between Cnut's two sons. The English councillors naturally decided to offer the crown to the surviving son of Cnut and their representatives met Harthacnut in Bruges *en route* for England. They quickly came to regret their welcome, however, when Harthacnut's first act in office was to impose a geld of £21,099, over half of which was used to pay off thirty-two ships, and this coincided with record grain prices, so a probable famine year.

Harthacnut's brief tenure of the throne clearly failed to impress his new subjects. His reputation was not helped by the subsequent change of dynasty, yet the little information available does nothing to improve it. At the instigation it was said of the Archbishop of York, he had his brother's body disinterred and treated dishonourably, and later ravaged Worcestershire as punishment for the killing of two of his housecarls when collecting taxes in the shire town. Lastly he allowed Earl Eadwulf – Uhtred's heir of the house of Bamburgh and leader of the long struggle fought in the far north against Earl Siward – to be slain while under his own safe conduct. Even so, the handful of surviving charters which grant lands to various churches do suggest another and less-disreputable side to the regime.

So too does his responsibility for the return of Edward from Normandy. The Worcester manuscript of the Chronicle contains the most detailed account:

And soon in that year [1041 following the punishment of Worcestershire] came from beyond the sea Edward, his brother on the mother's side – King

Aethelred's son, who had been driven from his country many years earlier, and yet was sworn in as king; and then he dwelled thus in his brother's court as long as he lived.

The Peterborough manuscript of the Chronicle confirms only Edward's arrival and his kinship with the king, but the *Encomium* also asserts that Harthacnut associated Edward with his own kingship, so what may on the face of it seem an unlikely story seems to be true. Precisely what Harthacnut hoped to achieve thereby is unknown, but it seems likely that he was attempting to stabilize his own kingship. He had already experienced the difficulties of attending to the political affairs of England and Denmark at the same time and clearly needed a loyal subordinate to take charge of England while he returned to confront the Norwegians in the north. Despite her undoubted loyalty, Emma's recent failure as regent perhaps undermined her candidacy for the task of deputy. None of the earls currently in post can have given Harthacnut much confidence. Siward was the individual least compromised by the power struggles of the previous six years but had only just detached himself – with the king's help – from a long, drawn-out war and his resources lay too far from the centre of government. As Harold I's principal supporter, Leofric was arguably an unreliable figure in Harthacnut's perspective, whose entire position was now likely to be put in question. In many respects, Godwine was the obvious candidate, but his eventual accommodation of Harold's kingship in 1036 had some potential to undermine the new king's confidence in his father's closest political associate. Furthermore, Godwine clearly had considerable responsibility for the fate suffered by Alfred and his companions, if not ultimately for the aetheling's actual death. Alfred was Harthacnut's half-brother, and this incident is likely to have cast a shadow over their relationship. Archbishop Aelfric reputedly accused Godwine and Bishop Lyfing of Worcester to Harthacnut, and he succeeded in having Lyfing temporarily deprived of his see in 1040 to his own advantage, so the issue was a sensitive one at that date. Godwine was said to have given Harthacnut's half-brother, Edward, a marvellous ship as a present at his accession, and it has been suggested that this was viewed by both parties in some sense as a wergild (compensation payment) for his treatment of Alfred.

Harthacnut had spent very little time, if any, in England during the last decade and is unlikely to have had the opportunity to form strong relationships with any member of the English aristocracy. His need to find an effective deputy capable of maintaining his regime while he returned to Denmark therefore left the king with no obvious candidate from among the officers whom he had inherited from his predecessor and enemy. It was in this circumstance that he invited his elder half-brother's return from Normandy, and had him recognized as 'co-king' in England. The chaos into which Normandy had by this date descended ensured that Edward would be unable to call in military support from the continent which he could then use to reinforce his own position *vis-à-vis* Harthacnut. Nor had he powerful connections inside England on which to build his own party. Edward was, therefore, a comparatively safe candidate from Harthacnut's perspective for the task of presiding over the royal council in his half-brother's absence. His close kinship with the senior king gave him the necessary status to referee the rivalries of the principal earls and his indubitable royal blood had the potential to add legitimacy to a regime which had quickly made itself deeply unpopular. All this was available without any significant threat to Harthacnut's kingship itself.

The potential of Edward's new position at court was not, however, ever put to the test since Harthacnut died suddenly only a few months later in 1042, 'as he stood at his drink, and he suddenly fell to the earth with an awful convulsion; and those who were close by took hold of him, and he spoke no words afterwards, and he passed away on 8 June'. The occasion may have been a society wedding, of Tovi the Proud to Gytha, the daughter of Osgod Clapa ('the rough'), both of whom were stallers at the royal court. The king's symptoms suggest that he may have suffered a brain haemorrhage, but his decease brought an end to Cnut's issue, all of whom, male and female, had died young and without producing children.

THE LAST OF THE CERDICINGS

Few men have succeeded to the English crown in such improbable circumstances as Edward in 1042. He was then aged about thirty-seven, unmarried and with no known offspring. Having been a prominent candidate in his youth for the succession to his father, King Aethelred, his chances seemed to have been overwhelmed by the political and dynastic crisis of 1013–16. Thereafter his candidacy was overshadowed first by that of his eldest surviving half-brother, Edmund Ironside, until his death in 1016, and then by the last survivor of that side of the family, Eadwig, until an unknown date in or after 1020. Edward then became the senior aetheling, but his absence from England enabled Cnut to consolidate his position without significant threat from the native dynasty. Only Norman support in the early 1030s offered any real possibility of reviving his claim. That interlude, however, degenerated into fiasco. Queen Emma's belated recall of her elder two sons in a last ditch attempt to deny Harold I the crown in 1036 likewise proved an expensive failure and cost the life of Edward's only full brother. The surviving aetheling's reputation may well have been damaged by these setbacks, and his very appearance of harmlessness may have encouraged Harthacnut to invite him to return in 1041.

Edward had little reason to turn the invitation down. His position as Harthacnut's closest surviving kinsman offered a degree of security and considerable status at the English court, and he was presumably cognisant of the role he was expected to perform there, whether or not that was as suggested above. At the same time, he had little reason to tarry longer in Normandy, where the ducal court was threatening to disintegrate under the competing claims of magnates, churchmen and rival members of William's family during a lengthy minority. His distant kinsman, the bastard child Duke William, was by now in frequent danger of his life. No further support for his ambitions in England could be expected for the foreseeable future from that quarter and Edward was already middle aged if not elderly by contemporary standards.

Not only Duke Robert had died on his ill-fated pilgrimage. Edward's brother-in-law, Drogo the Count of Amiens and the Vexin, likewise failed to return, leaving that court also to experience a minority. Countess Goda eventually married Eustace of Boulogne, a prominent client of the court of Flanders, but was in no position to aid her brother in 1041. Nor is there much trace of any positive interest in his candidacy as successor to Cnut in England. Harthacnut's invitation was, therefore, timely, from the viewpoint of an aetheling whose ambition to regain his father's throne had lost any real credibility.

Harthacnut's death soon after Edward's accommodation within the regime was a circumstance that was impossible to predict, unless that is the king had been showing signs of ill-health. Whether or not, his demise was the last of three within the same family in very rapid succession, beginning with Cnut's in 1035. All were premature inasmuch as those concerned were all comparatively young – with Cnut, at his death in 1035, about Edward's own age in 1042, Harold no more than twenty-five in 1040 and Harthacnut about twenty-two in 1042. Collectively their departures created a vacuum at the very heart of the English political establishment which must have taken all concerned by surprise.

The rapid succession of Harold, Harthacnut and Edward created considerable difficulties of adjustment for the English political classes. In 1035, it seems reasonable to assume that none of those holding senior offices either anticipated or desired the restoration of Aethelred's family. Each of the earls owed his own elevation to Cnut and none showed himself prepared to look beyond the previous king's sons for a successor. Of the bishops, only the aged Beorhtwald of Ramsbury and Athelstan of Hereford had been appointed under Aethelred. The two metropolitans – the West-Saxon aristocrat, Aethelnoth, at Canterbury and the more obscure monk of Peterborough, Aelfric Puttoc at York – were both appointed under Cnut, and the latter at least was apparently a supporter of Harthacnut after 1035. Aethelnoth died in 1038 and was replaced by Eadsige, who was described by one version of the Chronicle as the 'king's priest'. Archbishop Aelfric apart, none of them appear to have played a prominent part in the several successions of the period, although Eadsige's position required that he crown Edward. It may well be that the episcopal bench was made up at this time of comparative political lightweights, perhaps in part because no churchmen could compete with the landed wealth and political influence vested in the three great earls.

The Anglo-Danish political establishment had, therefore, by 1040, already had to dig deep into their reserves of flexibility to accommodate the demands of the two rival half-brothers. In 1042, it suddenly found itself without any obvious alternative but to rally behind the maternal half-brother of the last of them to die. Edward's position was apparently founded on four factors: his kinship with Harthacnut; his presence at court; the fact that no other potential candidate was then in England or seemed likely to arrive in the near future; and his very recent acknowledgement at Harthacnut's behest as 'co-king'. He was, of course, Cnut's stepson, so in some sense a member of the ruling house. Even so, it seems most unlikely that his succession was greeted with the effusive outpourings which the author of the *Vita Edwardi* was later to envisage.

Earl Godwine's part in the proceedings is the easiest to assess of all the great men of the realm. In the *Vita* he is portrayed as the 'father of all' who urged that 'they should admit their king to the throne that was his by right of birth' and bring him back to England, but the author failed to recognize that Edward was already in the country and then mistook the location of his consecration. His account of this episode was clearly as much purple prose as fact. In practice, Edward succeeded not by right of his descent from the English royal family but by his relationship to the last Danish king. Godwine, for one, is most unlikely to have welcomed the return of Aethelred's family. His commitment to the Danish royal house had been the central plank of an illustrious career and the return of Aethelred's kin had considerable potential to harm him. If this was true already in 1036, it was far more so in 1042, when the matter of Alfred's death could be raised against him at any time. One can be reasonably confident that Godwine would have supported another Danish candidate if there had been one, but Magnus of Norway immediately secured Denmark and Cnut's nephew, Swein Estrithsson, had considerable difficulty in establishing any sort of independent kingship there for himself. The role of Magnus and before him his father Olaf as an opponent to Cnut and his dynasty is unlikely to have endeared him to Godwine or reassured him that his candidacy was one which might benefit himself in England.

There is, of course, the rather later story of Harthacnut's treaty with Magnus, in about 1039, which enabled him to extricate himself from Scandinavia and set sail for England, which is told in *Magnus saga*. The terms reputedly included the establishment of each as heir to the other in the event of their dying without issue, but this was far more pertinent to Denmark than England, given that Godwine and the remainder of the political community had recognized Harold I as king when this treaty was made. Magnus certainly entertained ambitions thereafter to conquer Edward's kingdom, and may well have drawn moral support for his candidacy from the putative terms of the treaty, but his claim seems to have found little if any support within the Anglo-Danish establishment in England in the summer of 1042. Nor did the Norwegian king arrive to press his claim in person before Edward's coronation.

In the last resort, Godwine probably drove as hard a bargain as was available to him. Edward was consecrated king at Winchester on Easter Day (3 April) in 1043. The choice of site surely had important messages for participants and onlookers alike, since it emphasized Edward's descent from the West-Saxon kings of before, while at the same time connecting him with the sepulchre of both Cnut and Harthacnut, who were silent witnesses, therefore, of his coronation. It was also the spiritual heartland of Godwine's own earldom, and the site most closely associated with the dowager queen. The timing may also have been symbolic, with the promise of redemption so characteristic of Easter Day, but the delay of nine months between Edward's succession and his crowning may perhaps have been for other reasons as well. It seems likely that Edward had first to reconcile Godwine and the other leading magnates to his kingship and reassure them that their interests, and the Anglo-Danish political system over which they presided, were safe under a king whose natural instinct it was to resent his Viking predecessors and all their deeds. It may be relevant that the Abingdon and Peterborough manuscripts of the Chronicle refer to

Archbishop Eadsige's admonishing him during the consecration ceremony 'as to his own need and that of the people', and this erstwhile household priest of Harold I may have had good reason for concern on behalf of his friends and himself. To the extent that we can guess at the matters under discussion, Edward seems to have promised his patronage and amity to the existing political leadership in return for their commitment to his kingship and the defence of England against any new attack from Scandinavia, but such is obviously no more than hypothesis. It should also be noted that the delay in consecration of a new English king was not unusual.

Godwine had special problems concerning Alfred's death and this may have led him to hold out for a marriage alliance. Edward wedded Godwine's daughter, Edith, on 23 January 1045, almost two years after his coronation, but it seems very likely that the matter had already been agreed at the start of the reign. The delay between coronation and marriage could even reflect the king's disinclination to go through with it thereafter but his ultimate decision was to honour whatever agreements had already been made.

Despite the absence of alternative candidates, the nervousness of Edward and his closest advisors is attested by their treatment of Queen Emma shortly after the coronation. Her priest, Stigand, had very recently been appointed to the vacant see of Elmham, and the new king presumably took his mother's advice concerning this appointment. In mid-November, the king obtained information which made him so deeply suspicious of his mother's loyalty that he despatched all three of the principal earls from the court at Gloucester to Winchester to sequester her lands and treasure, and Stigand was similarly dispossessed. The reason given by the Worcester manuscript of the Chronicle, that Edward believed that 'she did less for him than he wanted before he became king, and also afterwards' is perhaps intentionally obscure, but there are intimations that she was accused of promising her support to Magnus of Norway. That this had much foundation seems unlikely and Edward later restored the dowager queen to court, and Stigand to his see. The latter was later promoted to Winchester itself and the immediate proximity of his royal patroness in 1047. The entire episode does, however, reveal an atmosphere of chronic insecurity at the beginning of the reign, with a novice king surrounded by advisors in whom he had little trust and who was vulnerable to the circulation of malicious rumours even regarding his own mother.

EDWARD AS KING

Edward attained the English throne, therefore, largely through a sudden dearth of more acceptable candidates, and because his recognition as 'co-king' had seemed to serve his half-brother's very different political needs in 1041. He found England under the control of a political establishment which was entirely reconciled to Danish kingship, within which some individuals, at least, had cause to fear that his succession would prove a threat to their own positions. Edward had several important tasks to achieve in the early years of the reign, which collectively had potential to stabilize his regime and convince the political community at large that his candidacy had been the right one for themselves:

1   He needed recognition from as many foreign courts as possible;
2   He needed to provide an effective defence for England against whatever threat Magnus of Norway was capable of launching;
3   He needed to reassure the bulk of the political classes that his regime would protect and promote their interests;
4   He needed to reward those who had stood by him during the long years of exile, and those who had reasonable claims upon his patronage, but without alienating the bulk of the possessor classes;
5   He needed to maintain the basic processes of government and patronage, head an effective council and make appointments to the church which went some way to satisfying the ambitions of the major power blocks within the country;
6   He needed to rule in a way that avoided accusations of injustice and tyranny – such as had characterized parts of Aethelred's reign and that too of Harthacnut. Harsh taxation, vengeful actions and summary execution were all actions which fitted this category;
7   He needed to establish the succession, particularly since he was already old by comparison with the three Danish kings before him.

Edward arguably had less room for manoeuvre than many of his predecessors. Unlike Cnut or Harthacnut, he could not call upon the armed forces of Denmark to sustain his rule, and pay them from unpopularly high levels of taxation in England. The establishment of the great earldoms under Aethelred, and more so under Cnut, had arguably been achieved only by alienating large amounts of crown lands. Such alienations were technically temporary and not hereditary, but Edward could hardly reclaim significant amounts without risking the wrath of the great earls, each of whom was better established as a patron and leader of men than was the king himself. Edward's foreignness and comparative friendlessness in England in 1042 was a fundamental weakness of his regime, and required that he ruled very cautiously and very much by consensus, initially at least.

RECOGNITION

The *Vita Edwardi* makes lavish claims for Edward's recognition on the continent, envisaging ambassadors rushing to England for example from the Emperor Henry III, whom it terms his brother-in-law, but Henry had not married Edward's full sister, but Cnut's daughter by Emma, Gunnhild, and she had died in 1038. Nor was Henry to be crowned emperor until 1047. Edward's kingship probably was recognized at an early date in Germany, where the prospect of Magnus establishing a powerful Norwegian-Danish-English 'empire' would have been unwelcome, but the incident itself is clearly embroidered. Edward's connections arguably made his accession comparatively welcome in some parts of Frankia, and the presence of ambassadors from King Henry I, Normandy, Brittany and the Vexin is credible. So too is that of representatives from Denmark, where Swein was already preparing to dispute Magnus's kingship. Indeed, it is not impossible that Swein offered to become Edward's client or vassal – presumably in return for military assistance against the Norwegians – as the *Vita* implied. Swein and he were distantly related, and the Dane was also a relative of his fiancée, Edith. There is, therefore, a possibility that Edward was offered the opportunity to ally himself with Swein as the senior partner in an alliance against Magnus, which would effectively revive the sort of forward policy towards Scandinavia that his father had last attempted in 1014–16 as well as the interconnected kingships which Cnut had probably sought to pass on to Harthacnut. If so, he did not accept the invitation, loath perhaps to commit his own untried kingship and England's ships to the unfathomable risks of campaigning in the Baltic region.

Edward had little knowledge of military leadership, no known experience of battle and no coterie of soldiery with a long commitment to himself. He inherited, however, housecarls from Harold and Harthacnut, and at least the nucleus of a fleet. If the support given by the shipmen to Harold in 1035–6 was characteristic of their wider perceptions of their own interests, then the new king could count on their willingness to uphold an English ruler against a Scandinavian. The general hostility to Harthacnut's great tax to pay the Danish fleet in 1040–1 is likely to have hardened attitudes on this score. Edward spent at least part of the summer of 1044 with a fleet of thirty-five ships at Sandwich, in expectation of the arrival of a Norwegian force in the Channel. None arrived but the following summer saw a repeat of that mobilization but this time apparently of a larger force: 'and there was gathered so great a raiding-army that no-one had even seen a greater raiding ship-army in this land'. Such was very profitable employment for his shipmen, who seem to have been paid out of an annual geld for doing what amounted to very little.

In the event, Magnus failed to arrive because he was occupied in war against Swein Estrithsson, who was seeking to make himself an independent king in Denmark. In general terms, Swein had the worst of this war, but maintained resistance throughout the bulk of the decade. In 1047, the Danish leader requested of Edward a fleet of fifty ships to succour him in his unequal struggle against the Norwegians but none was sent and Magnus successfully overwhelmed his defences and forced the Danes to acknowledge him as king. Only the death of the Norwegian king in October of the same year is likely to have saved England from full-scale invasion in 1048. This sudden death enabled Swein to regain Denmark, which he then ruled until he died in 1074. This is a period of Danish history which is relatively well documented in the near contemporary writings of Adam of Bremen, who lays stress on Swein's efforts to reorganize the Danish church and forge close political associations in Germany. However, Harald Sigurdsson, or Hardrada ('the ruthless'), Magnus's co-ruler, uncle and successor, continued his predecessor's war against the Danes and again Swein barely held his own.

England was saved, therefore, from a renewal of the Viking attacks of Aethelred's reign more by virtue of continuing warfare inside Scandinavia than by the reputation of its protector. A Scandinavian fleet did raid the south coast in 1048, taking advantage perhaps of Edward's sense of security in the summer following Magnus's death. Twenty-five ships struck at Sandwich and the Thames estuary and may have been responsible also for an attack on the Isle of Wight. They were pursued by Edward and the earls but seem to have escaped, and this failure will have done Edward's reputation little good, despite his resolute action. In 1049, a Dublin Norse fleet with Welsh allies took advantage of the estrangement of the king and Earl Swein to raid Monmouthshire, and the local English defenders were defeated.

ROYAL PATRONAGE

Edward does seem to have successfully avoided alienating powerful figures inside England during the first five or six years of his reign. His half-brother's invitation in 1041 does not seem to have been extended to numerous of his own associates from his years in exile. Even when king, Edward seems to have been circumspect in directing much patronage towards lay incomers. William of Poitiers envisaged Edward returning to England with a small band of Norman knights, and his nephew, Ralph the Timid, was perhaps among them and was elevated to the rank of earl in 1050 if not before. Others, not all of whom were necessarily his friends before 1041, arrived thereafter, and perhaps as many as thirty in all – comprising a motley crew of Normans, Frenchmen and Bretons – were established as lay landholders in England by 1066. Few, however, were well endowed, and only Edward's distant kinsmen Robert fitzWimarc, Osbern fitzRichard, Ralph the Staller, Baldwin fitzHerluin and Ralph the Timid could ever be described as wealthy. There is no real sign that he ever formed even a bodyguard out of exclusively Frankish or Norman soldiers. Such limited patronage of men who had followed Edward from France contrasts dramatically with Cnut's retention of a large Viking army from 1016–18 – and a significant fleet even thereafter – and appointment of Scandinavians to the majority of the great earldoms in 1016–23. Edward's far more gradual and low-key patronage of non-clerical outsiders can have caused little disquiet within the political establishment which he inherited from Cnut's sons.

Edward's surviving writs and charters are far more numerous than those of his immediate predecessors, although they have certainly been artificially inflated by forgeries. These survivors are not, of course, likely to be a representative sample, but the comparative scarcity of foreign interest in the early years is probably significant, and even the few courtiers of French extraction rarely signed surviving royal documents throughout the reign. Apart from a grant of land at the beach head of Mersea in Essex to the Abbey of St-Ouen, Rouen in 1046, which was perhaps associated with Robert Champart, once prior of that house but latterly Abbot of Jumièges, Edward's early grants were to a reassuring mixture of *ministri* or similar with English or Danish names, members of the clergy or churches. Such men included the housecarl Urk, for example, to whom Edward granted land in 1044.

His appointees to high office in the church betray a more substantial bias in favour of continentals, including the two Lotharingian royal priests, Hereman and Leofric, whom he appointed to Ramsey and Sherborne (later Old Sarum) and Crediton (later Exeter), respectively, but the suffragan appointed to assist at Canterbury in 1044 was an English abbot and was himself replaced by a succession of Englishmen. Edward's representatives at the papal synod of Rheims

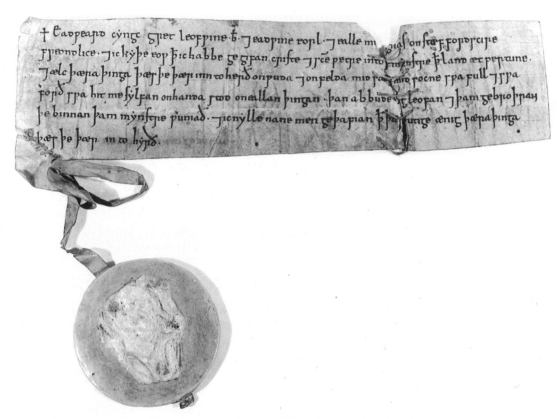

A writ supposedly of King Edward in favour of Westminster Abbey, dated 1065. In fact, this is one of a group of documents forged in the first half of the twelfth century, apparently to substantiate that house's claims to widespread lands.

in 1049 were similarly English, including Abbot Aelfwine of Ramsey who had only obtained that prestigious appointment in 1047. The first bishopric filled by Edward went not to a foreigner but to Stigand, his mother's priest. The only Norman whom he appointed at an early date was the distinguished but ambitious figure of Robert of Jumièges, whom he promoted to London in 1044. Robert had been responsible for massive rebuilding at Jumièges. Edward presumably already knew Robert from his years at Rouen and he seems to have established himself very early on as one of the king's more influential advisors. Even so, it was Stigand who obtained Winchester in 1047 and his brother Aethelmaer succeeded him at Elmham in the same year. Not until 1049 did Edward nominate another of his own Norman priests, Ulf, to the newly vacant see of Dorchester. Ulf's lack of the necessary qualities and training were remarked on, and resented, by contemporaries, and seem to have been substantiated by the hostility with which he was received at the synod of Vercelli the following year.

The door of All Saints' Church, Staplehurst in the Weald of Kent is a rare example of extant timberwork which is thought to date from the Conquest period. The decorative iron hingework depicts various sea creatures, including a two-headed serpent, and a boat.

The church which Edward inherited must have looked somewhat introverted and old fashioned to the new king, coming as he did from a region already being affected by the monastic reform movement. Although it was in parts intellectually competent, the English church was somewhat conservative, particularly as regards its architecture. This may well account for his patronage of Lotharingian priests and their rapid promotion thereafter to high office in the English church, but it is difficult to imagine that Edward was attempting to improve the quality of his episcopate by appointing Ulf, for example. Rather, this was probably an exercise in patronage unconnected with church reform, and it is perhaps noteworthy that it was this appointment, and not that of the Lotharingians, which English commentators actively criticized.

There were casualties, certainly, among the Anglo-Danish political establishment but – Emma and Stigand excepted – these were very few and exclusively from among the Danish members of the court, some of whom were evicted over the next few years. The Worcester manuscript of the Chronicle recorded the exile of 'the noblewoman Gunnhild, King Cnut's relative' in 1045 (corrected 1044), who was Cnut's niece, the widow of his close associate Earl Hakon, Erik's son, who had held power in Worcestershire until his departure to rule Norway on the king's behalf in about 1028. Thereafter she was also widow of

Earl Harald, probably Thorkell's son, who seems to have left England about the time of, and perhaps to avoid, Edward's succession and was murdered in Denmark late in 1042. Her second marriage, at least, seems to have associated Gunnhild with figures opposed to Edward, so her expulsion was perhaps inevitable. Another victim was the prominent courtier, the staller Osgod Clapa, who was outlawed in 1046. Osgod had enjoyed a lengthy and profitable career under Cnut and his sons, although his origins are unknown. Nor are the reasons for his expulsion, which may have been totally unconnected with his Danish connections. Osgod took refuge in Flanders and was probably still there when he died in 1054.

The departure of these two prominent figures had no obvious impact on the great earls. Indeed, it may well be that Leofric would have actively welcomed the removal of Gunnhild, who may well have held dower lands in the West Midlands which he coveted. Whether or not, Edward seems to have been at pains to preserve amity between himself and all three. Siward – the only Dane among them – was left in unchallenged supremacy in the north and Edward pointedly did nothing towards re-establishing the independence from his authority of the house of Bamburgh, which had proved a significant ally to Aethelred in the past but which had recently been savaged and effectively conquered by Siward and the Danish kings. Siward held rich lands in Huntingdonshire which may well have been granted him by Edward, presumably to help resource his rule in the north. Beorn Estrithsson, the brother of Swein in Denmark, held an extensive earldom elsewhere in the east Midlands. Leofric was left in control of western Mercia, but his family had arguably even there to counter the influence of Godwine's allies, with figures such as Lyfing and Ealdred promoted to the bishopric of Worcester. It is not surprising therefore that he and Lady Godiva were remembered there as despoilers of the church but elsewhere they were to become famous for their generosity as patrons – particularly towards Evesham but also Leominster, Wenlock, both houses at Chester and putatively Worcester itself. They were responsible also for the foundations of Coventry Abbey and the minster church of Stow St Mary in Lincolnshire. The several extant charters in favour of Coventry purport to date from 1043 but all are later forgeries, so it is not clear what date Leofric's most ambitious new foundation was established. Stow may perhaps reflect the family's desire to raise its profile in the eastern parts of Mercia, with which the family was comparatively poorly connected. The new church was the subject of dealings between the earl and Bishop Wulfwig of Dorchester early in the 1050s, so this initiative probably post-dates Beorn's death. The marriage of Leofric's son and heir, Aelfgar, to another Aelfgifu – arguably the daughter of that same thegn Morcar who had been killed by Eadric Streona at Aethelred's behest in 1015 – was probably undertaken for the same purpose but may have occurred earlier.

Leofric's rivalry with Godwine seems to have continued throughout the 1040s, but did not prosper until the end of the decade. From 1045 onwards, Earl Godwine was Edward's father-in-law, and was certainly the best-established of the English earls, with the added advantage of influence in Wessex where the court normally resided. He had, therefore, far easier access to royal patronage than his competitors. Godwine's involvement in the appointment of the Abbot of

The great cruciform church of Stow St Mary, Lincolnshire was founded by Earl Leofric in Lindsey in the mid-eleventh century. The transepts and lower part of the tower are pre-Conquest.

Abingdon as a suffragan to assist the infirm Archbishop Eadsige of Canterbury was specifically mentioned by the chroniclers and he may well have favoured the appointment of Cnut's erstwhile mass-priest from Ashingdon, Stigand, to the vacant see of Winchester in 1047. The two certainly seem to have been allies thereafter. Godwine seems to have continued his favoured pastime during these years of amassing land, wealth and influence, often at the expense of others including some churches and the king himself.

Godwine's eldest son, Swein, who was shortly to become Edward's brother-in-law, was given an earldom in Herefordshire in 1043, and his second son, Harold, had received East Anglia by 1045. Both appointments were arguably part of the settlement between Godwine and Edward which underpinned the latter's accession by conferring increased power on Godwine and his kin. The royal court cannot have been unaware of growing tensions in Wales at this time and the dangers such might pose along the march. The death in battle of Edwin, Earl Leofric's brother and sheriff of Hereford, in 1039, certainly required an English response, but the preferment of Godwine's son represented a significant encroachment into Leofric's sphere of influence. Swein's reaction is itself illuminating – he chose to ally himself in 1046 with Edwin's killer, Gruffudd ap Llewelyn of Gwynedd, against another Gruffudd, King of Deheubarth in south–

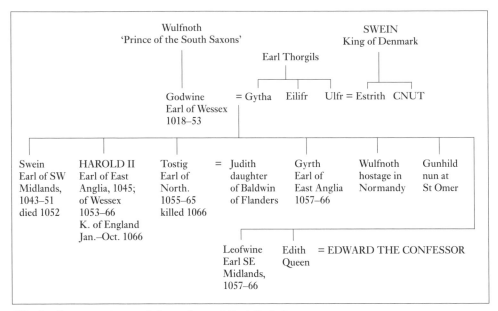

The family connections and descendants of Earl Godwine.

west Wales, and the two campaigned together. Swein's action is unlikely to have been acceptable to Leofric and the two comital families thereafter competed for influence among the Welsh. Leofric eventually secured a marriage alliance between his granddaughter and the northern Welsh king. Swein's abduction of the Abbess of Leominster, whose house was the object of Leofric's generosity and who was herself likely to have been of a noble family in the region, was similarly provocative. That deed certainly seems to have brought down the censure of the ecclesiastical establishment on him and arguably led to his banishment in 1047.

Edward also established his own nephew Ralph in the West Midlands as earl. The multiplicity of appointees in this region had good precedents under Cnut, and this was perhaps the obvious area in which to establish his own closest kinsman in England. Ralph eventually held Hereford and Oxfordshire. Taken together, Edward's new appointments to earldoms in the first part of his reign certainly advanced his own kinsmen but to nothing like the extent that they promoted his father-in-law's more numerous connections. Godwine's influence was clearly not absolute but it was extremely powerful, deeply entrenched and growing, particularly before Swein was forced into exile.

THE SUCCESSION ISSUE: DIVISION AND CRISIS

Edward had numerous reasons to resent the dominant position within the regime which he had been obliged to cede to Godwine at the start of the reign, but seems to have taken no action to retrieve the situation while he was still establishing himself during the first few years. Swein's departure may be what enabled him to begin to recoup lost ground. In 1049 he responded to the request of Emperor Henry III for naval support by mobilizing his fleet at Sandwich, 'and lay there with a great raiding ship-army until the emperor had all that he wanted from Baldwin'. The Count of Flanders had recently harboured several prominent English exiles, including Osgod and Earl Swein, and had proved in the recent past a firm friend to Scandinavian fleets on their way to England. He was also a close political ally of Earl Godwine. It is most unlikely to have been an accident that Swein overwintered there in 1047 before moving on to Denmark.

The underlying purpose of Swein's visit to the north has been convincingly connected with the English succession, although the matter is beyond proof. By that year, Edward was already in his forties and most unlikely to leave his throne to an adult son. Indeed, his marriage had so far proved barren, so Godwine was perhaps beginning to reconsider his future prospects. If he was unlikely to have the opportunity to secure a lengthy regency on behalf of his own grandson then he needed to reconsider his attitude to other candidacies for the succession. In the past, both he and Baldwin had supported the Danish royal house, but Swein Estrithsson gave every appearance in the spring of 1047 of facing final defeat – and that did in fact occur in the months which followed. Swein Godwinson may, therefore, have visited the Danish court to inform his namesake that he could no longer count on either Godwine's or Baldwin's support should Edward die without an heir of his body.

This is highly speculative until the events associated with Swein's return to England are examined. The exiled earl obtained access to the king on the south coast in 1049 and made his peace, 'and he was promised that he would be entitled to all those things which he formally possessed' – reinstatement to his earldom. This was opposed by both Earl Beorn and his brother Harold Godwineson, both of whom had apparently benefited from his expulsion. Thereafter, Swein and Godwine took advantage of fleet movements, including the departure of the Mercian fleet (which will have included Beorn's own vessels) and Edward's own campaigning against Osgod Clapa and a Flemish fleet in the Channel. They consulted together in Sussex and there abducted Earl Beorn. Swein and his men then ran westward away from the vicinity of the royal fleet and murdered their captive on the coast of Devon.

Beorn's violent and apparently premeditated death amounted to an international incident, owing to his being Swein Estrithsson's brother. As a prominent member of the Danish royal house who was in a position of influence in England, Beorn was also a significant candidate for the succession in his own right, and his murder looks very much like a pre-emptive strike by Godwine and his eldest son intended to deny both Swein and Beorn the English crown. It may well be relevant that Swein of Denmark was reputed to have joined the forces ranged against Baldwin in the summer campaign. There are signs, therefore, of a coalition of sorts between Edward, the Empire and Swein of Denmark, which Godwine and Count Baldwin sought to counter and disrupt. Either in or before 1051, these two allied themselves still more firmly by a contract of marriage between Godwine's third son, Tostig, and Baldwin's half-sister, Judith. Earl

Harold's ostentatious reburial of Beorn at Winchester suggests that he was seeking to detach himself from his father and elder brother at this date, and this is the first significant sign of division among Godwine's immediate family, but he held to his kin and shared their expulsion in the crisis which followed.

The death of Archbishop Eadsige of Canterbury in October 1050 proved a second flashpoint in relations between king and premier earl. Edward took the opportunity to advance his Norman Bishop of London to the archdiocese. The monks and clergy of Canterbury elected another candidate, however, a monk who was a kinsman of Earl Godwine, but the king held firm against all the persuasions of his father-in-law. The *Vita Edwardi* portrays the rift between king and earl as very largely Robert's responsibility, claiming that he poisoned the ear of the king against his loyal servant, and specifically that he brought actions against him over various estates, accused him falsely of complicity in Alfred's murder and even of planning Edward's own. The anonymous author had good reason to try to present both Godwine and Edward in the best possible light, since he was writing under Queen Edith's patronage. Archbishop Robert was from his perspective the obvious scapegoat, but he was certainly involved in bringing matters to a head on Edward's behalf.

There were clearly major issues at stake, which affected Edward's very ability to rule. First were the divided loyalties of earl and king in the matter of Flanders in 1049. Second was the murder of Beorn, Godwine's complicity therein, and the impact this had on Anglo-Danish affairs. Third was the outrageous behaviour of Earl Swein, Godwine's eldest son. Fourth was the matter of Edward's continuing inability to produce an heir by Godwine's daughter. By 1050, this must have seemed beyond hope, and Edward may well have planned to put away his wife and try again, in which case a pliant archbishop was an important asset and the prospect of one of Godwine's own kin securing that post a serious embarrassment. Although Edward did not actually remarry in 1051–2, he did consign his wife to the nunnery of Wherwell and probably then considered his marriage as much at an end as had been his paternal grandfather's in similar circumstances, when his wife retired to Wilton.

Even so, there seem to have been efforts made to effect a compromise between Edward and Godwine even at this late stage. Following the death of Magnus (1047) and the great mobilization of the English fleet in 1049, Edward paid off nine of his ships' crews in 1050, keeping back only five vessels as a basis for future royal fleets and so making himself more dependent on his earls. This allowed him to abolish the geld, the so-called 'raider-tax', which might be expected to enhance his popularity, but certainly weakened his regime. At the same time, Bishops Hereman and Ealdred (of Worcester) returned from the synod at Rome, and the latter may have been instrumental in organizing the return of Earl Swein from Flanders, since he was then reinstated to his earldom, so conceding one of Godwine's central demands. However, a Norman force had by then built at least one castle in Herefordshire, under Earl Ralph's authority, and this they retained. Early in 1051 there occurred a council meeting at London at which reconciliation looked likely. Robert was given Canterbury, Sparrowhawk, Abbot of Abingdon and arguably a protégé of Godwine's, the now vacant see of London, and

Dover was already a port in the mid–eleventh century, and the cliff-top site now occupied by the castle was already defended. The castle is, however, a product of successive developments dating largely to the period 1066–1280.

Edward's distant kinsman Rudolph, in exile from his Norwegian diocese, Abingdon. This compromise was, however, overturned as soon as Robert returned from Rome, since he refused consecration to Sparrowhawk on grounds of a papal prohibition.

The final confrontation was sparked off by a fracas at Dover involving Eustace of Boulogne, Edward's brother-in-law, and the men of the town, whom Godwine then refused the king's command to punish. The entire matter is omitted from the version of these events offered in the *Vita Edwardi*, which chose to concentrate on the perfidy of Robert to the exclusion of all else, but is dealt with in some detail in some but not all versions of the Chronicle, although in a manner which is generally sympathetic to the earl. Edward convened a council meeting at Gloucester on 8 September but mutual distrust had now risen to such a level that Godwine and his two eldest sons gathered forces at Beverston nearby, while the northern earls rode in to join the king. Perhaps in recognition of further efforts at compromise by Bishop Stigand, Edward ordered a second council meeting at London for 24 September but this was to coincide with a general mobilization. From a position of strength, the king once more exiled Swein and made demands on Godwine and Harold which neither felt able to accept. Faced with the king's intransigence, Godwine's support from the south west of his earldom melted away and Harold felt obliged to surrender his East-Anglian thegns to the king. Eventually, Godwine, his wife, Swein, Tostig and Judith, and another son Gyrth took ship from west Sussex to Bruges, while Harold and his brother Leofwine fled to Bristol, with Edward's soldiers in hot pursuit, and thence to Dublin.

The collapse of the power of Godwine and his family in 1051 was very dramatic, as the Worcester manuscript of the Chronicle points out: 'It would have seemed remarkable to everyone who was in England, if anyone earlier told them that it should turn out thus, because he was formally so very much raised up, as if he ruled the king and all England; and his sons were earls and the king's favourites.' Remarkable it was, but not entirely unlooked for, either at court or elsewhere. Robert and Edward took the opportunity to expel Sparrowhawk from London and substitute another French king's priest, named William, which further expanded the foreign contingent within the episcopacy; Queen Edith was dispatched to a nunnery while the old south-western province which had last been seen at the start of Cnut's reign was re-established under Earl Odda, a figure closely associated with Deerhurst in Gloucestershire. Earl Leofric received recompense for his troubles and encouragement to lend the new regime his full support by the grant of Harold's East-Anglian earldom to his son Aelfgar.

Therefore, 1051 witnessed dramatic changes to the balance of power in England. Leofric had probably benefited from Beorn's death by acquiring Lindsey but only now was he at last able to redress the northward expansion of the influence of Godwine and his family. His seniority and the acquisition by his family of a second earldom arguably projected him to the status of premier earl, although no royal charters exist from this year by which to clarify the matter and it seems most unlikely that Edward proposed to allow him the sort of influence at court that Godwine had wielded. Rather, his own newer appointees emerge as the dominant group, comprising Archbishop Robert and his clerical allies, and Earls Ralph and Odda. The death of Queen Emma in March 1052 completed this transformation, removing from the political scene a figure whose influence had rarely been negligible ever since her arrival in England a half century previously.

EDWARD'S INHERITANCE AND DUKE WILLIAM

The new regime is likely to have taken thought for the succession in 1051–2, although it need not have actually established an heir to King Edward. The Worcester manuscript of the Chronicle is the only English source for a putative visit by Duke William of Normandy with 'a great troop of Frenchmen' to Edward

Odda's Chapel, adjacent to St Mary's at Deerhurst, has long been incorporated into other buildings and has only recently been identified and opened for inspection. Unusually, a dedication stone inside names a senior political figure whom we can identify from literary sources as King Edward's earl and distant relative.

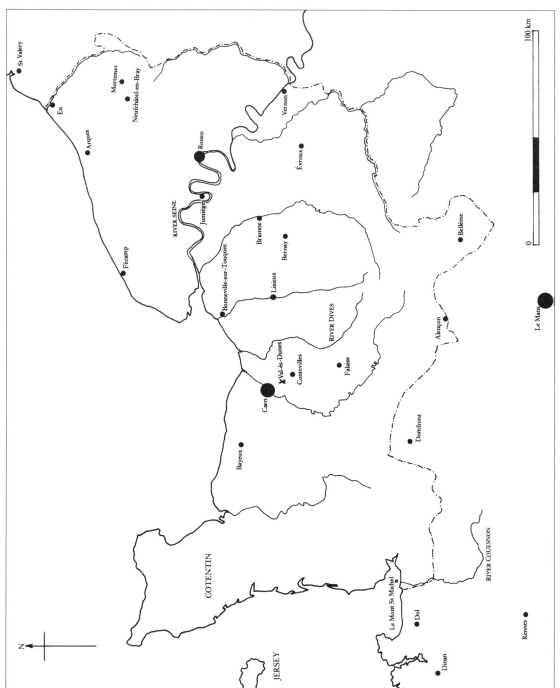

The Duchy of Normandy and its immediate environs.

in 1051. The matter is entirely ignored by the Godwine-centric *Vita Edwardi*, but finds some confirmation in the *History* of William of Poitiers. The latter, however, makes the implausible claim that Edward owed his throne in 1042 to the threat of Norman intervention, and that Edward:

> gratefully remembering with what generous munificence, what singular honour, what affectionate intimacy, prince William had treated him in Normandy . . . determined as a matter of honour to repay him in equal measure – and as an appropriate gift resolved to make him the heir of the crown obtained by his efforts. To this end, with the assent of his magnates, and by the agency of Robert archbishop of Canterbury as his ambassador in this matter, he sent him, as hostages of the most powerful family in the kingdom, the son and grandson of earl Godwine.

Much of this is, of course, highly charged rhetoric moulded so as to reinforce Duke William's candidacy in 1066 by portraying him as the first choice of Edward and the English aristocracy, to whom all concerned owed a debt of gratitude. In detail, parts are easily dispensed with. In 1041, when Edward left Normandy, William was probably thirteen and in no position to affect the career of his much older second cousin, although Edward did have good reason for gratitude towards William's father, Duke Robert. William had been titular duke since his father's death in 1035 but he was heavily dependent on the protection of his great uncle Archbishop Robert of Rouen (until his death in 1037) and King Henry I to preserve his position and even his life against the ambitions of several near relatives such as Mauger, the next archbishop, and William, who secured the lordship of Arques. The interregnum was characterized by civil insurrection and the construction of new castles. William finally fled in the face of widespread revolt in 1046, which was led by Guy of Burgundy, Lord of Vernon and Brionne, who apparently sought the succession for himself. The revolt was only suppressed through the intervention of King Henry I, who defeated William's enemies at the famous Battle of Val-ès-Dunes, south-east of Caen, but there followed a lengthy siege of Guy in Brionne, which only surrendered in 1050. William probably spent part of that interlude developing Caen as a major centre and it was there that he introduced the Peace of God to Normandy.

At the same time, both William and King Henry became embroiled in war against Geoffrey Martel, Count of Anjou, for control of Bellême and Maine. Late in the summer and on into the winter of 1051, William was engaged in a campaign to secure Domfront and Alençon and take control of the lordship of Bellême. He was then allied to King Henry. In the six months following, the French king dramatically abandoned his longterm friendship with his Norman client and allied himself instead with the Count of Anjou in support of William of Arques and other Norman opponents of the duke. The sudden realignment of the king against his erstwhile ward suggests some major difference of policy between the two, and the timing may well imply that the bone of contention related to England and William's ambitions there.

Whether William's movements late in 1051 permitted a visit to England is doubtful. Godwine only fled England in late September and William was by then

The walled town and Norman keep at Domfront emphasize the role of this site as one of several key fortresses on Normandy's borders.

busy laying siege to Domfront, far to the south. Robert did pass through northern France on his journey towards Rome that spring and may very well have visited William, but he is most unlikely then to have been able to hand over members of Godwine's close kin as hostages or make promises concerning the succession. However, the abortive negotiations between Edward and Godwine during September of that year certainly involved the issue of hostage giving and receiving, and it is quite possible that the earl's son Wulfnoth and grandson Hakon did come into the hands of the king. If the central thrust of William of Poitiers's claim is to be believed, Archbishop Robert then made a second visit to Normandy during the winter of 1051–2, and left Godwine's kinsmen with the duke at the same time as delivering to him an offer concerning the English succession. The earl's son and grandson would have been entirely inappropriate as hostages to Edward's good faith, so this detail of the account is arguably defective, but Normandy might well have been considered a good place to deposit them for safekeeping once Godwine had fled to Flanders, and they do certainly seem to have been in William's custody in the 1060s.

There is one further indication that Henry I supported Godwine and opposed Duke William in the 1051–2 crisis, and this comes in the claim made by the author of the *Vita* that the French king supported Godwine's requests to Edward

The new castle at Arques was constructed at the end of an exceptionally steep, narrow ridge, which was cut by a deep ditch. It was an ambitious structure, using what was then state-of-the-art military technology, and posed a serious threat to William's regime when it was held by his enemies.

while he was in exile to allow his return, 'both for love of him and in duty bound'. There can be no doubt that he thereafter ranged himself against William whenever possible and the duke found himself tied up in events in Normandy and unable to intervene on Edward's behalf, even had he so wished. In 1053 Duke William's uncle, Count William of Talou, rebelled in alliance with his brother, the Archbishop of Rouen, with the promise of French support. The duke invested William's grand new castle overlooking Arques and it fell to negotiation after a failed attempt by King Henry to relieve it in the autumn, but he had to face large-scale invasion by the king in the neighbourhood of Évreux in 1054, and a simultaneous assault via Neufchâtel-en-Bray towards Mortemer. The Battle of

Mortemer was a decisive engagement which at last stabilized Duke William's regime more securely and enabled him to have Archbishop Mauger solemnly deposed at a great ecclesiastical council at Lisieux. In 1055, William and his overlord were formally reconciled, but by that date England was firmly under the control of Earl Harold and William's candidacy for the succession must have seemed effectively moribund. The English regime and the French court arguably remained in contact thereafter, as is corroborated by Edward's grant of an Oxfordshire estate to St-Denis in the period 1053–7.

In retrospect, therefore, it is likely that Edward sent hostages whom he had received from Godwine to William and made him some sort of promise concerning the English succession. This probably occurred during Godwine's exile, so either late in 1041 or early in 1042. Closer rapprochement with Normandy at this point would certainly have commended itself to the English court, where there can have been little doubt that Godwine would launch an attack from Flanders and Harold another from Dublin in the next campaigning season. William's long coastline and his comparatively amicable relations with Flanders and Brittany may have been thought to offer Edward considerable advantages, particularly if Godwine were to place his support behind some other candidate for the throne, such as the Norwegian king. An offer of the succession may well have been considered necessary in order to obtain William's co-operation, given that his energies were then actively engaged on his own southern borders and in neighbouring Maine. Edward was, therefore, probably attempting to reconstruct the sort of strategic alliance which his father had long since sought with Normandy by marriage, in the hope that the duke might be persuaded to throw his own military weight into the scales against the king's enemies.

If this was the sort of calculation being made at the English court, it did not work. The council did what they could to guard the south coast against Godwine's expected attack, setting a fleet at Sandwich under Earls Ralph and Odda. These were politically reliable figures and two of those with most to lose should the exiles return but they are unlikely to have been experienced fleet commanders. A confused naval campaign ensued in late June, with Godwine using the havens at Dungeness and Pevensey, but the king's fleet then withdrew to London leaving Godwine free to obtain reinforcements from his family's long-standing associates – the sea-faring communities along the Sussex coast. With their help he then ravaged the Isle of Wight and rendezvoused at Portland with Harold's Irish fleet, which had already defeated the defending forces at Porlock Bay on the southern shore of the Bristol Channel. By the time Godwine returned to Sandwich, he had a formidable force capable of facing-down his enemies, and this time it consisted of the more committed groups of his supporters. No Norman fleet intervened and he led his ships northwards, probably via the Wantsum Channel, to Sheppey, where he burnt the royal vill of Milton Regis, then on to his great manor at Southwark. The Londoners joined him, thus providing Godwine with a very large force indeed.

Edward had also mobilized a large army and a navy and the two confronted each other in the Thames. As in the previous year, neither party was eager to press the issue to a trial of strength, mindful perhaps of the divisions in Aethelred's reign which had allowed in the Vikings. In consequence the two sides reached an accommodation, but most of the concessions this time were made by Edward rather than the earl. Godwine was allowed to clear himself by due legal process and he and Harold were restored to their earldoms in full and Countess Gytha and Queen Edith to their property. All sides 'affirmed complete friendship between them' and agreed 'good law', then expelled 'all the Frenchmen who earlier promoted illegality and passed unjust judgements and counselled bad counsel in this country, except for as many as they decided that the king liked to have about him'.

Archbishop Robert, Ulf of Dorchester and William of London all fled on 14 September, as soon as it became clear that resistance to Godwine had folded, and they took ship from Essex to the continent. The king was, thereafter, to retain only those Frenchmen to whom Godwine had no objection. These seem to have included the king's lay courtiers, almost all of whom survived this crisis unscathed, as did various royal officers such as the marshals Alfred and Roger, and the royal housecarl named Richard, who was active in Worcestershire at a later date in association with Earl Aelfgar. The principal casualties were the senior clerics who had already fled, but of these Bishop William was later recalled and reinstated. Archbishop Robert probably travelled on to Rome to appeal against his expulsion, but died at Jumièges soon after his return. Back in England, Stigand of Winchester succeeded him while he still lived, thus causing himself considerable difficulties thereafter. He held both sees – the two richest in England – in plurality for the remainder of the reign, despite the strictures of successive popes. Ulf too was replaced while he still lived, with Wulfwig. The only significant lay figure to be expelled was Osbern Pentecost in Herefordshire, apparently as punishment for sheltering those of the archbishop's men who fled to him, and he departed for a brief but exciting career in Scotland.

It may have been some comfort to Edward that Earl Swein did not return to England but instead died in September 1052 while returning from pilgrimage to Jerusalem, where he had apparently sought absolution for the murder of Beorn, but this was slight recompense for the reinstatement of Godwine and the remainder of his kin in England. Edward's personal rule was entirely undone and any prospect that he might still sire a son much reduced. Oversight of royal patronage henceforth was effectively ceded to his father-in-law.

It has sometimes been suggested that the appearance of a new coinage bearing a far more martial portrait of the king than previously provides evidence that Edward retained effective control of his own regime, but this 'pointed helmet' type is as likely to reflect the influence of Godwine's family as Edward himself, portraying a menacing face to foes within and without alike. The message may even have been intended for Duke William. This was in any case just one among a regular sequence of reformations of the coinage, which occurred in all ten times between 1042 and 1066 to the considerable profit of the regime.

For the remainder of the reign, Edward did not appoint his own priests to bishoprics as regularly as previously. Several candidates were abbots or monks, one was Harold's own priest, another was Queen Emma's, and only Giso,

Silver penny of Edward the Confessor. This example of the so-called 'Pyramids Type' – the last type of the reign – was minted at Oxford, probably in 1065.

appointed to Wells in 1060, was described as the king's chaplain. Several, including Walter of Hereford and Giso of Wells, were Lotharingians, but the Godwine family clearly had no objection to patronizing clerics from this region. Apart from his rebuilding of Westminster and grandiose endowment of that abbey, largely at the expense of several others, it is difficult to detect any effective political initiatives undertaken by Edward without the active approval of Godwine and his sons once they had forced their way back into England in 1052.

There was a need, however, to reconcile Leofric to the return of his rival, particularly since Harold's reappointment to East Anglia deprived Aelfgar of that earldom. It may well be relevant that Earl Leofric's nephew, another Leofric, was appointed Abbot of Peterborough in 1052. He was remembered as the man responsible for its extraordinary wealth in the last years of the Anglo-Saxon period, and this was largely a consequence of Edward's grant to him of the wealthy abbeys of Burton, Coventry, Crowland and Thorney. Coventry was the earl's principal new foundation in any case, and Burton had old associations with the family into which Aelfgar had married, but Edward seems to have been constructing a very wealthy monastic empire for Abbot Leofric, perhaps as compensation for the family's loss of the East Anglian earldom.

THE RISE OF HAROLD GODWINESON

Godwine died while attending the royal court at Winchester at Easter 1053: 'he sat at dinner with the king, he suddenly sank down against the footstool, deprived of speech and of all his strength; he was carried into the king's chamber and it was thought it would pass over, but it was not so; but he remained thus, unspeaking and helpless, through until the Thursday, and then gave up his life'. This comparatively detailed description suggests that he suffered a dominant hemisphere stroke. The old earl was buried in the Old Minster at Winchester, near the graves of his friend and patron, Cnut, Harthacnut and Earl Beorn. His political career had begun as an associate of Prince Athelstan some thirty years

Frontispiece to King Edgar's exceptionally lengthy charter to the New Minster, Winchester, which he refounded in 966. The king, bottom centre with arms raised and accompanied by the Virgin and St Peter, proffers his charter in book form to a Christ figure supported by the heavenly choir.

Malpas, Cheshire, from the air. A major estate and parochial centre before the Conquest, when it was held by Earl Edwin, this was one of many such foci to be transformed into a baronial caput after 1066. A Norman castle motte is visible immediately behind the church tower.

Mont St Michel. This island monastery was restored by Duke Richard in 966 and played a leading role in relations between England and Normandy in the eleventh century.

The tower of St Andrew's, Ashingdon. A church was constructed on this prominent ridge-top by Cnut as a chantry for the souls of those who fell in the battle in 1016 and its first priest was Stigand, the future archbishop. The fabric was substantially replaced in about 1300.

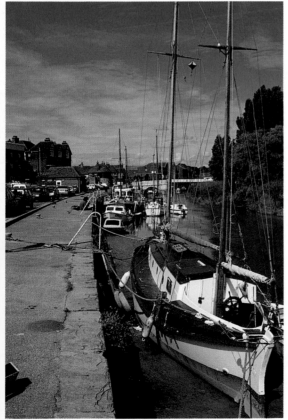

Sandwich. Despite its current role as a centre for amateur sailing, this was the principal station of the royal fleet in the eleventh century, guarding the southern approaches to the strategically vital Wantsum Channel as well as access to the south coast from the North Sea.

A retrospective medieval depiction of King Edward. Edward's strong resemblance to Christ in images of the Last Supper reflects the development of his sanctity during the later Middle Ages under a series of royal patrons.

St Oswald's Priory, Gloucester, under excavation. Founded by Earldorman Aethelred and his wife Aethelflaed (King Alfred's daughter) as a resting place for the remains of St Oswald, this tenth-century church was pivotal to the development of Gloucester as a royal centre for Mercia. Thereafter the town was often the scene of solemn crown-wearing ceremonies.

King Edward enthroned in conversation with two standing figures, the foremost of whom is Earl Harold, on the eve of his departure for France. (The Bayeux Tapestry – 11th century. By special permission of the City of Bayeux)

The foreshore at Dungeness. The beach has shifted considerably since the eleventh century but still offers an excellent haven for a fleet capable of being dragged up out of the water. It was used by Earl Godwine during his campaign to gain readmittance to England in 1052.

Porlock Bay on the south side of the Bristol Channel. Harold made land here in 1052 with nine ships from Dublin, defeated the local levies and revictualled his force.

The Wantsum Channel between Thanet and the mainland of Kent is today low-lying agricultural land around the picturesque River Stour. In the eleventh century it was, however, a strategically important waterway linking the south coast – and particualarly Sandwich – with the Thames estuary without the need to sail around the North Foreland, where fleets often suffered damage from the elements.

Bosham harbour. Bosham was a port and a large settlement in the eleventh century which was co-owned by the Godwine family and the Bishops of Chichester. The church remains the principal landmark – the west tower, nave, chancel-arch and parts of the chancel are all late Anglo-Saxon and the building has changed little since it was illustrated on the Bayeux Tapestry.

Harold's infamous oath to William. The Bayeux Tapestry indicates that it occurred at Bayeux although other sources prefer Bonneville-sur-Touques as the site. (The Bayeux Tapestry – 11th century. By special permission of the City of Bayeux)

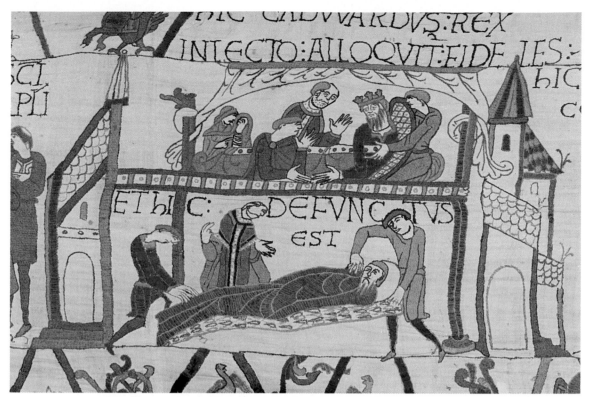

The last illness and death of Edward the Confessor depicted in a two-storey tableau. Stigand appears in both and Queen Edith and her brother, Earl Harold, are also among the figures around the old king in the upper scene. (The Bayeux Tapestry – 11th century. By special permission of the City of Bayeux)

King Harold II enthroned, supported on the left of the picture by armed figures and on the right by Stigand, the senior archbishop, with a throng of lay onlookers applauding. (The Bayeux Tapestry – 11th century. By special permission of the City of Bayeux)

King Harald Hardrada of Norway fights the northern earls at Gate Fulford on 20 September 1066, as depicted in a thirteenth-century French manuscript. Note the similarity with images of, for example, the third crusade, and in particular the entirely false assumption at this date that the battle would have been fought in part on horseback.

William's construction of a castle on a raised motte at Hastings. This is almost certainly the motte which still stands within the castle. (The Bayeux Tapestry – 11th century. By special permission of the City of Bayeux)

Hastings. The old town lies in a narrow valley running down to the sea; the castle is visible in the distance on the far clifftop.

Ferocious fighting between the English and Norman armies during the Battle of Hastings. (The Bayeux Tapestry – 11th century. By special permission of the City of Bayeux)

The death of King Harold. There has been some recent doubt whether the figure pulling the arrow from his eye was intended to be Harold, and caution is necessary given the amount of restoration that the tapestry underwent during the nineteenth century. The stricken figure overridden by the mounted knight may also represent King Harold. Note the collecting up of weapons and stripping of corpses after the battle depicted in the lower border. (The Bayeux Tapestry – 11th century. By special permission of the City of Bayeux)

Battle Abbey was constructed on King William's orders on the site of the Battle of Hastings. At the start of the conflict Harold's English forces occupied the hilltop while the Normans attacked up the slope.

Romney. Today the marshes are maintained as high quality pastureland by dykes and drainage channels, some of which date back to the Middle Ages. William ravaged Romney as punishment for earlier resistance to his soldiers once he had won the Battle of Hastings.

King William I receives the allegiance of one of his new subjects, from a later medieval manuscript. William is depicted dressed in a style more appropriate to the high Middle Ages, with a great, but highly inappropriate, beard added by the illustrator to give him an authentic, 'ancient' appearance.

previously but had risen to great and sustained heights as early as the 1020s under the first Danish king of England.

The earldom of Wessex went to Harold, Godwine's eldest surviving son, who surrendered East Anglia to obtain his father's key office. Leofric's son Aelfgar was thereby enabled to regain the earldom of East Anglia which he had briefly held in 1051–2, and he and his father then held authority over a great swathe of central England, from Ipswich to Chester, for several years. Leofric could not, however, compete with Harold for influence at court, and the latter's ability to manipulate royal patronage and decisions of the council eventually proved decisive in their struggle for power. Edith's role as a councillor to her husband is (understandably enough) emphasized by the author of the *Vita Edwardi* but there may be some substance to his claims, in which case the queen is likely to have cast her influence against the long-term rivals for power of her own family. The senior clergy were increasingly men who owed much if not all their preferment to the Godwine family. Excepting the Bishop of Lichfield, few of them are likely to have supported Leofric and his son in the scramble for influence in the royal council. Harold was assisted additionally by a fortunate sequence of events over which he had little control, but to which he reacted opportunistically and to his considerable benefit.

The first of these was Earl Siward's successful campaign in Scotland against Macbeth in 1054. The earl led a force which had been reinforced by some of the king's housecarls, and his army decisively defeated the Scottish king's force of local soldiery and Normans – this being the basis of the scene made famous by Shakespeare's 'Fear not, till Birnam Wood do come to Dunsinane' speech in *Macbeth*. As the bard noted, however, the earl's eldest son died in the battle and so too did his nephew. When Siward died at York in 1055, the extreme youth of his surviving son, Waltheof, enabled the court to make an appointment as his successor from outside his kin. It was arguably to facilitate this that Aelfgar was outlawed by the royal council in the same year. The rights of the matter were disputed by different chroniclers but his offence may well have been to object to the Northumbrian earldom being given to Harold's brother Tostig. In 1055, therefore, Harold arguably achieved two major objectives: to weaken the family of Earl Leofric and undermine its influence with Edward and in council; and to further the political careers of his brothers.

As an outlaw, Aelfgar was forced into open opposition not just to the Godwinesons but also to Edward and had little option but to fight his way back to power. He achieved this with the backing of an Irish Norse mercenary fleet and King Gruffudd of Gwynedd and Powys, but arguably he paid a heavy price – henceforth he was marginal to the court and without influence with the king, so what Harold lost by allowing his return he gained by consolidating his own influence over royal policy.

Fighting on the Welsh marches was nothing new in Edward's reign and hostilities had recently flared up once more between the English and Gruffudd's enemy and namesake, the king of Deheubarth in southern Wales. In 1055, Gruffudd ap Llywelyn finally defeated and killed Gruffudd ap Rhydderch, and it was as the king of all the Welsh that he threw his army behind Aelfgar and his

Hereford Cathedral and the site of the Norman castle, viewed from the south side of the River Wye. This was the core of the settlement refortified by Earl Harold in 1055 after being sacked by the Welsh.

Vikings. They then attacked Hereford but were met by a mounted force led by Earl Ralph. Sources are united in characterizing the outcome as a Welsh victory but divided as to the cause. The English chroniclers described it as an embarrassing rout for the English side which was due to Ralph's insistence that they should fight on horseback, and accused him of then leading the flight. The Welsh *Chronicle of the Princes* depicts it as a 'bitter-keen struggle' won by the Welsh. Certainly, the shire town and its great minster were pillaged and fired.

Had Ralph defeated the Welsh, then his standing would have risen within the regime but his discomfiture gave Harold the opportunity to mount an expedition to revive the situation, stage a limited invasion of Welsh territory and refortify Hereford with grand new banks and ditches. He then negotiated a peace on Edward's behalf which allowed Aelfgar back into his earldom. As part of the general pacification, Harold then obtained the office of Bishop of Hereford for his own mass-priest, Leofgar, who promptly launched his own invasion of Wales in 1056 – presumably on Harold's instructions – but was killed in the attempt and Earls Harold and Leofric with Bishop Ealdred of Worcester were left to negotiate a face-saving settlement with Gruffudd, who was now recognized as the king of all the Welsh by the English side in return for his recognition of Edward as his superior lord.

Harold arguably came out of this confused campaigning with an enhanced reputation both as a soldier and diplomat. Previously, his only known military activity was against the servants of the crown and even the king himself, when he beat up the coastal communities in North Devon and Somerset in 1052. In 1055–6 he demonstrated an ability to lead men on campaign and achieve strategic objectives and he was to be the senior commander of English armies thenceforth until his death in 1066. His role as a peace-weaver on behalf of king and council further enhanced his image, and comparison with Earl Ralph's military fiasco and Earl Aelfgar's illegal but effective activities can only have further improved his standing. Edward came out of 1056 with his ancestral 'overkingship' recognized in Wales, which had been infrequent, to say the least, since Edgar's day, so he too had reason to feel satisfied. Lastly, Harold himself was granted the south-west Mercian earldom which Swein had once held, focused on Hereford, so adding this important frontier region to his already substantial West-Saxon earldom.

There are important lessons herein for the balance of power between king and earl. Harold was increasingly the chief executive of the regime, dominant in its councils and earl of its richest and most populous territories, but he was very careful to portray himself as operating with, and on behalf of, the authority of the king and to cloak his own ambitions – whatever those were at this stage – under the guise of a loyal operative carrying out the collective decisions of Edward's council which had been endorsed by the king himself.

Harold's position was further strengthened by the deaths of two senior figures late in 1058, Earls Leofric and Ralph. Of the two, Leofric was by far the more formidable figure and had contested the supremacy of the Godwine family ever since the 1030s. His departure left his house short of adult figures and Aelfgar's succession to the Mercian earldom necessarily involved his relinquishing that of East Anglia, to which Harold persuaded the king to appoint his own brother,

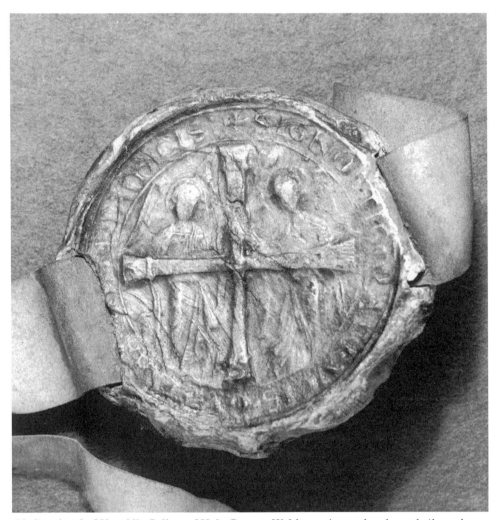

Medieval seal of Harold's College of Holy Cross at Waltham. A new church was built on the site in about 1030 by Tovi the Proud to house a figure of the crucified Christ which had been dug up on his estates, but Harold had an ambitious new secular college constructed with Romanesque nave and aisles in about 1060, one herring-bone wall of which is still visible.

Gyrth, in addition to his appointment to Oxfordshire of which Ralph seems to have been deprived by 1057. Aelfgar was again outlawed by the royal council in 1058, perhaps for objecting to the appointment of another Godwineson to a major earldom. Once more he returned with the aid of King Gruffudd, with whom he may by this point have contracted a marital alliance, and also of a large Norwegian fleet under the command of Magnus, the son of King Harald Hardrada.

Although Ralph was nothing like so potent a figure as Leofric, his death removed one of Edward's closest kinsmen, who, as a grandson of Aethelred, just might have become a candidate for the succession had he outlived the king.

Harold arguably had his own ideas concerning the descent of the crown, and these seem to have differed profoundly from those of Edward. Given that Harold and his father had expelled the king's French clerical allies in 1052 and then also successfully out-faced his attempted alliance with Normandy, Harold is most unlikely to have felt any enthusiasm for the prospect of a Norman succession. It was apparently in pursuit of a legitimate and sustainable alternative which would be compatible with the continuing dominance of the Godwinesons that Bishop Ealdred of Worcester journeyed to the imperial court in 1054 in the hope of making contact with Edward the Exile, the son of Edmund Ironside, who was in distant Hungary. Harold may also have made the journey himself on another occasion. The eventual outcome of this initiative was the arrival of Edward Aetheling, his wife and young son, at London in 1057, but he died almost immediately he had arrived (see below, p. 171). Ealdred visited Hungary on his way to Jerusalem in 1058, probably to report Edward's death to the court there. Although his diplomacy was presumably sanctioned by the council *in toto*, there can be little doubt that he was Harold's man. Appointed to Worcester back in 1046, he had administered Ramsbury diocese in 1055–8 and then Hereford – during Harold's early years as earl there – from 1056–60. His service was eventually rewarded with the metropolitan see of York (in 1060), which he held in plurality with Worcester until 1062, and thereafter until his death in 1069.

The initiative to bring back Edward Aetheling was ultimately abortive but it does provide valuable evidence that the English council was seeking an acceptable solution to the ever-growing problem of the succession when Edward should die, and there can be no real doubt that Edward acceded to their decisions. By 1057, the king was in his fifties so unlikely to live very much longer, although he still seems to have been a keen and active huntsman. The need to find a viable candidate for the succession who was less threatening to established interests, and particularly Godwinesons' interests, than Duke William could be expected to be, was becoming increasingly pressing from the viewpoint of the political establishment. That establishment had become used once more, over the previous fifteen years, to operating within a political context specific to England and its satellites, and without the need to acknowledge the interests of any foreign dynasty in English affairs.

Leofric's death removed the last senior layman whose appointment dated back to the Danish dynasty, and his family may well have been the last to seriously entertain the idea of a Scandinavian succession in England, given Aelfgar's debt to Hardrada's son for assistance in 1058. Aelfgar needed to devise his own solution to the succession problem, and his principal criterion is likely to have been his own self-interest as opposed to that of the Godwinesons. He may well have committed himself to the Norwegian candidacy but if so that fact is nowhere explicit. The Mercian earl and his Welsh allies apart, however, Earl Harold headed a regime which was increasingly insular in its perceptions, and an aristocracy which was likely to feel that its own interests were threatened by any successor to Edward coming in from outside with significant numbers of

The Norman motte at Rhuddlan. This important royal centre has been removed progressively downstream as silting of the River Clwyd has made it increasingly difficult to navigate. The earthworks of a probable Anglo-Saxon burh, which was perhaps the site used by Gruffudd, lie to the south of the motte, while Edward I's great castle and planned town lie to the north.

supporters expecting to be rewarded and resourced out of their treasures and their lands.

It was also a regime of unimpeachable legitimacy which was markedly successful at delivering peace and prosperity. Even Stigand's problems concerning the validity of his consecration to Canterbury were to an extent overcome by the recognition of Pope Benedict X, who sent him a *pallium* in 1058, but returned to plague him once again when Benedict was expelled and deposed in January 1059. Even so, the archbishop was immensely rich and a loyal ally of Harold and his position seems to have been secure within England if not outside. Additionally, the 1050s had witnessed the re-establishment of English overkingship throughout Wales and in 1059 Malcolm of Scotland visited Edward and made peace with him and Earl Tostig, following his raid on the north in 1058. Given his presence deep inside England, Malcolm presumably likewise

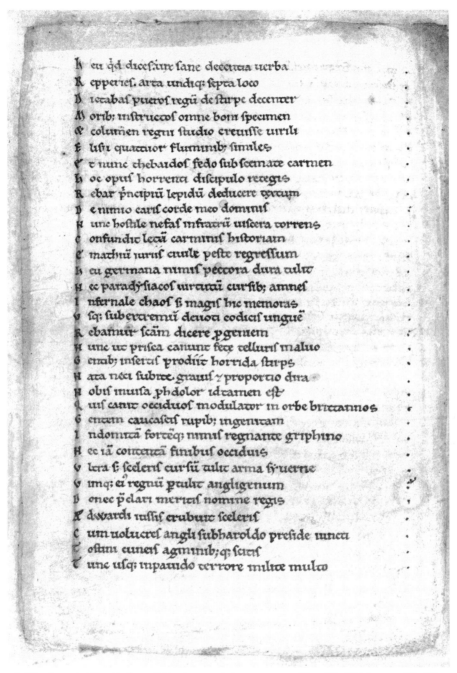

A folio from the Vita Eadwardi Regis *containing a poem on Harold's Welsh wars. The* Vita *was written for Queen Edith, perhaps in two episodes, probably during 1066 and provides a perspective on the events of Edward's reign which is profoundly that of a member of Godwine's family. This poem is in Book II. Its heroes are Harold and Tostig, whose feats were embellished by the poet with references to the work of Ovid and Virgil's* Aeneid.

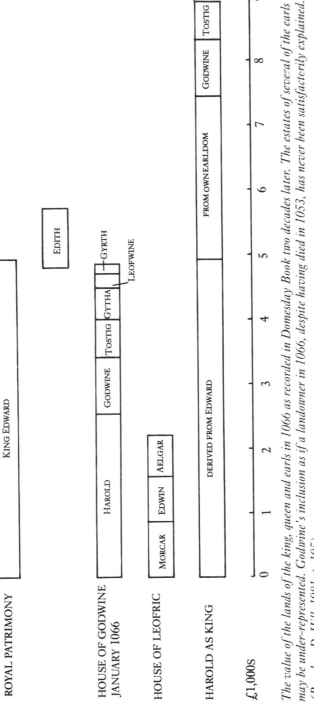

ROYAL PATRIMONY

KING EDWARD

EDITH

HOUSE OF GODWINE
JANUARY 1066

HAROLD | GODWINE | TOSTIG | GYTHA
GYTH
LEOFWINE

HOUSE OF LEOFRIC

MORCAR | EDWIN | AELGAR

HAROLD AS KING

DERIVED FROM EDWARD | FROM OWN EARLDOM | GODWINE | TOSTIG

£1,000S   0   1   2   3   4   5   6   7   8   9

The value of the lands of the king, queen and earls in 1066 as recorded in Domesday Book two decades later. The estates of several of the earls may be under-represented. Godwine's inclusion as if a landowner in 1066, despite having died in 1053, has never been satisfactorily explained. (Based on D. Hill, 1981, p. 105).

recognized Edward's supremacy. There had been a notable period of freedom from Viking attack. Relations with Flanders and the French court were arguably excellent. All this had been achieved by a partnership between the house of Cerdic and the house of Godwine, and most English observers outside Mercia are likely to have felt confident for the future provided that alliance could be maintained, or even in some way improved upon.

Although the deaths of both Henry I and Count Geoffrey Martel in 1060 significantly altered the balance of power against his interests in France, Harold's position in England was to be enhanced still further. Earl Aelfgar seems to have died in 1062. The event is nowhere recorded but his last known action was to participate in discussions concerning Wulfstan's appointment to the see of Worcester that summer. Harold and Tostig took advantage of the minority of his heir, Edwin, to invade Wales and destroy the power of Aelfgar's former ally, King Gruffudd. In a winter campaign, Harold destroyed Gruffudd's fleet base and halls at Rhuddlan, then in May of 1063 led a fleet along the Welsh coast from Bristol, while Tostig launched an invasion on the landward side, probably via the northern coastal plain. The Welsh surrendered under this unprecedented, co-ordinated attack, and themselves slew King Gruffudd on 5 August. Harold's reputation as an effective military leader and strategist was necessarily enhanced by this success, although he had to share the honours with his brother. Gruffudd's head and his ship's figurehead and trappings were delivered as trophies to King Edward, and the rule of Wales granted to the dead king's half-brothers on condition that they swear oaths and give hostages 'to the king and to the earl that they would be undeceiving to him in all things, and everywhere ready [to serve] him on water and on land, and likewise to pay from that land what was formally done before to the other king [Gruffudd]'.

The terms of this reported oath barely disguise the earl's position at the centre of the regime, and Harold was now approaching the zenith of his power and influence. Of the major earldoms, two were in his own hands and those of his brother Tostig, who was his companion in arms, and the other was sandwiched between them, without influence at court and under the control of a teenager with no military experience or reputation. East Anglia was securely held by his brother Gyrth and Middlesex and Hertfordshire by another brother, Leofwine. The much debated Herefordshire and Gloucestershire had been appended to his own great West-Saxon earldom. Siward's son Waltheof held authority in limited parts of the south-east Midlands, but cannot have been born before 1042 at earliest so remained a youth. Excepting only the earldoms of Waltheof and Edwin therefore, the Godwinesons dominated England. Scotland was ruled by Tostig's ally, King Malcolm, and most of Wales was under the authority of kings who owed their appointments to Harold.

Including Queen Edith's dower, the Godwinesons held lands in 1066 which collectively exceeded in value those of the king himself, and these were even greater before the Northumbrian rebellion deprived Tostig of the bulk of his estates in that region. The West-Saxon earl held estates valued at over £2,500, and the distribution of some of these still reflected appointments which he had held prior to his succession to his father's earldom in 1053. He had, for example, substantial estates in Essex and Norfolk, which had presumably been granted him in conjunction with his appointment as earl in that region for purposes of patronage and defence, but these had not been surrendered to his successor when he had relinquished that office. Aelfgar's rivalry with Harold over the East-Anglian earldom may well be the reason, but this is just one example of numerous discrepancies between assets and offices in the 1060s. Another was the group of estates held by Tostig in Hampshire (including the Isle of Wight), where he had perhaps been established by his father prior to his appointment to Northumbria in 1055. Likewise, Aelfgar was still credited in 1066 with lands in Essex and Cambridgeshire. Collectively such discrepancies suggest that Edward's government had been forced to alienate land which had previously been attached to temporary royal appointees, and this again points to excessive influence over the royal administration by an interrelated group of overmighty subjects.

EDWARD AND WESTMINSTER

Contemporary sources present a picture of Edward in the latter part of his life as a man devoted primarily to two things: the chase – and Edward was clearly often to be located at his hunting lodges and those palaces which had access to game – and the church. This latter focus was, of course, a conventional one in the eleventh century but Edward does seem to have placed considerable emphasis on his rebuilding and general redevelopment of Westminster Abbey, which was at that point a comparatively undistinguished tenth-century Benedictine house. Visitors to the site today cannot see anything of the fabric of Edward's monastery, since it was rebuilt thereafter in the Early English style and then further embellished with a Perpendicular chapel at the east end by Henry VII. They see even less of the idyllic rural ambience which the author of the *Vita Edwardi* claimed for it: '. . . it both lay hard by the famous and rich town and also was a delightful spot, surrounded with fertile lands and green fields and near the main channel of the river'. Edward's was to be a major rebuilding which was funded 'out of the tithes of all his revenues' and from the grant of numerous estates in Essex, Kent, Middlesex, Hampshire and Hertfordshire and a London wharf. It was presumably undertaken by his 'churchwright', Teinfrith, who was granted land at Shepperton in Middlesex in the last decade of the reign.

The new abbey church was the first in England to be built in the Romanesque or Norman style, which had become standard over the previous generation or so in Frankia. The principal hallmarks of the style are rounded arches, simple vaulting, the semicircular or polygonal apse and vigorous carving of detail, and particularly of capitals. Edward will have been familiar with the style from his long sojourn in Normandy, where we can be confident that he knew the magnificent and influential house at Fécamp (founded by Richard I in 1001), the several monasteries at Rouen, and Robert's new works at Jumièges, which was eventually consecrated in 1067. The latter was perhaps Edward's greatest inspiration and provides important insights to the sort of building he commissioned, although the rather earlier abbey church of Bernay today provides the only complete example of this genre still surviving in Normandy.

The interior of Jumièges Abbey – the columns along the north side of the nave of the abbey church looking towards the crossing.

Jumièges Abbey Church, which was eventually consecrated in Duke William's presence in 1067, was under construction during Edward's reign and, through Archbishop Robert, was arguably the principal inspiration for the rebuilding of Westminster. Although now ruined, the twin towers still stand some 60 m high.

The interior of Bernay Abbey, completed in about 1040. This is now the most complete of Normandy's greater eleventh-century churches and perhaps provides the best idea of what the interior of Edward's Westminster would have been like.

Both Edith and Edward commissioned new churches, with Edith rebuilding along far more conservative lines at Wilton. The foundation of twin monasteries at Caen by William and Matilda in 1063 provides an obvious parallel, but Edward's work was clearly already underway by then. The scale of his building was to be grandiose, with the church in excess of 98 m (320 ft) in length. The enthusiasm of the author of the *Vita Edwardi* was probably justified:

The princely house of the altar, noble with its most lofty vaulting, is surrounded by dressed stone evenly jointed. Also the passage round that temple is enclosed on both sides by a double arching of stone with the joints of the structure strongly consolidated on this side and that. Furthermore, the crossing of the church, which is to hold in its midst the choir of God's

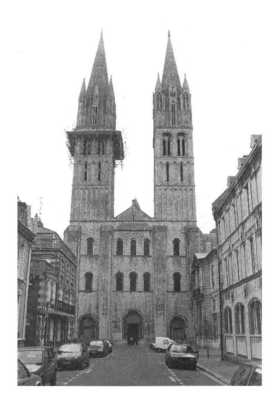

Caen was virtually founded by William, and he and his wife built two great abbeys, the Abbaye des Dames and the Abbaye des Hommes. The church of the latter, dedicated to St Etienne, is seen here and was designed to be his sepulchre.

choristers, and to uphold with like support from either side the high apex of the central tower, rises simply at first with a low and sturdy vault, swells with many a stair spiralling up in artistic profusion, but then with a plain wall climbs to the wooden roof which is carefully covered with lead.

What messages should be read into this great enterprise? Edward's commitment to the construction of a great Norman church like no other then in England to act as his own sepulchre necessarily invites interpretation as a barely disguised statement of his own continuing commitment to the philo-Norman policies which had characterized his brief emergence from the influence of the Godwinesons in 1051–2. Perhaps he still hankered after the succession of his distant kinsman in Normandy. The design of his great architectural achievement was clearly immutable long before its consecration on 28 December 1065, just days before Edward's own nomination of Earl Harold as his successor in the hours immediately prior to his own death.

FOUR

1066: Succession and Crisis

If the story of the succession crisis precipitated by King Edward's death has a sensible starting point in political events internal to England, then that lies in the autumn of 1065, when the Northumbrians rebelled against their earl and demanded that Edward replace him with their own nominee – a demand which is quite exceptional in the history of late Anglo-Saxon England. There is, however, one slightly earlier event which perhaps sheds some light on the reaction of Edward's regime to the demands of the Northumbrians, and particularly reveals something of the concerns and ambitions of Earl Harold Godwineson, who played a central role in bringing the northern crisis of late 1065 to a peaceful settlement. We must, therefore, turn first to the difficult matter of Harold's putative visit to Normandy and the events surrounding that, before discussing the rebellion of the Northerners.

HAROLD AND WILLIAM

This journey of Earl Harold across the seas is a curious episode: it is undated in any source; the English chroniclers are entirely silent concerning this event, despite their notice of other diplomats who crossed the Channel during Edward's reign; yet the entire issue was so central a plank of Norman efforts to justify William's invasion and conquest of England that it had to be credible in the late 1060s and early 1070s. The Bayeux Tapestry focuses on it to the exclusion of all else before the death of King Edward. It likewise occurs in *Haralds saga hardrada*, although that is a far from contemporary source. We should be in no doubt that the Norman sources do collectively describe an historical event, and one which William's apologists were later able to present as the crucial flaw in the legitimacy of Harold's candidacy to the succession. They do not, however, set out to describe this small piece of history with any degree of objectivity, or to date it, since their collective purpose was merely to underpin William's comparatively weak claim to the English throne by undermining that of his principal rival.

The story is a simple one and is told most graphically in the Bayeux Tapestry. Harold bade farewell to King Edward at one of his palaces and took ship from his

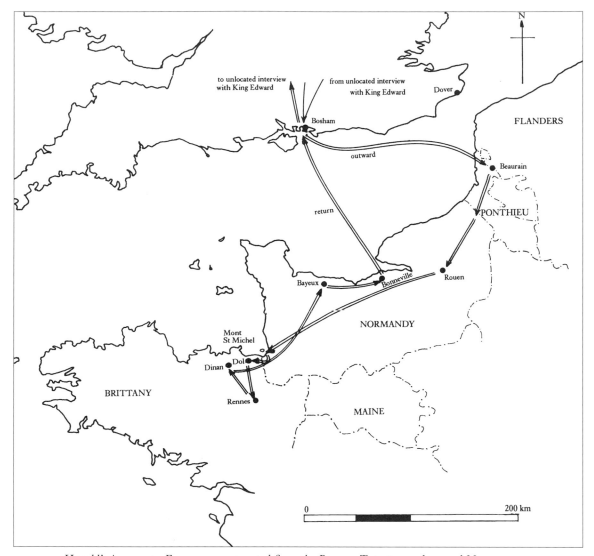

Harold's journey to France, reconstructed from the Bayeux Tapestry and several Norman histories, but not securely dated.

own family's port of Bosham in Sussex to cross to France. Coming to land north of the Somme, he was captured by Guy, Count of Ponthieu, and taken to Beaurain in the Canche valley where he was imprisoned. Thereafter he was released and handed over to Duke William on the latter's insistence, and taken to the ducal palace at Rouen where they discussed matters of mutual interest. Harold then joined William's army at Mont St Michel and went into action

Harold at Bosham Church, Sussex immediately before embarking for France. (The Bayeux Tapestry – 11th Century. By special permission of the City of Bayeux)

against Count Conan in eastern Brittany. The Englishman was represented as having distinguished himself by virtue of his great strength, since he is depicted carrying Norman knights and shields across the River Couesnon. William attacked Dol and Dinan with some success and there knighted Harold, giving him arms. There then occurred the famous oath-taking ceremony, which the Tapestry placed at Bayeux but William of Poitiers at Bonneville-sur-Touques. Wherever it occurred, Harold was represented as having committed himself on oath to Duke William's candidacy for the English succession. Only with that done was he allowed to depart back to England.

William's campaign against Conan in Brittany seems to fix Harold's visit to a period of 1064–5, and it has to have occurred by August 1065. Some slight confirmation of this comes from *Harald's saga*, which associates Harold's visit with his activities in Wales, which climaxed in the summer of 1063, but the notion

Harold about to set sail from Bosham. (The Bayeux Tapestry – 11th Century. By special permission of the City of Bayeux)

that Harold was blown off-course on his way there and landed up in Normandy entirely by accident seems less than plausible. The purpose of Harold's journey is very unclear. To William of Poitiers, it was King Edward's initiative intended to reinforce William's candidacy as his successor, which the old king still fervently supported:

> To confirm his former promise by a further oath he sent to him [William] Harold, of all his subjects the greatest in riches, honour and power, whose brother and nephew had previously been accepted as hostages for the duke's succession.

This account is clearly based on the slightly earlier and shorter version of William of Jumièges, and both reap from this episode the maximum rhetorical advantage for their hero as Edward's chosen successor. The Tapestry is, however, not entirely consistent with this interpretation, and this is significant since it too conveys a generally supportive view of William's candidacy. The critical scene is

Harold being given arms by William. This act amounted to his becoming William's man and may account for the anger of King Edward depicted in a later panel (see page 158). (The Bayeux Tapestry – 11th Century. By special permission of the City of Bayeux)

Harold's return to the presence of King Edward. The earl is depicted as adopting an exceptionally obsequious demeanour and being reprimanded by the king, with the support of others portrayed almost as if they were a theatrical chorus in a Greek play. The latter were apparently included for the purpose of reinforcement of the point being made in this cameo. Had Harold just returned from the Norman court having carried out Edward's instructions as the account of William of Poitiers has it, there would have been no reason to depict the king as anything but entirely contented with his earl, but that is certainly not the impression given. Unless the Tapestry itself is straying from historicity at this point, there must be something amiss in William's account – and it seems sensible to prefer the source which deviates from the generally self-justificatory and propagandist vision of the past portrayed by the Norman political literature. If Edward was displeased with Harold's behaviour in Normandy, this must imply disapproval of the earl's willingness to bind himself on oath to Duke William as heir to the English throne, in which case this was not Edward's policy at all at this point but something agreed by William and Harold themselves. In practice, Edward's views on the succession in the early 1060s may not even have been common knowledge within the political elite of the early post-conquest period – some of the English bishops alone perhaps excepted – so William's several propagandists were comparatively free to place on events the construction best suited to their own purposes.

Bishop Odo's crypt in the Cathedral of Notre-Dame at Bayeux is the only part of the current structure which is virtually unchanged since 1066.

There are two further explanations of Harold's journey in near contemporary sources. According to the Canterbury cleric, Eadmer, writing after 1090, Harold purposed to visit Normandy in order to persuade Duke William to set free his brother and nephew who had been hostages at the ducal court since perhaps the early 1050s. This would have seemed advisable within England only if both Edward and Harold were agreed that William's candidacy was no longer viable, although Eadmer has Edward express serious reservations concerning the advisability of Harold's proposed course of action; the Bayeux Tapestry itself offers another view but only in cartoon form. Harold is depicted as engaged in excited conversation with the seated figure of Duke William in the context of their initial meeting inside his palace – therefore after his release from captivity in Ponthieu. Harold is pointing with his left hand past the several retainers who stand behind him in the hall towards the next panel, wherein the figure of a tonsured priest is depicted as reaching out to the face of a single female figure who is standing indoors, beneath the comment, 'where one cleric and Aelgyva'. Beneath the principal figures, two naked and well-endowed male figures are depicted in lewd poses, one using what may be an adze on a piece of timber. Aelfgifu, the priest and these naked figures are presumably connected in some way with Harold's speech. It is possible that Harold had come to William to

Harold is received back by Edward – note the representation of Edward as reprimanding his earl and of Harold as a supplicant. (The Bayeux Tapestry – 11th Century. By special permission of the City of Bayeux)

protest at the sexual molestation of some highborn English lady – since Aelfgifu is an English name which was common at this date – at the hands of a priest who is diplomatically unnamed but within the duke's jurisdiction. If so, then this offers a further possible explanation of Harold's visit to Normandy. However, it may be that this conversation concerned the historical Aelfgifu of Northampton, who was the mother of Harold I of England and that Prince Swein to whom Cnut entrusted Norway. The suggestion that Swein was the son not of Cnut but of a clerk has a bearing on the succession crisis which was expected to break out at Edward's death, since it had some capacity to undermine the candidacy of the Norwegian king of the day, Harald Hardrada, as Swein's ultimate successor. If William and Harold Godwineson could agree on nothing else regarding Edward's throne, they were surely united in opposing the Norwegian claimant.

These several sources therefore suggest that Harold may have had more than one reason to travel to northern France. That he had expected to fall into William's power seems improbable and he may well have felt that he could rely on his own status as a senior aristocrat to avoid any undue pressure during his own visit. If so, then he seriously miscalculated.

There are, of course, other possibilities regarding Harold's purposes, but none have even a shred of contemporary support. His arrival in Ponthieu might imply that his intended destination was never Normandy at all, in which case he may have hoped to build up some sort of anti-Norman party among the principal

The panel depicting Harold in conference with William in his hall is followed immediately by this enigmatic tableau, explained by the words 'one priest and Aelfgyva [Aelfgifu]'. (The Bayeux Tapestry – 11th Century. By special permission of the City of Bayeux)

powers of north-west France to include his family's old allies in Flanders and the Counts of Ponthieu and Boulogne – whose interests certainly did not coincide with those of William as regards the English succession. Had the Frankish king been of age at this date, there can be little doubt that some sort of diplomacy would have been in progress between Wessex and Paris, designed to oppose the possibility of a Norman succession to the English throne. Harold's detention in Ponthieu may have been more protective than the Norman sources suggest, and Guy's apparent unwillingness to release the English earl into William's custody is at least indicative of some separate but now veiled agenda. Harold may have been not so much rescued by William as extracted by him from the count's protection under threat of war. This is, of course, little more than speculation, but the possibility of some rather different purpose should be borne in mind.

That Edward had by this date in practice given up any hope that William would prove acceptable as his heir to the English throne is confirmed by the efforts which the English regime made in the mid- to late 1050s to engineer the return of Edward the Exile – Edward the Confessor's half-nephew and a direct descendant of Cerdic – from Hungary. His reappearance must mean that he was being considered as a potential heir to the throne, and that would surely have been anathema to the old king had he still entertained serious hopes of a Norman succession. In such circumstances, the narrative offered by Duke William's closest sympathizers writing with all the advantages of hindsight certainly looks to have exaggerated the English king's commitment to William's candidature in the mid-1060s, and it seems safe to assume that the ostensible reason for the earl's journey was other than to bolster William's claim to the succession.

However, Harold did visit the Norman court, whether by accident or design. To suppose that he did so without any interest whatsoever in the future descent of the English crown is to ignore his famed subtlety and the importance of the succession as the major political issue of the day. Earl Harold was a consummate politician, as the author of the *Life* avowed. He was also the senior English power broker. His meeting with William provided an opportunity for each to explore the position of the other, to seek advantage and share any areas of mutual interest. It is not surprising that they took the opportunity to forge an alliance behind an agreed policy for the succession. William's propagandists focused solely on those aspects of the relationship between Harold and their patron which portrayed the latter as the injured party in the context of Harold's taking the throne in January 1066 – Harold's oath, therefore, and William's unrewarded generosity towards, and patronage of, the Englishman. It is Eadmer's account which expands this limited vision: William sought from Harold his active support for his own candidacy, the stronghold of Dover with a well of water and a marriage alliance; Harold's sister was to be married to one of William's great Norman nobles, while Harold should himself marry one of the duke's daughters (who is generally identified as Agatha). Further to this tie to the new king – which would have paralleled his kinship by marriage with King Edward – Harold would obtain the immediate release of his nephew and that of his brother when William should succeed, and 'everything which you ask of me which can reasonably be granted'. Harold was, therefore, to retain his prominent position in England but under the rule of King William. The much later *Harald's saga* certainly emphasizes the proposed marriage alliance and fails even to note Harold's oath to William, and this may have been the more important part of the entire procedure which had some potential to bind together the policies of two powerful figures whose interests were not obviously nor entirely compatible.

Harold's departure for England was conditional on his agreeing to William's demands. As the author of the *Life* remarked, the earl was inclined to be 'rather too generous with oaths', but he had discovered much to his own advantage concerning the situation in Normandy, and now knew the strength of William's resolve concerning the English succession. He may well have considered that a little duplicity, and even perjury, was therefore warranted. Furthermore, Harold needed to cover all possibilities. Should, on Edward's death, his own best interest dictate that he support William's candidacy, the Bonneville Accord provided a basis for such a policy that had some potential to guarantee his own future under a Norman king in a role which differed little from that which he enjoyed under

Edward. This was a comparatively low-risk policy which had obvious attractions. It would be a great mistake to imagine that Harold had a clear vision at this point of precisely what stance he should adopt in the coming succession crisis, since so many factors remained outside his own control. Most of all, he could not guarantee that Edward would nominate himself as successor. Harold Godwineson was an astute politician, and one who played his hand so close to his chest that it is now extremely difficult to discover just what was in it.

As King Edward's man, his premier earl and *sub-regulus*, Harold did not, of course, have the right to commend himself to Duke William or take oaths to him concerning the succession, since any such commitment cut across the old king's right of nomination of his own successor. To put it at its simplest, the English succession was not Harold's to give, and his sworn support to a particular candidate was valid only if that candidate was also King Edward's choice. A generation earlier, Edward himself was perhaps the focus of a general oath of the English nobility as successor to King Aethelred, but such was initiated only at the king's instigation. For one great nobleman to make his own commitment on the matter of the succession without reference to the king was another matter, although one that was far from uncommon in late Anglo-Saxon England. The propriety and validity of the oath are, of course, articles of faith among the Norman apologists but this rests entirely on the currency of Edward's initial recognition of William as his heir, a decade and a half earlier (see above, p. 136), and that problematic nomination looks to have long since died the death by the early 1060s. It may well be that it was Edward's anger at Harold's contravention of his own prerogative that the Tapestry attempted to depict – which would certainly have been recalled among the well-connected Canterbury clerisy in the half-decade or so after the conquest. Whether or not, the futility of the entire episode in English opinion, once, that is, Edward's opposition had effectively nullified the manoeuvrings of his senior earl, may have been what kept it out of the English sources. The Bonneville Accord was incapable of influencing the succession, to the extent that that remained in Edward's gift.

What is equally important to us in attempting to unravel these matters is the insight which it provides: whatever the exact detail of the exchanges between duke and earl, the English succession was very clearly at issue. And that is an important lesson, if only because it confirms what we would otherwise expect to be the case. Harold's power and influence as premier earl in England was threatened by the imminent prospect of Edward's death, and the person of his successor was a matter of profound importance to himself. Indeed, his very survival was likely to depend upon supporting the successful candidate before the event. It is in this light that his dealings with William make sense, although he found himself negotiating with the Norman duke from an unexpected position of weakness. Harold had no right to be making promises and swearing oaths concerning his support without regard to his king's prerogative, but, *de facto*, the entire matter was too important for him to ignore. Harold was in turn too important for William to let go the opportunity to attempt to secure his support.

Whenever Harold's visit to Normandy occurred, it was necessarily before the Northumbrian rebellion. Harold had, therefore, already by that date been involved in high-level discussion concerning his own attitude towards the descent of the English crown, and had very good reason to ponder his best policy on the matter. He is most unlikely to have proceeded without reference to his own perception of this same issue when the northern crisis broke upon him in the autumn of 1065, and there is some evidence that he attempted to influence its outcome in ways intended to assist himself in the matter of the succession.

THE NORTHUMBRIAN REBELLION: CONTEXT AND IMPACT

Before the rebellion of the northerners, the house of Godwine dominated almost all England beneath the king, even to the extent that in circumstances when the several brothers were united there is little doubt that Edward was powerless to oppose them. Harold had been Earl of Wessex since his father's death in 1053, and had added to that earldom south-western Mercia (Hereford, Gloucestershire, and perhaps Oxfordshire) thereafter; Tostig, the eldest of his surviving brothers, was made Earl of Northumbria following the death of Siward in 1055, and seems to have also held Northamptonshire in addition; their two younger brothers, Gyrth and Leofwine, later obtained earldoms in the south east. This disposition represented a vast accretion of power and responsibility to the Godwinesons since 1042, when their father had held just England below the Thames. Siward's family had been all but eliminated. His son Waltheof may have held a small earldom in Middle Anglia in 1065, but was of little real account, and Leofric's grandson, Edwin, held the north Midlands, stretching from his 'capital' at Chester to Lincolnshire, but had lost the family's earlier predominance in southern Mercia and the West Midlands around Coventry. Earl Edwin was himself barely adult, bereft of the Welsh alliance which had sustained his father's struggles with the Godwinesons, and marginalized by the far greater power and influence of the rival house, whose territories and vassals (in Wales) by 1065 surrounded his earldom on all sides.

If Edward had died in 1065 and Godwine's sons had then agreed that Harold should reign after him, there would have been no one in England to contradict them. That is not, of course, to assume that they were necessarily united over something as important to them all as the succession, but this does provide an indication of their effective power. That power and their potential for unity of purpose suffered a damaging blow in the autumn of 1065. The story of the Northumbrian rebellion as recounted in the several different Chronicles is well known, but a rather more detailed treatment is offered in the *History of the Kings of England*, by Simeon of Durham, and in chapter seven of the contemporary but anonymous *Life of Edward*.

'Soon after' St Bartholomew's Day (24 August), or on 3 October – depending on the source – a rising of the Northumbrians of Northumberland and Durham and the men of Yorkshire combined swept away Tostig's regime at York, where the Anglo-Danish Copsig seems to have been his lieutenant. Tostig was often absent from his earldom, as were others of the earls – he is recorded as a pilgrim to Rome in 1061 and was at war in Wales in 1063. When the northerners rose against him he was with King Edward deep inside Wessex at Britford in Dorset,

Detail of a pre-Conquest door jamb at St Peter's, Britford, Wiltshire, where both Tostig and King Edward are likely to have attended services in the late autumn of 1065, during the northern revolt.

'detained by his love of the king and while he dealt with some palace business which had been put on him', but perhaps also hunting with a monarch who still lived as much as anything for the chase.

The grievances of the northerners seem real enough – the *Life* described his rule as 'a heavy yoke because of their misdeeds'. Simeon blamed Tostig's murder of Gospatric (a northern nobleman of the house of Bamburgh) – carried out by order of his sister Queen Edith on 28 December 1064 – and of Gamel son of Orm and Ulf son of Dolfin at York. Tostig had therefore struck down several senior figures among the native aristocracy of northern Northumbria and the deed clearly provoked a new blood feud with the semi-detached leaders of furthermost England. In addition to these murders were his demands for increased taxation, which affected the Anglo-Danish inhabitants of Yorkshire perhaps more than the far north, and his misuse of justice to acquire the wealth and lands of his opponents.

These were local issues, of course, rather than national ones, and it is important to recognize how limited the objectives of the Northumbrians were. Unlike their struggles against the West-Saxon kings a century earlier, the rising of 1065 was not an attack on the monarchy but on its principal local agent. Their objective was not independence but their own choice of earl and a less oppressive rule still under a single English kingship.

Given that their purpose was to dispossess Tostig Godwineson of his earldom, the Northumbrian rebels had little option but to ally themselves with the house of Leofric, since no other family had the political or military potential or the self-interest to assist them. They proposed, therefore, Edwin's younger brother (or perhaps half-brother) Morcar as their new earl and were joined by Edwin and his Mercian and Welsh soldiery as they marched south. A similar combination of forces from Mercia and Northumbria had decisively influenced several recent succession crises and had enabled Edward to expel Godwine and his sons in 1051, so the rebels were following a well-trodden path in 1065. Having reached the environs of Northampton, they ravaged that region, probably because it had helped to finance Tostig's unpopular regime at York.

Earl Harold was the mouthpiece of the king in his dealings with the rebels. The critical meetings were variously represented as occurring at Northampton and Oxford, while Edward himself held council, probably still at Britford near Wilton. In the several Chronicle accounts, Harold receives some credit for his attempts to reconcile the two parties and make peace, but less so in the fuller description of these events in the *Life*. Therein, Tostig was characterized as the archetypal good governor of an unworthy and vicious people:

> this distinguished earl, a son and lover of divine peace, had in his time so reduced the number of robbers and cleared the country of them by mutilating or killing . . . that any man, even with any of his goods, could travel at will even alone without fear of attack.

This pre-emptive exoneration of his conduct places in a very different light those who complained of his cruelty and cupidity in the king's presence at Britford, and leaves no doubt that Queen Edith supported Tostig in this crisis.

It is only the *Life* which refers to rumours which would connect Earl Harold with the northern rebels. The author artfully distances himself from such slander and declares himself convinced that the accusations were false, but the impact of his words certainly places a question mark over Harold's attitude as the crisis unrolled, and was clearly intended so to do. There seems little reason to doubt that Tostig himself charged Harold with complicity before the king, and that Harold cleared himself with oaths. It is this occasion which led the author to remark that 'Harold was rather too generous with oaths (alas!)', which is generally assumed to be an oblique reference also to his dealings with Duke William and particularly the Bonneville Accord.

What should we make of the crisis of 1065? And more particularly, what part did it play in the succession crisis which followed so soon after? Whatever else it did, it demonstrated the ineffectiveness of Edward as king and his over-dependence on a single lieutenant – Harold. The forces which the northerners had raised and which then confronted Edward's government were clearly significant, but the *Life* leaves us in no doubt that Edward proposed to confront them with even greater force rather than see his own appointment as earl overthrown. From Edward's perspective, the Northumbrians had rebelled against his own authority and there is no reason to doubt that, of the several Godwinesons who held office beneath him, it was Tostig whom he preferred and who offered some opportunity to counterbalance Harold's overriding influence. According to the *Life* again, Edward 'stirred up the whole population of the rest of England by a royal edict and decided to crush their impudent contumacy by force', and there is no obvious reason to doubt the veracity of this statement. The proposed mobilization did not, however, occur, for several reasons: one was the imminence of winter and the impact that might have on the assembling of a credible force; a second was a general horror of civil war, and the same factor was considered by the chroniclers to have undermined Edward's capacity to resist the return of Earl Godwine and his affinity in 1052; the last was the effort of some of his councillors to argue against the king's policy of confrontation. The *Life* asserts that 'they did not so much divert the king from his desire to march as wrongfully and against his will desert him'.

This is, of course, a version of events told from the perspective of Queen Edith and there is no doubting her partiality for her brother Tostig. Yet there is circumstantial evidence which offers some support. The result of the rebellion is entirely consistent with this vision of Edward's response and its failure. The northerners were not opposed in arms and ultimately obtained the earl of their choice – Edwin's brother Morcar – and effectively ruled themselves under a titular earl who was little more than a boy during the Conquest period and had only minimal effective patronage inside Northumbria. Tostig, his wife Judith, and his closest followers went into exile at the Flemish court – the court that is of Judith's half-brother, Baldwin V – laden with treasure by a chagrined King Edward. Harold rose to the kingship a matter of weeks after the crisis was resolved, and emerges at an unknown date as the brother-in-law of earls Edwin and Morcar.

Two powerful dynasts, therefore, emerged from the Northumbrian rebellion with their power much enhanced. Earl Edwin loosened the encirclement established by the Godwinesons of his own earldom during the 1050s, regained a second earldom for his house, re-established a semblance of balance between the great comital families in his own favour and restored the capacity of the Midlands and the north to act in conjunction at times of crisis, as they had in the days of his grandfather. He resurrected, therefore, the political influence of his house from its marginalization of recent years. At some point, he also became Harold's brother-in-law, and therefore regained some influence at the centre and considerable reassurance for his own position under a Godwineson king. Earl Harold obtained the greatest plum of them all – the English crown. His marriage to Edwin's sister and the support which he received during 1066 from Leofric's grandsons does imply that their alliance of mutual self-interest stemmed at least from the late autumn of 1065. Then Earl Harold acted as go-between for the king in his dealings with the insurgents and Earl Edwin is likely to have been their mouthpiece by virtue of his seniority and the legitimacy which an earldom carried. There is good reason to think, along with Tostig and his sister, that Harold then developed his own agenda and pursued that instead of the interests of his king and brother in dealing with the Northumbrian rebellion in the closing weeks of 1065.

Had Harold been committed to military efforts against the rebels, a campaign could probably have been attempted. If some of Edward's advisors successfully opposed his determined stance against the rebels, then Harold must necessarily have been their leader. It would be far too much to suggest that Harold played any part in instigating the northern rebellion. That clearly emerged out of local circumstances and the excesses of Tostig's rule. Harold did, however, use the opportunity when it presented itself to strengthen his own candidacy for the succession. He avoided the opprobrium which would have been his had he attempted to put down the rebellion by armed force, and all the venom which that would have let loose in the Midlands and the north. Instead he sacrificed his brother's interests in Northumbria as the price of his own reconciliation with the house of Leofric, obtaining the support of two brothers-in-law as a replacement for one brother whose objectives may have been far from compatible with his own. Harold's marriage is undated, of course, and may well have occurred in 1066, but there seems little reason to doubt that he had laid the foundations for his new alliance in the course of his negotiations with Edwin, Morcar and their supporters in the early winter of 1065. If it occurred before his own succession, then this was the moment when he decisively rejected the Bonneville Accord and the Norman marriage alliance which had supposedly been agreed there.

This raises, of course, the question of Harold's ambitions and the point at which he decided to pursue his own candidacy for the throne. His protracted dealings with the rebels in 1065 provided the likeliest period when his views on this subject finally crystallized. Harold may also have welcomed an opportunity to marginalize the most powerful of his brothers, whose support for his own candidacy is likely to have been at best equivocal. Tostig was himself a successful general with a decade's experience of rule of the most independent and turbulent of the English earldoms. His wife was a member of a leading continental family, giving him connections with the Duke of Normandy as well as the wealthy and politically powerful ruler of Flanders, who was at this stage guardian of the young King Philip I of the Franks. The friendship of both Edward and his queen may have encouraged Tostig to harbour his own ambitions concerning the succession. His claims were certainly no weaker than those of Harold. If Tostig was in the event to oppose Harold's ambition then some compromise candidate – such as Edgar Aetheling – might have emerged in the search for a figure on whom the principal earls could agree. Whatever his exact thoughts – and these remain a matter of unsupported speculation – Tostig's departure removed the second most powerful figure in England beneath the crown and had the effect of freeing Harold to consider a wider range of options concerning the succession than might otherwise have been possible. The position that he adopted in 1065 certainly suggests – but does not of course prove – that he considered Tostig's exile a small loss compared with the potential consequences of supporting him in arms. It was in pursuit of his own agenda, therefore, that he undermined King Edward's response to the rebellion and imposed his own terms on the outcome.

KING EDWARD'S DEATH

King Edward, later known as the 'Confessor' or 'the Good' (in the sagas), 'languishing from the sickness of soul which he had contracted' as a consequence of being 'deprived of the due obedience of his men in repressing the presumption of the unrighteous' died on 4 January 1066 – the eve of twelfth night. His last known act as king had been to journey 'towards midwinter' to Westminster and the abbey which he had refounded just outside London, and on which he had lavished much energy and the wealth previously reserved to several other monasteries. The magnificent new abbey church – which was described in glowing terms by the author of the *Life of King Edward* – was hurriedly consecrated on 28 December 1065 and the king buried in state there on 5 January, the very day after his death. According to his biographer – if one dare use the term for the author of this semi-hagiographical but near-contemporary piece – his last illness stemmed from the anger and frustration that welled up in him at having to give way to the demands of the Northumbrians and outlaw his brother-in-law, Earl Tostig, during the November of 1065. This, however, may give too much credence to the opinions of a cleric who was writing under the patronage of the widowed queen, Edith, and who was naturally keen to portray the relationship between herself, her husband and Tostig – clearly her favourite brother – as peculiarly close. Whatever the nature of his last illness, King Edward was by contemporary standards an old man of about sixty by the winter of 1065–6, who had reigned as king over the English for an improbable twenty-four years.

Edward died childless, and he did so at a time when one of the fundamental duties of a king was to provide for the succession, to ensure the continuation of proper authority and patronage within the body politic. At least one adult son of sound body and mind provided the easiest solution to the problem of royal

The burial of Edward the Confessor in Westminster, as visualized by an illustrator of Matthew Paris's History of St Edward the King. *The original was written in about 1236–45 and this copy also dates from the thirteenth century.*

succession in Anglo-Saxon England, as in many other communities during this period. It seems clear that the political community at large expected the English crown to pass down the generations within a relatively tight-knit royal dynasty defined by paternity. This occurred from father to son where it was possible, or from one brother to another and then to son or nephew where circumstances favoured it. Disputes might occur between a nephew and the son of a previous king (as at Alfred's death), or between half-brothers (at the deaths variously of Eadred, Edgar and Cnut), but more distant members of the royal kin seem to have been either unable or unwilling to mount a challenge for the kingship.

Edward the Confessor's subsequent reputation for sanctity has encouraged some speculation – during the Norman period as well as later – that he was a virgin king and chose so to be, and his *Life* certainly portrays his relationship with

Queen Edith in later life, at least, as one between father and daughter rather than husband and wife. Of course, one might wonder just how keen Edward may have been to make Godwine the grandfather of a king of England if he considered the earl in part at least responsible for the mutilation and death of his own brother Alfred. Even so, there is no firm foundation in contemporary sources for the view that he had never intended to sire children once he had become king in 1042 and his attempt to put away his wife in 1051–2 into the nunnery at Wherwell may well have been as much out of a desire to replace her with a more fertile partner as on account of her membership of Godwine's family. Indeed, as was suggested above (p. 128), Edward's need to dispose of Edith so as to have another attempt at producing an heir may have been as significant a factor as any other in the breakdown of relations between king and earl in 1051. The needs of the succession were paramount and many previous English kings, from the seventh century onwards, had disposed of unwanted wives and contracted new alliances even while their spouses still lived, and the examples of Edward's own grandfather, King Edgar, and Cnut – his stepfather – are likely to have been known to Edward and his advisors.

Whatever his earlier intentions, however, Edward eventually died leaving no heir of his body. Nor were there brothers, nephews or first cousins available. Yet a comparatively restricted definition of royal descent had long been a *sine qua non* of candidacy for the English throne, and indeed for the various kingships among the English prior to the ninth- and tenth-century consolidation of England into a single kingship. As Alfred's chronicler proudly announced, the West-Saxon kings of the ninth century claimed descent, one and all, from the mythical Cerdic who had putatively led the first English conquests in the region in 494. Cerdic in turn had a pedigree stretching back to the god Woden and he to Adam. The earlier names in this genealogy are entirely unhistorical but that was totally irrelevant to its political utility in the late Anglo-Saxon period. Legitimacy in the matter of the succession was confined to Cerdic's descendants. Since Edward the Confessor was a direct descendant in the male line of Alfred (he was his great-great-greatgrandson), he was a *bona fide* member of the Cerdicings, and that fact was an important feature of his own legitimacy as king. In the past, the kings of his lineage had confined their nominations to other close members of the same royal kin.

Yet the house of Cerdic was very poorly represented in 1066, despite Aethelred's great brood of offspring by two wives at the turn of the century. Edward was the only male of his generation of the royal family who survived to this date. He had two full nephews: from Aethelred's second marriage to Emma of Normandy, of which Edward himself was the eldest child, only his sister, Goda, had produced children via her marriage to Count Drogo of the Vexin. One was Walter, who succeeded his father. He also attempted, with local support, to make himself Count of Maine in right of his wife early in the 1060s, but there fell foul of Duke William's ambitions. William captured Le Mans in 1063 and with it his rival and his wife, who were both later reported by Orderic Vitalis to have perished by poison soon after while 'guests' at the duke's castle of Falaise. This certainly removed a possible candidate for the English throne who might have brought external forces to England in support of his claim, but it seems unlikely

Falaise Castle. William's supposed birthplace – the rectangular keep – is Norman, but a massive circular corner tower was added by English defenders during the latter phases of the Hundred Years War. The whole has, however, been massively restored since the destruction of the town during the Battle of Normandy in 1944.

that either Edward or any other group within England had given his candidacy serious consideration even before his death as he was so firmly embedded in Frankish politics. The other son of this marriage, Ralph the Timid, had followed Edward to England at the beginning of the reign and been promoted to the earldom of Hereford, but he died in December 1057. Ralph's reputation seems to have been much damaged by his failure to protect Hereford from the Welsh in 1055. He left a son, Harold, born to his marriage into a prominent East-Midlands family, but this cannot have occurred before the 1040s and his father's tempestuous marcher earldom understandably did not descend to the young son but to the ever acquisitive Harold Godwineson. Edward's great-nephew survived to 1066 but his father's unexceptional career, poor reputation and premature death had conspired to rob him of any significant support as a candidate for the crown and the pragmatic Edward does not appear to have taken any particular interest in him in the closing years of the reign, at least as far as we can now judge.

There remain for consideration the descendants of King Aethelred by his first marriage, who were Edward's half-brothers and sisters. Of his numerous sons by Aelfgifu, only Edmund Ironside produced heirs and just one of these grew up in exile, distant from Cnut's baleful interest in potential rivals for the English crown. This was Edward the Exile, whose return to England from Hungary, with his immediate family, was engineered in 1057 (see p. 143). The author of the Worcester manuscript of the Chronicle remarked that:

> We do not know for what cause it was arranged that he might not see his relative King Edward's [face]. Alas! That was a cruel fate, and harmful to this nation, that he so quickly ended his life after he came to England, to the misfortune of this wretched nation.

This somewhat ambiguous comment has on occasion been interpreted as suggestive of chicanery on the part of some figure such as Earl Harold, whose own ambitions might be thought by this stage to have overlapped with those of a returning prince of the royal house, but this is arguably to misunderstand the author's meaning. Harold seems to have been fully supportive of Edward's return and one of his closest associates was the principal ambassador to Germany who secured it. There is no suggestion that Edward was murdered or even that he died in suspicious circumstances, in the manner of Edward's brother, Alfred, in a *cause célèbre* a generation earlier. Rather, Edward apparently died a natural death on 19 April in London, having only just set foot in England, and the chronicler – who was writing after the Norman conquest – interpreted his end as a significant factor leading to that conquest. The responsibility was surely God's and this comment should be read in conjunction with the assumption that the Norman conquest was a manifestation of divine displeasure at the English, to which this Chronicle refers under the year 1066 and elsewhere. England was, therefore, robbed of the figure of Edward Cerdicing and thereby laid open to the great dispute between Harold Godwineson and William for the succession, through which God punished His people for their sins.

Edward the Exile died, therefore, before his candidacy for the English throne could really gather momentum. He left a widow, one Agatha, who was a relative of one of the German emperors but without family or influence in England which she could deploy on behalf of her young son, Edgar the Aetheling, who seems to have been about fourteen in 1066, so was only a young child when his father died. Without committed kin in high places, large estates or a powerful affinity, there was little prospect that this juvenile and comparatively alien descendant of the house of Cerdic could be promoted as a serious contender for the succession merely by the efforts of his immediate associates. His chances of emerging as the agreed candidate of Edward and his council may have been seriously weakened by the political changes in the north during late 1065, which enabled Harold to ally himself with the house of Leofric and to drive Earl Tostig abroad.

Edgar was the only candidate who was a *bona fide* member of the English royal dynasty when Edward died but none of those gathering at Westminster early in January 1066 were certainly committed to his cause. This may owe something to our ignorance of his condition. We do not, for example, know in whose household he and his two sisters were being raised. What is more, the precedents for a minority were far from good. The last occasion on which a royal prince of tender years had been raised to the throne was the succession crisis of 975–8, when Edward the Martyr and Aethelred were successively promoted to the kingship. The subsequent decades of foreign attacks will have been recalled in England in 1066, when similar attacks could once again be expected. All must have anticipated that Edward's heir would need to lead armies in the field and in that circumstance Edgar's candidacy was clearly deficient. Only Harold's uncompromising support could give Edgar's candidacy a reasonable prospect of success, and that was unavailable once Harold had emerged as a candidate for the succession.

In January 1066, there was not, therefore, a member of the Cerdicings descended from any of the last few kings who was both adult and well established in England, who could be promoted by the old king as his chosen heir and who could hold out the prospect of a credible shield for the realm of England. There were, admittedly, more distant members of the royal family. Various figures were described as related to Edward – for example, the Domesday Book referred to both Siward, a landholder in Herefordshire, and Swein of Essex, Robert fitzWimarc's son, as 'kinsman of King Edward', but the family ties were both distant and obscure. Moreover, in many instances such blood links were not a matter of common paternal descent from the West-Saxon dynasty – and Edward's friend and courtier, Robert fitzWimarc, was clearly his maternal relative since he was also related to the Norman ducal house. He was probably illegitimate, since he is known as the son of his mother, and this cannot have helped him.

The Danish royal family was at this point headed by an adult male, Cnut's nephew via his sister, Swein Estrithsson, but Edward is most unlikely to have favoured the heir of that dynasty which had so ravaged his father's kingdom and forced himself and his brother into exile for a quarter of a century. If there was anything consistent about his foreign policy between 1042 and 1066, it was his opposition to the Vikings. Late reference to a supposed promise by Edward of the succession to Swein early in the reign is likely to have been an invention in the

Baltic region on behalf of the claims of the Danish kings, which Swein and his sons sought to make effective only after 1066. It seems clear that there was no significant body of opinion in southern England at least which favoured Swein as a candidate in 1066, and the impossibility of Danish invasion while the powerful Norwegian king still threatened Denmark must discount any theoretical claim he might have mounted. King Harald of Norway could lay no claim to a connection by blood with the English dynasty, and was an unlikely candidate to find support within Edward's own household and council.

Yet the descent of his crown was clearly a matter of pressing concern to the dying king, and the key issue to those he left behind. It may be that Edward had already made and communicated his views but it is at least as likely that the king had remained silent until the very end. The deathbed scene is graphically – and arguably accurately – illustrated on the Bayeux Tapestry, which depicts the old king, distinguished by his crown as much as by his shaggy hair and beard, sitting up in his bedchamber. He is in the act of extending his hand to a kneeling and deferential figure of a man, who is clearly intended to represent Harold. Robert fitzWimarc is supporting him on the right, Archbishop Stigand bends over him, ministering to him and perhaps in the act of offering the last rites, and the distraught figure of the queen sits, or more probably kneels, at the foot of the bed, her face half hidden as if in tears. The identity of the individuals concerned is confirmed by the author of Edward's *Life*, whose source was presumably the queen. The text above the scene in the Tapestry reads, 'Here King Edward in bed speaks with those he trusts', and it is highly significant that those responsible for the detail of this work, commissioned by a Norman patron after William's succession, felt that both the scene itself and this commentary were appropriate.

Edward conversed, therefore, with those whom even post-Conquest commentators were prepared to describe as his closest and most trusted associates shortly before he died, and it was this group interaction out of which an agreed solution to the succession crisis finally emerged. That is not to suppose that Edward had much enthusiasm for the course that he adopted. Rather, his final nomination of that figure who had so frustrated his efforts against the northern rebels only weeks before looks very much like Edward's caving in to the collective advice of his councillors. Even so, his nomination was of fundamental importance to those gathered at the bedside and was accepted by all concerned as a valid statement of his intentions as he died. In English law, this took precedence over all other dispositions which he may have made in the past.

The lengthy and detailed treatment of this episode in the *Life* suggests that on his deathbed Edward harangued his associates concerning their immorality and his concern for the future – and this may be so, although this passage occurs in the second half of this work, which was written in the knowledge of Harold's subsequent downfall and the destruction of all that had been agreed at this very meeting. The wrath of God, therefore, comes into play once more, and Edward was being depicted as beloved of God and so as capable of prophecy concerning His treatment of a less-worthy successor and the unworthy race over whom he reigned. More importantly, it has Edward making provision for the future protection of the queen, his friends and his people:

stretching forth his hand to his *nutricius* [which probably means 'protector' or 'governor' but could even carry the meaning of 'adopted heir'], her brother, Harold, he said, 'I commend this woman and all the kingdom to your protection. Serve and honour her with faithful obedience as your lady and sister, which she is, and do not despoil her, as long as she lives, of any due honour got from me. Likewise I also commend those men who have left their native land for love of me, and have up till now served me faithfully. Take from them an oath of fealty, if they should so wish, and protect and retain them, or send them with your safe conduct safely across the Channel to their own homes with all that they have acquired in my service.'

This is an entirely clearcut and near contemporary vision of events which can leave us in no doubt that Edward nominated Harold as his successor. Each and every version of the Anglo-Saxon Chronicle likewise has Edward committing the kingdom to Earl Harold in terms which mark the appropriateness and rectitude of the act, and it was considered worthy of inclusion in his epitaph, beside notice of his generosity, blamelessness, and role as England's protector:

> However, the wise man committed the kingdom
> to a distinguished man, Harold himself,
> a princely earl, who at all times
> loyally obeyed his superior
> in words and deeds, neglecting nothing
> of which the nation's king was in need.

The chronicler's message is straightforward: Edward's wisdom encompassed even his management of the succession, in the problematic circumstances which resulted from the default of close kin of adult age who might normally have been expected to have followed him on the throne. His selection of Harold is justified by reference to his previous loyalty, conscientiousness in governance and personal virtues. We are offered, therefore, a vision of a successor made worthy by personal qualities, close association with the king and career success, and recognized as such by the dying king whose responsibility it was to nominate a successor. It does not mean that Edward was entirely happy at the prospect.

It is Edward's nomination of a successor from outside his own dynasty over the head of his own great-nephew, Edgar Aetheling, which is the most exceptional feature of the first part of the succession crisis of 1066. In the past, with the solitary exception of the Danish usurpation, the connection between blood relationship and succession had been immutable. In some respects, it was Edward's nomination of a non-Cerdicing which opened up the entire question of the descent of England's crown and served to legitimize the interference of other great men whose credentials were little more compelling than the large numbers of warriors prepared to support them. Yet Edward's dilemma was a very real one, since William's intention to contest the succession was necessarily well known and must have overshadowed the deliberations of the old king and his councillors around the deathbed. Whether or not Edward himself still favoured William's candidacy, that was entirely unacceptable to all his advisors. The expectation of invasion and the need to appoint a competent soldier as king may well have finally destroyed any lingering chance that Edgar Aetheling then retained of Edward's nomination.

This was not, of course, the end of the matter, since Harold needed far more than Edward's nomination as heir to the throne, however important that was considered to be. To achieve the crown he needed additionally the support of a substantial section of the secular community and their acclamation, the active assistance of the clergy and consecration at the hands of a metropolitan bishop. The next scene in the Bayeux Tapestry clearly suggests that all this occurred rapidly after this; it is captioned: 'And here they gave the king's crown to Harold'. This features the figure of Harold holding a great battleaxe – thus he is depicted as England's protector – being offered the crown by a secular figure whose right hand points back to the deathbed scene in the previous panel. Another layman in the foreground deferentially proffers Harold another battleaxe. It was perhaps the embroiderers' intention to link the presentation of the crown to Harold with Edward's dying wishes and the conversations at his deathbed, and it may even be the king's kinsman Robert, steward of Edward's household, who is depicted once more. The armed figure symbolizes the support of the English nobility and their soldiery in Harold's promotion to the throne.

The following panel reinforces these themes. It is probably not a depiction of Harold's coronation, as has often been suggested, but of his holding court in state. The caption reads: 'Here resides Harold King of the English', so the building is arguably a royal palace rather than Westminster Abbey, where he was crowned. The closest parallel is with Harold's taking his leave from King Edward in the opening panel of the Tapestry, wherein the old king is seated on an animal-headed seat reminiscent of a hog-back tombstone (the closest modern parallel would be a piano stool), with the sceptre in his left hand. Harold is, however, portrayed in more regal circumstances. He sits elevated above those standing around him, on a higher, stepped and backed throne and in full regalia as king – with orb and sceptre in his hands and a crown on his head – towering over the figures which flank him. On his left (to the right of the panel) stands Archbishop Stigand, with his name blazoned around his head and in his archiepiscopal robes with his *pallium* in his left hand. On his right are two deferential lay figures proffering the king a great sword. The entire panel represents Harold as king in majesty, presiding over and supported by the twin foundations of the English church and by the nobles and their soldiery, and is a crucial confirmation of the legitimacy of Harold's accession as king.

This legitimacy finds some admittedly rather later support in the text commonly ascribed to 'Florence' (John) of Worcester: 'After the burial the underking [*subregulus*] Harold, Earl Godwine's son, whom the king before his death had appointed successor to the kingdom, was elected to the royal dignity by the magnates of the whole realm and on the same day was honourably consecrated as king by Ealdred, Archbishop of York.'

Norman literature written in support of William's claim is the only significant body of contemporary comment which disputes this vision of Harold's accession.

Harold is offered the crown. (The Bayeux Tapestry – 11th Century. By special permission of the City of Bayeux)

William, a monk in the ducal Abbey of Jumièges, wrote his popular continuation of the *Deeds of the Dukes of the Normans* in support of William's claim to the English throne in 1070–1: 'Harold immediately [as soon that is as Edward was dead] usurped his kingdom, perjured in the fealty which he had sworn to the duke [William]'. William of Poitiers, the well-connected and well-informed Norman cleric who had previously served William as a knight but was by now his

Harold in majesty, holding court: 'here resides Harold King of the English'. (The Bayeux Tapestry – 11th Century. By special permission of the City of Bayeux)

chaplain, writing in the 1070s, similarly depicted Harold's succession in far from complimentary terms:

> Not for this insane Englishman the decision of a public choice, but, on that sorrowful day when the best of kings was buried and the whole nation mourned his passing, he seized the royal throne with the plaudits of certain iniquitous supporters and thereby perjured himself. He was made king by the unholy consecration of Stigand, who had been deprived of his ministry by the justified fervour of papal anathema.

These versions of events were for post-Conquest consumption, and it was the intention of both authors to legitimize and so reinforce William's succession. One important means of so doing was to undermine the legitimacy of Harold's kingship. Reference to Stigand as the archbishop who consecrated him, for example, was clearly included for precisely that purpose since he had been deposed in 1070, and this is likely to be a deliberate misrepresentation. The well-reputed and uncontroversial Archbishop Ealdred of York is by far the likelier figure to have actually crowned Harold, as he did William, since all involved were conscious of the controversies surrounding Stigand's authority, and several bishops had already gone to Rome to avoid consecration at his hands. William of Poitiers even asserted that Duke William was the candidate preferred by Queen Edith in 1066, over against her own brother – 'this man defiled by luxury, this cruel murderer insolent in stolen riches, the enemy of justice and good'. Harold was later, therefore, portrayed by William's propagandists as a usurper promoted only by a faction, whose coronation was undermined by Stigand's participation, but their purposes in so doing are transparently rhetorical and the means used far from subtle. Only the later Welsh Chronicles shared the Norman perception of Harold's kingship, portraying him as one who had 'through oppression after the death of King Edward, unlawfully gained supremacy of the kingdom of the English', but their hostility to Gruffudd's nemesis and dependence on later Anglo-Norman sources is sufficient explanation.

Not all post-Conquest writers from within the Norman establishment followed this line. Eadmer, an English monk at Canterbury who became one of the closest associates of Archbishop Anselm, was entirely comfortable with Harold's legitimacy as king. In his *History of recent events in England*, he remarked: 'Shortly after this [Harold's return from his adventures in Normandy] Edward died; and, as he had before his death provided, Harold succeeded him on the throne.'

It is the body of Norman-derived, post-Conquest literature and the Bayeux Tapestry which together provide that evidence of significant contact between Earl Harold and Duke William prior to the succession crisis of 1066, which William's apologists then used as a major plank in their efforts to justify the conquest, and it is important to bear in mind their treatment of that episode when evaluating their comments on Harold's succession. That succession was considered deficient only outside England, and most particularly in Normandy where it cut across William's own long-held ambition to secure the English throne. In the last resort, it was more inconvenient than illegitimate.

We can, therefore, be reasonably confident that Harold was Edward's own nominee for the succession in 1066 (whatever his earlier plans may have been), that he had substantial support within England, and that he was properly consecrated as king on 5 January, in the afternoon following, and apparently in the same church as, Edward's funeral. Edward and his closest associates had adopted a course which offered what must have seemed to them the best solution available at the time to the difficult problem of the succession, in the light of the demands which were likely to be made on the new king by outside forces. It was presumably the prospect of external attack – particularly from Normandy – which led Edgar's far superior dynastic claim to be overlooked in favour of Harold. In the latter's favour was his maturity – he was at least in his thirties – his membership of a powerful kin, the existence of sons, his own longstanding political pre-eminence as the foremost earl and his military experience. Harold was the only senior figure in England in 1066 with a military reputation of any consequence, following his Welsh wars, so the one figure who inspired confidence in the role of protector. Furthermore, Harold comes over in the *Life* as an ambitious man and even a subtle schemer. It seems likely that he had, by January

1066, set his own sights on the crown and was unwilling to step aside from the main prize in favour of a boy without significant backing, whatever his dynastic claims. It would probably be fair to say that he manipulated the English court and the king during the few months prior to Edward's death, with the specific purpose of securing the throne. On 5 January 1066, he succeeded, and there was no obvious reason why he should not have held it for a long time to come.

Harold's lack of royal blood was his only significant weakness from an English perspective, but it should be stressed that this was a failing shared by each and every adult candidate in 1066. Harold could claim kinship with Edward by virtue of his sister Edith, Edward's queen, and this may have served him well in gathering support and legitimizing his position. When Edward the Elder had taken control of the kingdom of Mercia in 919, he apparently did so in part at least by virtue of his close kinship with the recently deceased 'Lady of the Mercians' – Aethelflaed, his sister, whom the Mercians apparently thought of as queen. Athelstan marched into and secured Northumbria at the death of King Sihtric, in 927, who had likewise been his brother-in-law as well as his subordinate as king. The succession of a brother-in-law was not, therefore, unknown in late Anglo-Saxon England. Indeed, on these two occasions the connection had been used by the West-Saxon royal house alongside superior kingship and military power as if it had some value as a legitimizing mechanism to what were essentially in both instances usurpations by force of arms of hitherto separate kingdoms. We should not necessarily assume that such instances were unknown in 1066, and Edith's role as Edward's queen may have been considered to have leant Harold a degree of legitimacy as his successor. Harold could also claim membership of the Danish royal family, but not royal blood, via his mother, Gytha, the sister of that Jarl Ulf who had married Cnut's sister, Estrith, and fathered King Swein of Denmark (1047–76). His kin was, therefore, illustrious, without being precisely royal by descent. Contemporaries stressed his princely qualities as if those legitimized his candidacy while keeping discreetly quiet concerning his lack of kingly forebears.

Harold's membership of the English royal family was somewhat less equivocal than that of William, whose sole connection with it was by virtue of his great-aunt, Emma, Edward's mother, who had married Aethelred two-thirds of a century before. This made William and Edward cousins, but the link was a distant one. William certainly had no advantage over Harold in this respect, and the connection was ancient history in the circumstances of Edward's death, however useful it may have seemed to both Edward and William earlier in the reign. That William was also illegitimate cannot have strengthened his case, although this was less a bar to kingship in the eleventh century than it was to become in the twelfth.

Harold's candidacy was arguably strongest as regards the support of many of the more influential sections of the political classes. Archbishops Stigand and Ealdred and many other senior churchmen were close associates of the Godwinesons, in and out of government, and had enjoyed the patronage of the West-Saxon earls and their kin over a period of forty years. Similarly, many of the landholders of southern and south-eastern England had commended themselves to Harold himself, his sister, his brothers or, in times past, to his father, and

(Tostig's affinity perhaps excepted) could be expected to welcome his elevation in the expectation that they could only benefit from better access to royal patronage. Recent history had demonstrated that the family had particularly strong support among the seafaring communities of the Kent and Sussex coast, and particularly from what would later be known as the Cinque Ports, and these ship-owning and ship-using localities were of particular importance to the protection of England against Scandinavia or Normandy. Harold's own core family estates seem to have lain predominately in Sussex, and here the connection between the Godwinesons and other landholders arguably went back at least three generations. The connection of the family with Bosham was clearly a very close one.

Harold was, therefore, the preferred candidate of the bulk of the southern landholding classes and the English church. If Edward had scruples about placing his own support behind his premier earl as his successor, they were arguably dispelled by the arguments of his intimates and friends, and their concern to promote a credible successor. Indeed, Edward's apparent concern, as voiced in the *Life*, concerning the future well-being of his wife and continental friends, implies that he did have reservations and was seeking assurances from Harold. As king, Harold seems to have honoured the obligations which he then undertook, there is no hint that Edith was despoiled by her brother, as Queen Emma had been by Harold I and then even Edward himself in 1043. Only one authentic writ of King Harold survives and that is a commonplace confirmation of the judicial and financial rights of the Lotharingian Bishop Giso of Wells, which was probably just one of numerous similar statements likely to have been sought from and sanctioned by a new king. Yet it may not be entirely irrelevant that Queen Edith was a benefactress and associate of this very same bishop, who had been a royal priest before his promotion. The *Life* is silent on the subject of Harold's treatment of Edith and this may be significant since it could reasonably have been expected to have voiced any grievances which the dowager queen entertained against her brother following his death.

Some at least of Edward's French and Norman friends did stay on under Harold and apparently prospered. Robert fitzWimarc received further lands in addition to those which Edward had granted him. The story told by William of Poitiers concerning the advice offered by an English-domiciled Norman called Robert son of the lady 'Guimora' to William in the early stages of the Hastings campaign may refer to him, in which case his loyalties then lay primarily with the English king.

There were, of course, sections of the English provincial community who habitually opposed the Earls of Wessex. In 1035 the leaders of Mercia and Northumbria had supported the candidacy of Harold I, in opposition to Earl Godwine and Queen Emma, and Edward's reign had been characterized by rivalry between the three senior comital families of Godwine, Leofric and Siward. Godwine's sons had all but displaced Siward's. Harold's resolution of the northern rebellion had, however, brought this era of dynastic competition to an end by allowing Leofric's grandsons to add the Northumbrian earldom to their core Mercian office. They owed this very much to Harold himself. At some stage – although whether before or after his succession is unclear – Harold consolidated this new alliance by marrying their sister, Ealdgyth, and by so doing he presumably confirmed their tenure of both northern earldoms. Just as Edward's succession in 1042 had been cemented by a marriage alliance with his most powerful earl, so too was Harold's and this too has all the hallmarks of a political treaty between two dynasties. Indeed, Ealdgyth had been the wife of King Gruffudd of Wales until Harold's campaigns against him had brought about his death. Her marriage to the new king of the English who had previously widowed her must necessarily be interpreted as a political match, designed to heal tensions between two powerful dynasties in their mutual self-interest.

Morcar held Northumbria in 1066 and the political accord apparently agreed by the two brothers with Harold and sealed by marriage was necessarily at Tostig's expense. It was very largely this division between the Godwinesons which the anonymous author of the *Life* believed had brought down the Anglo-Saxon state, but in practical terms Harold had no other course of action open to him – the acquiescence of the Mercians and Northumbrians in his kingship was essential to his prospects and that could not be obtained while at the same time readmitting Tostig to power in England. Even with the support of Edwin and Morcar, Harold's kingship seems to have been less than welcome at York, and the new king felt it necessary to hold court there before Easter in his first regnal year.

Something which Edwin and Morcar gave up was the option of supporting some other candidate for the throne. There is no evidence that they favoured Edgar's cause at this stage but their father, Earl Aelfgar, had been restored to England after his outlawry in 1058 by a Norwegian fleet commanded by Magnus the son of Harald Hardrada, in alliance with King Gruffudd. This alliance of the house of Leofric, the Welsh and the Norwegians was a powerful one which is likely to have had its own plans for the succession. Two of the three principals had, of course, died by 1066, but without an alliance with Harold Aelfgar's sons might have considered reserving their support for Harald Hardrada. Their determined effort later in the year against Harald's invasion clearly implies that the earls were committed to the new deal. They seem, therefore, to have accepted Harold as king without reservation and to have sought power within the new regime rather than via opposition to it. The outcome was a pragmatic drawing together of the several leaders of the English to present a comparatively united front to invaders. Within England, the candidacy of the young Edgar was the principal victim of this political brokering, but the unanimity of purpose achieved by the English elite in the opening months of the new year was impressive.

Even so, the setting aside of Edgar Aetheling – a *bona fide* candidate of the house of Cerdic – in favour of another candidate without his genealogical credentials constituted a dynastic revolution at the very heart of the English polity. Despite Edward's nomination and his widespread support, Harold was in that sense a candidate whose legitimacy was suspect. This was something likely to send a wave of unease through the political community at large if events should turn against him, since the tenure of the throne by the royal kin was hallowed by antiquity. Should Harold fail, the regime was dangerously exposed to the charge that his accession had been contrary to God's will, as eventually in fact occurred.

HAROLD'S RIVALS

The summer of 1066 was dominated by the expectation within England that foreign attack was imminent, and in parts of Europe by preparations for the same. Harold returned to Westminster from York at Easter, and perhaps there put in place his strategies for the defence of England. He had by this point successfully committed to himself all the senior figures in England and had every prospect of making a successful defence of his new kingship. Harold had one more very substantial advantage over his predecessor. Edward's freedom to pursue his own policies as king had been hampered by the impact of Godwine and then Harold on the immediate political and personal loyalties of the West-Saxon landholding classes, which had made the king uncomfortably dependent on non-West-Saxon support in any attempt to oppose their interests. Harold, by contrast, was able to combine his own massive influence and affinity with that which he had inherited from Edward himself, so ending the duality of king and earl – and near equality of power and patronage – in the heartland of the kingdom. This had obvious advantages for the massing of housecarls, who formed the backbone of any late Anglo-Saxon army, under a single command structure, and for the new king's ability to distribute largesse on an unprecedented scale. King Edward's capacity to field an army had depended heavily in latter years on Harold's willingness to throw his own resources behind royal policy. By contrast, Harold himself could now field an armed following which dwarfed those of the other earls – excepting perhaps the affinities of the Mercian and Northumbrian earls combined.

He was also accounted a wealthy prince by contemporary writers, who used his wealth in defence of his kingship. The combination of his own vast estates and great office with the resources of the crown was significant in this respect as well. It may be entirely unhistorical, but it is interesting to note that *Harald's saga* was later to imagine Harold Godwineson as the principal financial officer of Edward's regime, while the role of commander of the armed forces was Tostig's rather than his brother's. This connection between Harold and the politic use of money may well not be coincidental. Certainly, the recovery of coins of King Harold II from approximately half the English mints points to the rapid and efficient adaptation of the English coinage to the new reign. This may have been a matter of administrative detail, but Harold arguably used the output of his mints as part of his armoury for the struggle ahead, as well as for their considerable value as propaganda on behalf of his kingship.

Late spring saw Harold poised to defend the shores of southern England, having 'gathered a greater raiding ship-army and also raiding land-army than any king in the land had ever gathered before', to oppose Duke William. The same period saw the coming too of Halley's Comet, which the Bayeux Tapestry illustrated so graphically in conjunction with Harold's ceremonial crown wearing, and if that occurred at Easter (16 April) that was not so far removed from the appearance of the comet, which was visible in England between 24 and 30 April. What men made of that omen when it first appeared is unrecorded, despite its later interpretation as a portent of Harold's downfall and the collapse of Anglo-Saxon England, but there was a very obvious biblical parallel in the nativity which

Silver penny of King Harold II from the mint at Chichester. Harold's only type carried the 'Pacx' motif. Edward the Confessor's first issue was similarly a 'Pacx' style and the message – 'peace' – and the unusual depiction of Harold crowned both imply a political manifesto put out by an insecure regime which expected resistance.

Halley's Comet. (The Bayeux Tapestry – 11th Century. By special permission of the City of Bayeux)

might have encouraged the English to think Harold's regime unusually blessed by God, until that is his sudden defeat and death the following October. A not dissimilar comet had been recorded by Anglo-Saxon chroniclers under the year 995, and that had not coincided with any major dynastic upheaval, although it could be associated with Viking attacks.

THE RETURN OF TOSTIG

Tostig and his immediate household and following had taken refuge in the closing weeks of 1065 with Count Baldwin V of Flanders. Baldwin housed the exiles and resourced them with apparent liberality at St Omer, effectively enfeoffing Tostig with that town, at least in the view of the anonymous author of the *Life of King Edward*, who was probably a monk of St Bertin at St Omer.

In practice, Count Baldwin's position on the English succession is ambiguous and was perhaps always so. Baldwin had been very close to the Godwine family early in Edward's reign, and Tostig's marriage to Judith occurred either soon before or when Godwine, Swein, Tostig and Gyrth had all sought refuge in Bruges in 1051. A few years earlier, their amity probably found a common political cause in their joint commitment to an agreed policy on the English succession in favour of Cnut's descendants in Denmark, but the murder of Swein's brother, Earl Beorn, in 1049 apparently signalled the end of that intention (see above). Even so, Flanders offered the Godwine family a valuable counterweight to Edward's alliance with Normandy in the early 1050s. Baldwin's marriage to the sister of King Henry allied him to the French king in the late 1040s – when Henry was acting as if guardian of the young William's duchy. This may help explain the marriage alliance between Baldwin's daughter, Matilda, and the Duke, which had certainly been canvassed by 1049, when it was forbidden by Leo IX, but which only occurred about 1051. In 1052, Baldwin's marital alliances were thrown into disarray by the estrangement of king and duke, and their subsequent hostilities in and after 1053.

By 1066, however, the political utility of these connections was long worn out and Baldwin must be assumed to have been preoccupied with his own interests as he perceived them at that date. It is generally thought that he gave diplomatic support to William's candidacy for the English succession and William certainly retained Flemish knights in some numbers in his army of invasion, but Baldwin was probably more involved with his championship of the young King Philip I, whose uncle and guardian he was, until his own death in 1067. Philip's interests certainly did not encompass any further advancement of the power of William of Normandy. Baldwin was probably also mindful of the pact which the Normans had recently made with Henry IV of Saxony, Baldwin's own rival for parts of his territory. In 1066, therefore, relations between Baldwin and William are unlikely to have been particularly amicable, and Flanders had much to lose should her southern neighbour succeed in adding the crown of England to his existing pre-eminence in Atlantic Frankia.

Baldwin restricted his own active intervention in the English succession to his support for Tostig, who crossed the Channel at the head of a small flotilla of

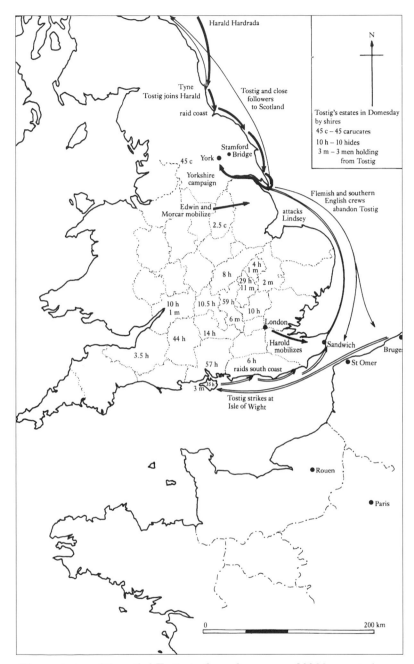

The campaign of the exiled Tostig in the early summer of 1066 seems to have initally targeted areas where he had held estates up until the previous autumn. The value of his estates in each shire are given in terms of their liability to geld, in either hides or carucates, plus the number of landholders described as his men. Even this minimalist assessment of his assets demonstrates that Tostig had been a wealthy man prior to his expulsion.

Flemish ships, manned in part at least by Baldwin's men. Tostig had an unimpeachable claim on his support by kinship, but the expedition was a comparatively small one and its objectives were probably limited. Whatever else it was, Tostig's venture was not a full-blown invasion of England but he was at least exploring the possibility of rallying English forces to his standard. His foray is described in some detail by two of the Anglo-Saxon Chronicles. First he descended on the Isle of Wight. Tostig was listed in Domesday Book as the holder of numerous estates in southern England, such as Fishbourne near Chichester, but this was the one area of the south where he held a predominance of coastal estates and could expect a sympathetic reaction from the local thegns. He was given money and provisions there, then ravaged along the coast as far as Sandwich, where he recruited some local seamen and press-ganged others. News that Harold had set out against him from London with a great army reached Tostig here and he departed northwards to the Humber with a force reputed to be sixty ships. There he struck at Lindsey – a province under the protection of Edwin and Morcar where their maternal kin were perhaps still influential – but the northern earls mobilized forces and ejected him in turn.

Tostig's force was clearly inadequate to mount a full blown invasion, despite some success in recruiting men and ships in England. His tactic was perhaps modelled on those used by other political exiles during Edward's reign, who had repeatedly made sufficient nuisance of themselves to persuade the ruling group to readmit them to positions of power and influence. This did not always work, of course, as the case of Osgod Clapa demonstrates, but Tostig had himself been involved in a very similar attack in 1052 which had culminated in his family's full reinstatement. His objective was, therefore, very probably a position of power within England commensurate with the Northumbrian earldom from which he had been ejected. It may be significant that he ravaged Earl Edwin's Mercia rather than his own old earldom in Yorkshire, and this may imply that he sought to be reinstated to the north.

Unfortunately for Tostig, his readmission to the English elite was the one thing capable of dissolving the new-found political consensus between King Harold and the house of Leofric, so it is unsurprising that he found himself resisted at all points. Put simply, Harold just could not afford to accommodate his brother.

That is not to say that Tostig was without influence with lesser men: some provisioned his forces; some paid him cash; some actually volunteered to fight for him, and it seems unlikely that all did so under duress. It seems clear that others besides the queen favoured his cause, therefore, and he could presumably call on deep-seated and long-standing associations with a portion of the political community of southern England in the furtherance of his ambitions. To take just a single shire, Tostig was named in Domesday Book as the *TRE* holder of three manors in Buckinghamshire, assessed for tax at fifty-nine hides and including the great forty-hide estate of Haddenham. A further six landholders were described as his men, with nineteen hides and one virgate. In 1066, Tostig was not enjoying the income and status commensurate with these holdings. A clue to what had occurred to his estates is given by several Domesday entries, including the ten-hide manor of Bayford near Hertford, which notes that 'Earl Tostig held this manor but King Edward had it in lordship at the time of his death.' If such manors had fallen to the crown when Tostig had been exiled, the same was presumably true of the remainder of his estates. Tostig was therefore landless in 1066 and, unless he could somehow engineer his reinstatement, entirely dependent on the charity of his Flemish brother-in-law.

Tostig's circumstances offer one more reason for Harold to deny him. The new king had, of course, taken over the landed assets of his predecessor. If these included rolling acres which had very recently been held by Earl Tostig, then his reinstatement in England would necessarily involve his readmission to his estates. Some of these went with the office of earl and would have been held by Morcar in 1066. Such were, however, exclusively in the north, where both Morcar and Tostig occur in the folios of Domesday Book as landholders in the 'time of King Edward'. In that context, we can safely assume that Tostig had lost his estates in Yorkshire (including districts which were eventually to become Lancashire and Westmorland) and that these had passed to Morcar as the new earl. Some at least of Tostig's considerable estates south of the Humber were, however, quite separate from his office of earl and it was these lands – including great manors like Haddenham (above) – which Harold was in a position to profit from or grant out at will to his own supporters at the beginning of his own reign. He would retain control of these assets only provided Tostig remained in exile, and this factor may have added to his resolve to resist his brother.

It is little wonder that contemporaries felt some sympathy for Tostig. His treatment by the chroniclers is comparatively even handed and factual in tone and his activities were ignored by the Bayeux Tapestry – the focus of which is William's claim and its fruition – and later by Eadmer in his comparatively brief sketch of the year's events, which also omits any reference to Harald Hardrada and the furious fighting which occurred in Yorkshire. William of Poitiers does, however, refer to his grievance against his brother: 'Nor is it to be wondered at that his brother, driven by the injuries done to him and striving to regain his lost honour, brought alien arms against Harold . . .'. William was, of course, using this episode to blacken Harold's character, but even so this vision of Tostig's plight is a credible one.

Having been driven out of Lindsey by the northern earls, Tostig's options had narrowed considerably. If his purpose had been to make sufficient nuisance of himself to persuade King Harold to reinstate him then he had manifestly failed. In these circumstances, his Flemish and southern English crews refused to follow him any further. Tostig could either abandon his mission and accept exile or seek some alternative path back to power and influence in England. He and his closest associates chose the latter option. When his shipmen abandoned him, Tostig went on to Scotland with twelve small boats. During his period as Earl of Northumbria, Tostig had forged close personal links with King Malcolm which he now exploited, remaining in Scotland for the summer. He did so presumably in the hope that he might be able to exploit the situation in England to his own advantage as events unfolded during the summer months. Tostig cannot have been ignorant of Duke William's preparations in Normandy and may even have had some contact with him before leaving Flanders in April or May. It would hardly be surprising if he had at least sounded out the attitude of this kinsman by marriage to his own ambitions. In the event, however, his opportunity came not from Normandy but from Scandinavia, whence Harald Hardrada arrived on the Scottish coasts in the autumn.

HARALD HARDRADA AND THE NORWEGIAN CANDIDACY

That King Harald of the Norwegians should have entertained ambitions regarding the English throne comes as no surprise, since his predecessor, King Magnus, had been the principal external threat to Edward's kingship for the first half decade of his reign. Neither king had any claim by descent from a previous ruler of England, whether or not the Danish royal line be included as a potential source of legitimacy, although Magnus could pose as the successor of Swein Cnutson in Norway, so in a sense to Cnut himself. Stories circulated in Scandinavia of an accord between Harthacnut and Magnus I of Norway (otherwise known as Magnus the Good or Magnus Olafson) in about 1040, by which each recognized the other as heir if either should die childless; Harthacnut did just that, of course, in 1042, when he was king of both the Danes and the English. If such a treaty occurred – and that seems likely given Harthacnut's need to secure Denmark before invading England – then that and that alone legitimized the ambitions which Magnus entertained regarding Edward's realm. That threat was certainly taken seriously in England, where the king found it necessary to station himself with a fleet at Sandwich during the summer months in the mid-1040s. In practice, however, the Norwegian fleet was interminably delayed, first by the war of conquest by which Magnus purposed to wrest control of Denmark from Swein Estrithsson and then by Magnus's own death in October 1047.

Magnus was succeeded by his uncle, Harald Sigurdsson, better known as Harald Hardrada ('the ruthless'), who was the half-brother of King (St) Olaf but who had fled Scandinavia following the Battle of Stilkestad in 1030, in which Olaf was slain. He was then fifteen. Harald and his retainers spent the next seventeen years as mercenary soldiers and Vikings in the Mediterranean and Asia Minor, where they entered the service of the rulers of Byzantium. *Harald's saga* depicts him as rising rapidly to become leader of the Varangians and a captain in numerous minor campaigns in the Aegean before leading what amounts to a freebooting raid in strength on Muslim Africa and Sicily, the profits of which he deposited for safe keeping with King Jaroslav at Novgorod (now in Russia, south of St Petersburg), who had formerly been Magnus's patron and protector. He became deeply embroiled in the palace revolution at Byzantium of 1042, which resulted in the public blinding of Emperor Michael Calaphates, but thereafter retired to Novgorod, married King Jaroslav's daughter, Elizabeth, and took charge of his own massive war chest. This and his great reputation as a warrior made Harald a force to be reckoned with throughout Scandinavia, and he forced Magnus to share the Norwegian throne with him and then took control of the whole when his nephew died.

Harald's reign was dominated by his attempts to make himself king also of Denmark in succession to his nephew, but that claim was doggedly resisted by

Swein Estrithsson, who could count on considerable Danish support. The contest came to a climax at the great naval battle of the Nissa – the River Nissa in southern Sweden – fought in August 1062, at which King Harald and his ally Earl Hakon proved victorious. Swein survived, however, and the two kings finally made peace in 1064. This treaty enabled Harald to crush his rivals within Norway itself and also to give thought to the English crown.

Upon his own accession, Harald was said by the author of the Worcester manuscript of the Chronicle to have sent an embassy to Edward to make peace. The outcome of this diplomacy is unrecorded but the English certainly gave him a free hand in Denmark, sending none of the aid which Swein sought, and this may indeed have been the *quid pro quo* of England's comparative security from Viking attack during the 1050s. Indeed, both Edward and Harald may have considered their own interests well served by the resurrection of the Anglo-Norwegian alliance which Aethelred had forged in 1014 with Olaf. Harald did, however, retain an interest in the English succession. Welsh annals suggest that a large Norwegian force under Harald's son Magnus was active in the Irish Sea in 1058 and then helped King Gruffudd of Wales to restore Aelfgar, Edwin's father, to the earldom of Mercia and attack the English. As already suggested, interference in England on behalf of a bitter rival of the Godwinesons is likely to have involved some commitment from Aelfgar that he would favour Harald's candidacy when Edward died, but, unsurprisingly, no notice of the detail of their alliance has survived. It is possible, of course, that Magnus backed Aelfgar for money, much as Dublin shipmen had done in 1055, but this has at least the appearance of a more serious enterprise than that, and it may even have started out as a direct attack on Edward's England.

Harald may, therefore, have been building up support for his own candidacy for Edward's inheritance in Dublin, Man, the Islands, Mercia and Wales. If so, the disappearance from history and presumed death of Earl Aelfgar in about 1063 and the subsequent defeat and death of his son-in-law King Gruffudd were severe set-backs for Hardrada. So too was the accord reached by Harold Godwineson and Aelfgar's two young sons in 1065–6, which deprived him of the support of any substantial figure already in a position of real power inside England. Even so, his pacification of Scandinavia in 1064 and his alliances among the Vikings of eastern Europe provided him with a platform from which to launch his own candidacy by force of arms, and his military record will certainly have made that of Harold Godwineson pale into insignificance by comparison, in the eyes of well-informed contemporaries.

Harald Hardrada seems to have spent the summer making preparations for a descent on England. There is no memory of any diplomacy between him and Harold II of England, and the surprise which he apparently achieved on arrival implies that little or no contact occurred. It is difficult to imagine that the fact of his mobilization was something which can have remained secret for long on the busy seaways of the North Sea but that prospect will have benefited from his sailing from Norway direct to the British Isles via the Shetlands and Orkneys, rather than taking the coastal route via his rival's Denmark then Flanders to the Channel. Harald's route may have been influenced by various factors: passage of the Danish coastline might have tempted Swein to intervene and Harold Godwineson was probably known to have taken up guard on the southern coasts of England, and Hardrada had a long history of attacking his enemies where he was least expected. Alternatively, it may have been his intention to gather further reinforcements from the islands and Scandinavian Scotland and reach England not via the Godwineson heartland of the south but through Viking Yorkshire. Knowledge that the northern rebellion of 1065 had succeeded in outfacing the leaders of the south may have been relevant to this.

Whatever his thinking, Harald arrived in the mouth of the Tyne shortly after Harold Godwineson's dispersal of his forces on 8 September, and the English chroniclers considered that he achieved surprise in so doing. He was reputed to have had with him 300 vessels (the later Worcester annals give 500). This was, therefore, a massed levy of warriors and warships from the Viking world in excess even of the armies with which Swein of Denmark, and then Cnut, had captured the throne of England a generation earlier. According to the Abingdon manuscript of the Chronicle, he was joined by Tostig in the Tyne by prior arrangement, but the Worcester manuscript implies that they actually joined forces in Scotland. Whichever, Tostig now harnessed his own prospects in England to the possibility of a Norwegian victory over Harold Godwineson.

The later *Harald's saga* gives Tostig a far more central role in Harald's decision making than other sources, representing him as visiting both King Swein in Denmark and Harald in Norway between going into exile at the end of 1065 and attacking England in the following April/May. The story is, however, at best unconfirmed and the earl's initial solo effort against England may imply that he had as yet not allied himself with either of the Scandinavian kings. Only after he had failed to fight his way back did Tostig reach Scotland and it was presumably there that he and Harald came to agreement. The centre-piece of their accord was the earl's recognition of Hardrada's lordship: 'he submitted to him and became his man', but the forces which Tostig is likely to have added to the Norwegian host were negligible. Far more important was his status as a leading English earl and member of the Godwineson family. It seems reasonable to imagine that it was that which Harald valued, for, from his perspective, Tostig was a key figure within the English elite such as his cause had hitherto lacked. Although Tostig's assistance could make no difference to the fragility of his dynastic claim, it could go some way to legitimizing his candidacy among the political classes – and it should be remembered that Tostig had been a core member of Edward's regime for a decade before his very recent exile and was, like Harold, the old king's brother-in-law. He also knew his way around northern England, and his local knowledge – both geographical and political – could be of great benefit to the Norwegians. His adhesion was, therefore, of considerable value to Hardrada, and it is not surprising that they are portrayed thereafter as acting like allies in joint command of operations. They may even have intended to share the kingship once they had defeated Harold Godwineson, with Earl Tostig the resident viceroy and Harald the itinerant royal fleet commander – much like Cnut and Godwine before them.

THE YORKSHIRE CAMPAIGN

Harald Hardrada and Tostig led their armada from the Tyne to the Humber and then up the Ouse towards York. Some later writers state that they landed at Riccal, and since Simeon of Durham is numbered among them they are likely to be providing local detail still circulating in the north a generation or so later, but his reconstruction of the campaign is at times somewhat confused. Their disembarkation should probably be dated to about 16 September, and Harold Godwineson is represented by the chroniclers as ignorant of their arrival until news of the actual landing reached him in the south. King Harold's location at that point is unknown, since he was recorded as having 'ridden inland' once his forces on the coast had disbanded on 8 September. If Harold was up until then still on the Isle of Wight, then he could well have been in Hampshire a week or so later, although the storm losses suffered by the fleet as it returned to the Thames may well have drawn him back to London to assess the damage. He clearly had relatively few men around him, however, when the news of the Norwegian attack reached him, so had to mobilize once more before and during his ride north to confront Hardrada and Tostig. Despite the speed with which King Harold reacted, he was unable to reach Tadcaster before Sunday 24 September.

Hardrada's first objective was presumably York, since that would give him control of the only substantial fortress in the north, a large and comparatively successful urban community of well over 1,500 households and several markets, and the governmental capital of a third of England. It was still the centre of Anglo-Scandinavian culture in England, where Cnut's lawcode had only recently been restored to use – a concession on Edward's part to the northern rebels in 1065 – and its inhabitants were more likely than others to empathize with his candidacy and back him against Harold II, with whose kingship they had little reason to sympathize. York was also a prominent mint and the second metropolitan see of England. The presence of Archbishop Ealdred at this point seems far from certain, given his central role in English governance, but even the archdiocesan seat and the minster with its canons were important foci within the region and there were several more churches besides.

Simeon suggested that Hardrada took York early on in his campaign and, only with that achieved, fought against the northern earls. The briefer accounts in the nearer contemporary Chronicles are less than supportive of this interpretation. According to the Worcester manuscript, Harald and Tostig 'both went into the Humber until they came to York, and there Earl Edwin and Earl Morcar, his brother, fought against them, but the Northmen had the victory'. The Abingdon manuscript is less circumspect in placing the battle before Hardrada's entry to York. Given that Earl Edwin's battle at Gate Fulford occurred on 20 September, Hardrada seems likely to have secured the walled city only once the English army had been defeated outside the walls – perhaps that same evening – and the logic of the battle field would certainly suggest that the Norwegians, not Earl Edwin, attacked from the south.

Despite the undoubted political value to the Norwegian king of Tostig's support in a broader context, this was arguably an asset of the most dubious value

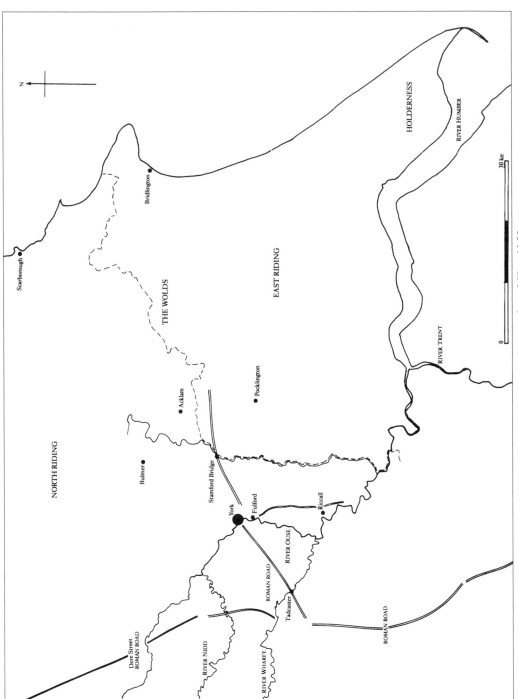

Yorkshire at the time of the campaigns of Harald Hardrada, the northern earls and Harold II.

A late Anglo-Saxon sword found in the Thames at Wallingford, where William's army crossed in the late autumn of 1066.

when it came to wooing the Yorkshire nobility to his cause, since it was their rebellion against his rule which had forced Tostig into exile less than a year before. This may help to explain a detail of this campaign which is otherwise incomprehensible, which is Hardrada's apparent failure to persuade York to surrender to him before his own victory over Earl Edwin's forces. Riccal lies a mere 14 kilometres (less than 9 miles) from York, a distance which could easily have been covered by part at least of the Norwegian army on the same day as they disembarked. What is more, there seems no very obvious reason why the entire fleet should not have tied up at York itself, other than reservations concerning its welcome there. The presence of Morcar's housecarls might be one consideration, but his military household is unlikely to have been particularly impressive on its own considering his very recent elevation to high office, and it seems improbable that he was actually there in person. Rather, the army of both Edwin and Morcar probably reached York and its vicinity some days later than Harald. More important to attitudes in York itself was arguably the presence of the hated Tostig with the Norwegian king. It seems most unlikely that his initial reception there will have been other than hostile, and this may well be why the citizens of York initially closed their gates to the Norwegians and awaited the arrival of those who had been their allies in the autumn of 1065. York witnessed, therefore, in

September 1066, a renewal of the common front mounted by the Northumbrians and Mercians in October 1065, once again against Tostig.

In the circumstances, Earl Edwin and his brother raised a substantial force extremely quickly. They are unlikely to have learnt of Hardrada's arrival very much before messengers set out to warn King Harold, but they may have received information from further north about the time the Norwegian fleet entered the Humber, so perhaps a day or too earlier. *Harald's saga* suggests that the Norwegian forces raided Cleveland, Scarborough and Holderness as they proceeded southwards, in which case they may have taken four days or so to make the journey to the Humber from the Tyne, but this may be less than entirely accurate. Edwin's forces were presumably made up in part of his own military retainers and those of his brother, and the house of Leofric arguably kept as large a force of housecarls as it could afford throughout this period. But, he needed also to mobilize the thegns and landholding classes of his earldom, and particularly its heartland in Cheshire, Staffordshire and Shropshire and neighbouring parts of Wales. These forces then had to travel to York, a distance of some 200 km by road from Chester. They probably advanced on the city from the south-west via Tadcaster, keeping the Ouse between themselves and the Norwegians and then entering the city via the bridge across the Ouse. Harald Hardrada was presumably encamped not far south of York, somewhere between Riccal and Fulford.

The earls fought Harald Hardrada, according to Simeon, 'at Fulford, near York, on the northern bank of the river Ouse'. The battle occurred on Wednesday 20 September – 'the Vigil of St Matthew the Apostle' – and was hard contested with substantial casualties on both sides. The opening of the conflict was characterized by a ferocious attack launched by the earls on the invaders but the Norwegians were the eventual victors, and all accounts suggest that more of the English forces were drowned in the retreat than had been slain in the actual conflict – presumably in an attempt to regain the west side of the Ouse. The earls, however, survived.

The political context of the Battle of Fulford is of some significance. Harold Godwineson reached York during the morning of 25 September, having spent the previous night at Tadcaster, to the south-west, so had arrived in Yorkshire during 24 September at latest. A delay of just four days would have allowed Edwin and Morcar to combine their own forces with those of the king and given them a far better prospect of victory. It does not seem plausible to imagine that the earls were entirely ignorant of King Harold's movements. Their forces could presumably have held the walls of York against the Norwegians for the necessary few days, particularly since he already seems to have been kept at bay by the townsfolk without their assistance for at least a day or two. They did not, however, and one must conclude that the earls elected to fight rather than to wait.

Several factors may have contributed to their resolution. One must surely be the presence in the Norwegian host of Tostig, their arch-enemy and Morcar's rival for the office of Earl of Northumbria. The possibility that the ever-subtle King Harold II might negotiate with his brother may have spurred them on. Furthermore, his presence was the one thing giving their Mercian and

Northumbrian following real cohesion. Secondly, if they had themselves reneged on an understanding previously reached between Hardrada and their own father, Earl Aelfgar, Edwin and Morcar could expect little sympathy from the Norwegian king should he become king. In such circumstances, resolute opposition may well have seemed the preferable option. Thirdly, the outcome of this battle had the potential to alter the whole balance of their understanding with King Harold II. Victory by the two earls over the Norwegians and Tostig would have given them invaluable prestige, and enabled them to emerge from the crisis as virtual kingmakers. Such thinking perhaps underlies the boldness with which Edwin and his brother undertook to fight against Harald Hardrada and his great army.

The two earls did not, however, achieve their primary objective. Instead, they were defeated and lost a significant part of their soldiery in the rout. The battle at Gate Fulford effectively finished Morcar in the north and it must have fundamentally undermined the reputations of both brothers as military leaders – reputations which had perhaps begun to grow on the strength of the successful northern rebellion in 1065 and their campaign against Tostig in Lindsey earlier in the year. This reversal and its outcome was to be of considerable significance after Hastings, when the matter of the succession had once more been thrown into play. The risk must, however, have seemed worth taking when they made their plans on 19 September, and talked over their prospects for the morrow from the comparative safety of the city walls.

The immediate consequence of the Battle of Gate Fulford was York's surrender to Harald Hardrada. The Abingdon manuscript of the Chronicle notes that 'Harald king of Norway and Earl Tostig went into York with as great a force as seemed to them [necessary] and they were given hostages from the town, and also help with provisions, and so went from there to ship, and spoke of complete peace provided that they would all go south with them and win this land.' For Tostig, entry to York for the first time in twelve difficult months must have tasted sweet, and fully justified his decision to lend his support to the Norwegian candidate for the throne. For Harald, this was the beginning of a piecemeal recognition of his kingship over England, province by province, of a kind that he was familiar with from his campaigning in Denmark and even Norway itself. If he and his friends sought English precedents, such were available in the crisis of 1013, when Swein of Denmark had gained the support of the north and eastern Mercia, and used that as a platform for the conquest of all England with an army the core of which consisted of Scandinavians.

From the ships at Riccal, Harald journeyed to Stamford Bridge on the River Derwent, quite probably travelling via York once more. His purpose was to wait there on the boundary between the North and East Ridings, and between the Wapentakes of Pocklington, Acklam and Bulmer, for hostages to reach him from the whole shire. This boundary location has all the characteristics of a well-used hosting place, and this may well explain its selection. It is very important to recognize that Harald was there for purposes that were primarily political. He had no immediate intention of fighting Harold Godwineson.

Harold II and the army which he had raised in great haste in the south reached Tadcaster on the Sunday following Edwin's defeat at Gate Fulford. The

Abingdon Chronicle remarks that he there 'drew up his shipmen' and this has often been taken to refer to the presence of English ships there. If so, these must necessarily have entered the River Wharfe before Harald brought his great fleet into the Ouse, since Riccal lies between Tadcaster and the sea, in which case this is a reference to English ships which had retreated in the face of the Norwegian fleet at the start of the campaign. However, this is perhaps to read too much into the technical meaning of the word *lid-mann* as 'seaman', since English and Scandinavian soldiers were effectively marines and equally at home on board ship and on land. The likelier interpretation of the passage is that Harold paused at Tadcaster to marshal all the forces available to him, and these may well have included companies which had arrived at this rendezvous independently of his own main force. It may well be that significant groups of survivors from the Battle of Fulford had retired on Tadcaster to await his arrival, and either or both of Earls Edwin and Morcar may well have joined him, although their presence is unrecorded. It may be of some significance that Hardrada had placed himself in a location suited to the arrival of hostages only from the North and East Ridings, and it seems quite likely that the earls and their surviving forces were somewhere in the West Riding, where they could at need retire on western Mercia.

Harold already seems to have known of the outcome of Gate Fulford before he arrived and will have obtained fresh information of events at Tadcaster. Given the nature of his activities, Hardrada's location was necessarily well known. On Monday 25 September Harold advanced through York and onward up the Roman road towards Bridlington. It was a march of about 26 kilometres (16 miles) to Stamford Bridge but the English army arrived in time to launch an immediate attack on the Norwegian host. It seems quite clear that Harold's rapid advance had taken Hardrada completely by surprise and the Norwegians were unprepared for battle. A later addition to the Abingdon version of the Chronicle described a single Viking warrior holding the bridge against the entire English army, but this scene may owe as much to the classic story of Horatio as anything else. *Harald's saga* seeks to explain the Norwegians' defeat by reference to many of them being without body armour, and such is entirely possible in the circumstances of surprise. The later Welsh annals, *The Chronicle of the Princes*, similarly depicts Harald as taken unawares and unarmed, 'in an unexpected battle through native treachery'.

Whatever the precise circumstances, Stamford Bridge proved a resounding victory for Harold Godwineson and the English army:

There were killed Harald Hardrada [numerous near contemporary texts follow the Worcester manuscript of the Chronicle in misrepresenting him here as Harald Fine-hair] and Earl Tostig, and the Northmen who remained there were put to flight, and the English fiercely attacked them from behind until some of them came to ship, some drowned, and some also burnt, and thus variously perished, so that there were few survivors, and the English had possession of the place of slaughter. The king then gave safe-conduct to Olaf, the son of the king of the Norse, and to their bishop, and to the earl of Orkney, and to all those who were left on the ships. And they then went up to our king, and swore oaths that they would always keep peace and friendship in this land; and the king let them go home with twenty-four ships.

So ended in sudden and violent death two of the great men of the age, Harald Hardrada and Tostig Godwineson, and with them fell away any prospect that the succession to Edward's English throne would, in the short term at least, be decided by dint of Scandinavian arms. From the perspective of both Harold Godwineson and Earl Edwin, Tostig's death removed a significant loose cannon from play which had some capacity to harm both. However, Harold's great victory contrasted dramatically with Edwin's defeat by the same invasion force, and the result must have had dramatic consequences as regards the reputation of each and the balance of power between them. Harold II had justified his consecration as king in the previous January, and his triumph will arguably have been viewed by contemporaries – particularly in England – as proof of the legitimacy of his kingship. He had emerged as just the sort of effective protector-figure that they had anticipated, and his nomination over the head of a youthful descendant of the royal house was vindicated. In contrast, Earl Edwin and his brother had sought to establish themselves as major players in the political arena by virtue of defeating the Norwegians. Their failure relegated them to the second division thereafter, and they would find it extremely difficult to restore their reputations after such a major defeat as had occurred at Gate Fulford.

Stamford Bridge, therefore, rescued Northumbria from the Norwegian king but it did nothing for the northern earls, whose presence in the battle was not even noted by contemporaries and must remain unproven. It was Harold who gained the kudos and his kingship was the stronger as a result.

DUKE WILLIAM

William was born in 1027–8, at Falaise in Lower Normandy, the illegitimate son of Duke Robert I ('the Magnificent') and a tanner's daughter in the town, whose family hailed from the countryside south of Caen at Conteville. His father's death in 1035 brought him to the office of Count or Duke of Normandy while still a child. It was the period 1035–40 during which he presumably came into initial contact with his great-aunt's much older English son, Edward the Confessor, who was then in exile at the Norman court. William was, therefore, of similar age to Harold Godwineson and Queen Edith and in his late thirties in 1066. The child-duke was long beset by the conflicting ambitions of his own nobility and paternal relatives, and his survival owed much to King Henry of France, who comprehensively defeated William's enemies at the Battle of Val-es-Dunes, in what are now rich grain fields between Conteville, Billy and Caen, in 1047. By 1050 William had emerged as a capable young soldier and leader of men, although still beset by wars at home. It was the Norman duke to whom Edward the Confessor seems to have turned in his search for allies to help him exclude the family of Earl Godwine in 1051, and the Worcester manuscript of the Chronicle refers to a grand but apparently brief visit by William to Edward's court at that time. Edward's putative nomination of William as his heir was probably designed

Falaise townscape. Duke William's mother, Arlette, was supposedly a seamstress from a family of tanners resident in the town, but originally from the countryside south-east of Caen.

to engage the duke's self-interest but it failed to deliver any active assistance since he immediately became embroiled in a new war with Henry I. By the time peace was restored and William had fought off his enemies, the Godwinesons were securely back in England and in control of the royal court. Although members of their family remained as hostages at the Norman court, William had lost the opportunity to establish himself as Edward's heir.

Edward's nomination in 1051–2 was, therefore, the basis of William's claim to the throne and his apologists insist on its significance and contempory relevance even in 1066. The difficulty is that we have no independent record that Edward still then harboured the wish to be succeeded by his Norman cousin and in practice there are good reasons to suppose that he may have long since abandoned the notion as impractical. William was clearly perceived by the English elite as an outsider and as a threat to their own interests. It is certainly difficult to see why else Edward should have brought back his half-nephew from Hungary in 1057 other than to install him as heir to the throne. At the last he nominated Harold Godwineson, not William. Whether or not William's candidature remained his own preference, therefore, Edward was pragmatic enough to recognize the political needs of his own people and on his deathbed to legitimize Harold Godwineson's bid for the crown. From an English perspective, Edward's nomination of Harold at the point of death necessarily destroyed any lingering currency which William's candidature might still retain from the king's much earlier promise.

This left William, like Harald Hardrada, without political support within England in 1066, when the elite, Tostig excepted but Edward included, closed ranks behind Harold's candidacy. It was this circumstance which rendered Harold's dealings with William just a year or two earlier so important: what the Bonneville Accord had seemed to offer the Norman duke was the prospect of the support of the old king's brother-in-law, senior earl and leading general. Certainly, both sides must have been conscious that the agreement which they reached was conditioned by William's temporary advantage by reason of Harold's presence in his court, but the prospect of a dual marriage alliance and the promise of increased power in England just might have kept Harold to his bargain.

When news reached William of Edward's death, it was, according to the Bayeux Tapestry, via a messenger sent by Harold himself, and the single ship is pictured on a suitably mountainous sea, as might be expected in early January. William of Jumièges represented the duke as responding to the news of Harold's consecration by sending envoys to Harold to urge him to honour the Bonneville Accord and his own oaths, but the duke can hardly have been surprised when this approach failed. Harold's coronation was a *fait accompli* by this point. Since the author referred at this juncture to Halley's Comet, the diplomatic exchanges had apparently been completed already by 24 April. Duke William responded to Harold's accession by mobilizing forces for an assault on England and by a diplomatic offensive designed to isolate Harold and reinforce his own candidacy.

According to William of Poitiers, Duke William laid his case before Pope Alexander III and received his support and a standard under which to fight. One must assume that the story of his claim and Harold's contumacy as told by William himself and the Bayeux Tapestry provided the substance of his appeal to Rome, evidence of which does not otherwise exist, and Alexander's support obviously did no harm to William. Indeed, it may have made it easier to raise support inside Frankia and particularly among the rich and influential churchmen and their tenants. However, the papal court had no authority to determine the descent of the crown of the English. Harold's position was undefended so went by default and the entire event had little efficacy or potential for such inside England. That William should have laid his claims before the papal court underlines the subtlety of his political mind, but it also reveals the fragility of his claim. It arguably did the standing of the papacy more good than the duke himself.

The same author reported a pact of friendship also made in recent times between Normandy and the Emperor Henry IV, by which the latter would come to the duke's aid against any enemy at his request. Henry himself had no direct interest in the English succession, but did have ambitions in the Low Countries where the powerful Count Baldwin of Flanders had secured the guardianship of the kingdom of France during the minority of the young Philip. An alliance between the principal rival of Paris inside Frankia – Normandy – and the feudal superior of the current guardian of the kingdom did, therefore, have a certain logic. There is no reason, however, to imagine that the agreement bound Henry to support a Norman attack on England, nor any evidence that he did.

The other figure whom William of Poitiers alleged to have given the Norman claim some support in 1066 is King Swein of Denmark. Swein himself had a far better right to the English crown by descent than Duke William and he was later to pursue that claim by force, in and after 1069–70. In 1066, however, the Danish king faced the prospect of a Norwegian descent on the English shores. No one knew better than the embattled Swein the military effectiveness of Harald Hardrada and one might excuse him if he anticipated a Norwegian victory. If Harald succeeded, then Swein's own future looked bleak. Caught between the hammer of the Norwegian soldiery and the anvil of English cash reserves, the Danes would have had little option but to recognize Harald Hardrada as king. Until Stamford Bridge, therefore, Swein had good reason to hope that William of Normandy would act as an effective counterweight to Harald Hardrada, and enable himself to retain Denmark. His own attitude towards Harold Godwineson may have been poisoned by the responsibility of that family, in the person of Harold's older brother Swein, for the death of his own brother Earl Beorn, back in the first half of Edward's reign, and this too may have influenced the Danes to side with Duke William.

When all is said and done, however, William's diplomacy provided him with no significant military assistance for his campaign in 1066, and its impact on events was extremely limited. Of far greater importance was his freedom to take large forces out of the duchy in 1066 with little prospect of external attack, and this was due very largely to circumstances outside his own control. Had the county of Anjou and the kingdom of France had adult rulers at this date, then his invasion would have been far riskier, even despite the superiority which William had painstakingly established over the several counts along the seaboard to the north and west of his own territories.

Even in the unusually advantageous circumstances which prevailed in 1066, it is clear that many of the Norman elite considered his expedition foolhardy in the extreme and beyond William's powers to resource. The fullest account of these discussions, by William of Poitiers, is illuminated by the retrospective knowledge that the conquest would be successful. Had it been otherwise his account would have been very different – had it been written at all. Clearly, Normandy did not have even ships enough to carry Duke William's armada, and the entire project had to await the construction of numerous vessels, responsibility for which was divided among William's less than willing vassals. The discussions part way through preparations which William retrospectively reconstructed may well be apocryphal but nevertheless are far from irrelevant. He supposed the Norman magnates to have been alarmed by the entire enterprise and in despair at the comparison of Harold's strength to that of Normandy:

> He abounded in riches whereby powerful kings and princes were brought into alliance; he had a numberless fleet with expert crews long experienced in maritime dangers and battles; the wealth and therefore the military resources of his country far exceeded those of our land. Who could hope to have a ship

Building William's fleet on the Dives in Lower Normandy. (The Bayeux Tapestry – 11th Century. By special permission of the City of Bayeux)

completed within a year as required or find crews for those that were thus completed? Who would not be afraid that this new expedition would reduce the prosperous condition of Normandy to penury? Who would not affirm that the power of a Roman emperor would be insufficient for so hazardous an undertaking?

If the Duke's vassals were indeed expressing alarm at his adventure, one can hardly blame them, since at this point its prospects must have seemed poor. What is more, Duke William could only put such an enterprise in motion once, since it traded heavily on his reputation in war and a serious setback would have undermined his credibility. The duke had to go for broke or not at all.

Duke William's reputation has, of course, gained considerably from the accounts of his propagandists concerning the mobilization and management of the fleet and army of invasion, and this has encouraged comparison to his advantage with King Harold in a wide variety of modern publications. Take for example the duke's oft-quoted achievement in keeping his army and fleet supplied without looting the neighbourhood while they awaited the necessary wind to carry them to England from the mouth of the Dives, which has been contrasted with the dispersal of Harold's army on 8 September because their food had given out. King Harold had mobilized at or around Easter, so in April, and

The Dives estuary, which is now a popular venue for recreational sailing. William's fleet moved eastwards and northwards to Ponthieu soon after it was constructed.

had succeeded in maintaining large forces – and one might reasonably guess very much larger forces than William's at this point – for five months or more when they disbanded. The Normans, by contrast, had arguably mobilized much later in the year. William of Poitiers suggests that they were delayed for just a month at Dives, but there is also the matter of their ultimate location; in this account the duke is identified first at the mouth of the Dives in Lower Normandy but then as moving eastward to the Somme. The Bayeux Tapestry makes no reference to the locality of either ship building and supply or embarkation, but William of Jumièges represented the new fleet as having been built and anchored at St Valery-sur-Somme, which is not in Normandy at all but in Ponthieu. In seeking to reconcile these several accounts, modern scholars have generally accepted William of Poitiers's interpretation, that the fleet was blown by westerly winds from the Dives to St Valery, and there awaited with considerable impatience a wind that would take them to England.

The grainfields of the coastal plain of Lower Normandy. This area would initially have been burdened with provisioning William's mobilization.

What is at issue, however, is William's ability to resource his armada, and this was obviously enhanced by its use of two bases. Supposing that his new ships were built in territory firmly under his own control, so in Lower Normandy, they remained there only four weeks after preparations were concluded, and comments on his firm control apply only to this period. He was then able to mobilize the entire force before invasion in distant Ponthieu, where responsibility for its supply could be diverted to Count Guy. Certainly, Normandy was itself protected from any deleterious impact, but the wholesome praise which the Duke receives from Norman intimates should surely be treated with some caution and not extended to cover the fleet's sojourn in Ponthieu.

So too should we treat the well-known vision of William's fleet impatiently immured in port by contrary winds with some caution. This story has one major advantage to William's candidacy in that it places responsibility for the timing of his enterprise in God's hands. If William was delayed in Frankia by the winds,

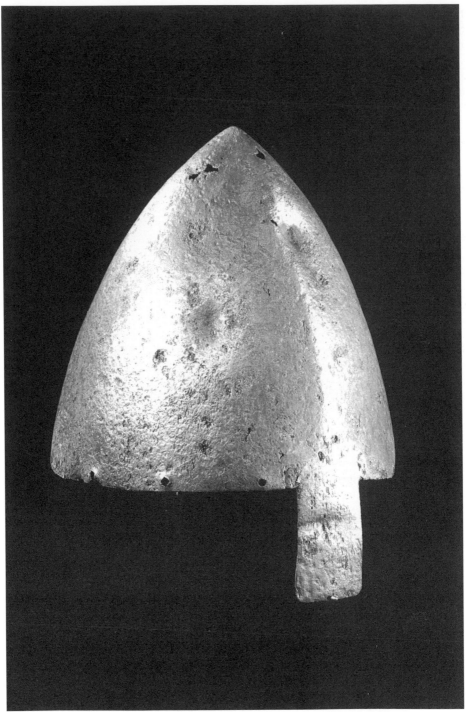

A Norman helmet of the period, which closely resembles those illustrated in the Bayeux Tapestry.

then he was like a pawn within God's divine plan for the destruction of Harold's iniquitous kingship and its replacement by his own as Edward's true heir. He is represented, of course, as offering prayers at the church of St Valery, for favourable winds, and the arrival of that wind is of course further proof of William's position as an instrument of God, yet the duke had very good reasons to delay his crossing of the Channel. In the first place, he could not risk an engagement with significant English forces at sea, since his soldiers were primarily cavalry and had none of the experience of the English and Scandinavians in sea battles. That numerous ships were carrying cavalry mounts would have made them vulnerable to attack while still in open water. William had, therefore, to await the disbanding not just of Harold's land army but more particularly his fleet, and it was not until that had retired to London, battered by the autumnal weather, that he could risk his army on the Channel. His removal from Dives to St Valery may have been in part at least an attempt to distance himself from Harold's ships based in the Solent and to shorten the hazardous crossings.

Secondly, the ultimate timing of the invasion suggests that William was not even prepared to set out while he knew that Harold was in the south. Rather, his descent on Sussex coincided with the Viking attack on Yorkshire. From St Valery, William will have had little difficulty in gathering information from coastal traders and others concerning fleet activity in the North Sea, and he probably knew of the descent of Harald Hardrada on the Humber in the middle of September, not much later (if at all) than Harold Godwineson himself. He seems also to have known of Harold's mobilization and march northwards, and it would be very unwise to forget the close contacts of the port of London and the north-Frankish coastlands during this period. Harold had left the south before Gate Fulford was fought on 20 September, to ride the long and weary miles to York. His temporary absence was the opportunity for William to arrive in England unopposed. He seems to have set sail, therefore, on 26 September, once final preparations were complete, and his departure from France signals the opening of the Hastings campaign.

HAROLD, WILLIAM AND HASTINGS

Expectation of William's arrival was the principal factor conditioning Harold's deployment of the English armed forces throughout the summer of 1066. There could be little doubt in his mind concerning William's intentions: he had himself conversed with William only two or three years earlier; the two had exchanged embassies concerning the course of events and the issues separating them between January and Easter, and William of Poitiers reported on the spies in Normandy itself whom Harold had employed to keep him informed. When Harold marched north against the Norwegians he must have known that William's armada still lay in a state of near readiness at St Valery, and his haste throughout the entire campaign was conditioned by the need to return to the south before William could launch himself across the Channel. Given the time needed, the odds were heavily against the English achieving this objective, despite Harold's almost legendary speed of march.

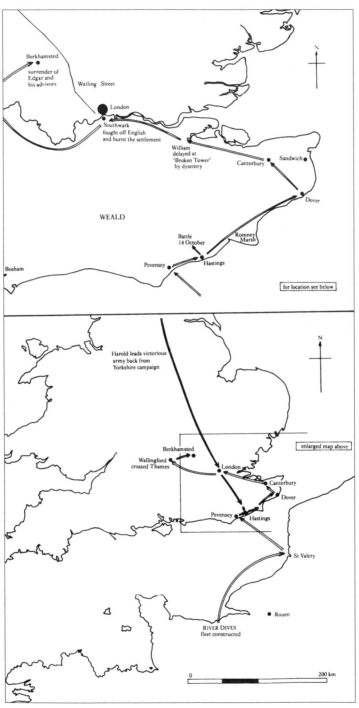

William's preparations for invasion and his campaign in England in the autumn of 1066.

William's fleet arrived after an overnight crossing at Pevensey, probably on the 'eve of the Feast of St Michael' – 28 September. Any harbour in western or central Sussex would have made a logical enough landfall from the Dives, but one might have expected William to have been aiming further east than Pevensey when sailing from St Valery. The nearest English beaches where a large fleet could disembark troops were about 90 kilometres (55 miles) distant at Dungeness, and the suitability of the 'Ness which is to the south of Romney' for such enterprises had already been demonstrated by Earl Godwine in 1052. Alternatively, Sandwich was the port most favoured by England's fleet commanders during the eleventh century. William seems already to have expressed some interest in Dover, which featured in the Bonneville Accord, and his superiority over Count Eustace of Boulogne meant that he could have crossed on the narrows. It is quite possible, therefore, that one of these was William's objective. If so, he was off course during his night crossing. He apparently missed the harbours of Rye and Hastings at the first attempt then came ashore at Pevensey, just a few miles short of the famous cliffs which form Beachy Head and which stretch from Eastbourne to Newhaven. At this point he had traversed something like 112 km of sea. His rapid departure from Pevensey eastward to Hastings on the dawn of his arrival certainly suggests that he had landed further westwards than he had intended.

Pevensey has changed out of all recognition since the eleventh century, with the silting up of the great bay which then stretched inland almost as far as Hailsham and Wartling. The Saxon Shore fortress had been constructed some seven centuries earlier on a promontory jutting out into the Bay from the west, and the substantial remains of this massive fortification now provided William with a secure base, within which he constructed his first castle in England, probably a motte thrown up in the south-east corner of the Roman walled enceinte, where the later stone castle still stands.

The following day, William moved the bulk of his forces eastward some 18 kilometres along the coast to Hastings, where he likewise threw up a castle mound, which is, unusually, still extant within the later Medieval castle which still perches on the cliffs above the town. The Bayeux Tapestry makes it clear that this advance was by land, so much of the fleet was perhaps initially left at Pevensey, although it seems likely that it was thereafter marshalled at Hastings once that site had been secured. William's reason may well have been the strategic nature of Pevensey itself, which was an excellent haven for a large fleet and which could provide shelter from storms in the Channel, but he had to provision his forces and Pevensey was small and cut off from the hinterland to both north and east by the Bay itself, so less well suited to the looting of the farmers of coastal Sussex than was Hastings. The Tapestry makes it quite clear that the duke's first concern at this point was to revictual his forces, and they were depicted at Hastings seizing and consuming the livestock and other provisions of the local community.

Even Hastings was not easy as regards access, and William discovered this by hard experience in the extended account of his namesake, William of Poitiers, who described the duke as personally leading a reconnaissance from which he

Pevensey Castle. First fortified as a Roman-Saxon shore fort, the site was re-used in the late Anglo-Saxon period as a burh or fortified town. William briefly occupied it and built a castle there in 1066 before shifting his forces to Hastings.

found himself returning on foot because of the difficulty of the way. The steepness of the roads northwards and eastward – into and around Fairlight, for example – remains a fact of the geography of this picturesque corner of England, which lies at the south-eastern end of the great knot of broken woodland and pasture which comprises the Weald of Kent and Sussex. William was not, therefore, seeking a route inland, but sustenance and shelter for himself and his troops within easy access of his ships, and the trading site and walled *burh* of Hastings itself had obvious advantages in this respect over the smaller Pevensey. William of Poitiers remarked that the duke later punished the men of Romney for attacking some of his men, so they were presumably raiding up to 30 kilometres along the coast in search of provender and booty.

News of the Norman invasion of 28 September will have reached Harold within four or five days, even if he had not by that date set out to return south from York and his great victory of the Monday previous at Stamford Bridge. According to William of Poitiers, news of Stamford Bridge reached William at Hastings quite soon after his arrival there, so perhaps in early October, via a messenger sent by Robert fitz 'Guimora', who seems likely to have been Robert fitzWimarc. Robert's purpose was putatively to advise William not to risk combat against Harold Godwineson but to retreat behind his defences, since Harold had a

Hastings old town occupies a narrow break in the chalk cliffs which provides access to the beach.
It was a late Saxon burh and an important fishing port. William built his castle on the cliff
above the town in the middle distance.

great force with him and was come from the slaughter of the Norwegians and
Hardrada – 'the doughtiest warrior under Heaven'. There is a powerful rhetorical
element in William's writing, of course, but events do suggest that the duke was
prepared for Harold's arrival.

William of Poitiers also describes a diplomatic exchange before the battle, via
an English monk and Duke William's representative from the Abbey of Fécamp,
by which the two principals rehearsed their respective grievances and their claims
to the throne. An interesting feature of this is the admission in Harold's reputed
challenge of the fact that it had long been 'the common custom of this nation that
a gift made at the point of death is held as valid' and took precedence over all else,
and it is difficult indeed on the available evidence to fault this argument. Duke
William is, of course, portrayed as winning the war of words via Harold's reputed
dismay at a challenge to single combat, but a retrospective reconstruction had
little option but to deliver this result in favour of a triumphant patron. Whatever

Hastings Castle motte is the most complete survivor of those thrown up by William in 1066, despite being incorporated in the later medieval, stone-built fortifications.

the precise exchanges, therefore, they certainly did not deter either leader from trial by battle.

It has often been suggested that William controlled the course of the Hastings campaign and that his generalship was in various respects superior to that of Harold. In particular, Harold has been criticized for his speed of advance and apparent failure to collect a larger army, and his tactics on the actual battle field. Hastings is often additionally hailed as a victory of the 'new' over the 'old' – of mixed forces of cavalry, infantry and archers over the housecarl. Some of these judgements may be apt, but we compare and criticize the leaders and their various forces at our peril given the comparative poverty of our knowledge and also its highly retrospective nature.

First the campaign itself. William landed in, and was busily despoiling, the core of Harold's own family estates, murdering his men, stealing their cattle and crops and burning their homes, as the Bayeux Tapestry testifies. To all intents and purposes, therefore, William was behaving like a Viking. Harold's responsibility was to protect his people and drive him out, since he was both king and also the more immediate lord of these coastal communities, whose association with his own family dated back at least three generations. Any remaining doubts among the English concerning Harold's own legitimacy as king required that he act in as

:LD:) ℏIC DOMVS:IN CEN DITVR:

Burning a house at or near Hastings. Norman ravaging of the Sussex coastal plain can only have hardened English attitudes against William, but it may have hastened Harold's march south against him. (The Bayeux Tapestry – 11th Century. By special permission of the City of Bayeux)

kingly a way as possible when his kingdom was attacked, and that required a prompt assault on William.

What is more, Harold was operating inside his own kingdom, and not, like William, in hostile territory. He could not, therefore, maintain a large force for long during the winter months and expect to be able to feed both troops and riding horses. By contrast, William could continue his plundering all winter if necessary. Additionally, William of Poitiers claimed that Harold had dispatched the English fleet to cut off the retreat of the Norman ships. Harold clearly sought a decisive victory and this was one way of making that more likely, but he could not play a waiting game which might endanger his fleet as it circumnavigated the Kent coast in mid-October, well outside the normal season for sailing. He had no guarantee that he would be able to maintain contact with his ships. Harold had, therefore, to agree a plan of campaign with his captains at London, then abide by it.

In the circumstances, Harold had very little option but to launch a rapid attack on the Norman invaders, and his reasons were both political and tactical. Both English and Norman authors represent his forces as large, and there seems no obvious reason to think that Harold went into battle with fewer men than he needed. He obviously had the pick of England's warriors with him in his own large companies of housecarls, his brothers' men and those of other magnates, and he probably called out the levies of the nearer shires. The number of top quality soldiers who were absent is unlikely to have been very great, even despite the delay which kept Edwin and Morcar absent. It seems most unlikely that Harold intended that the northern earls should fight on the south coast. They had after all spent the whole of 1066 from Easter onwards guarding the shores of the Midlands and the north while Harold himself awaited William, and their battle-depleted forces can have been fit for little more in October. The presence of their first cousin, the prominent and influential Abbot of Peterborough, demonstrates that Leofric's house was represented at Hastings and fully committed to the king.

Harold's army was, therefore, a credible host, and arguably as large as he could reasonably expect to provision during even a short campaign. The troops would themselves probably have been expected to march carrying enough food to see them through, but their horses still had to be pastured and that posed difficulties in a war-ravaged landscape in an English October. If many of his troops were travel weary and some carrying wounds from Stamford Bridge, they were also buoyed up by their great victory over the Norwegians and confident of destroying the Norman host in turn – and morale was perhaps the most important single ingredient of victory at this date.

What is more, the English were not entirely ignorant of Norman tactics. Harold had himself joined in William's campaigning in Brittany and could make his dispositions accordingly. The English more generally had knowledge of the French via several episodes during Edward's reign: there was Earl Ralph's performance at Hereford in 1055, for example, and the presence of a group of Norman mercenaries among the forces of Macbeth when he confronted Earl Siward and the English in 1054. In neither event had Norman tactics impressed the English, who arguably believed that they could and would overcome William's army when the two finally came to blows.

The final battle occurred on 14 October, some 10 kilometres as the crow flies along the London road north of Hastings (now the A2100). Harold probably marched south from London, reaching the vicinity of Battle on 13 October and overnighting there, but was discomfited by an unexpected Norman advance out of Hastings to confront him. The Worcester manuscript of the Chronicle – which is the sole surviving English account of the battle with any claim to contemporaneity – concurs with the view that the English army was taken by surprise and engulfed in battle even before it could fully form its front. Harold perhaps anticipated that his rapid advance southwards would be as successful in surprising his enemy as had been his march from Tadcaster to Stamford Bridge. He may also have been advised by such as Robert 'son of Guimora' that Duke William feared his approach and was unlikely to fight, but this was not to be the case:

> Nevertheless the king fought very hard against him with those men who wanted to support him, and there was a great slaughter on either side. There were killed King Harold, and Earl Leofwine his brother, and Earl Gyrth his

brother, and many good men. And the French had possession of the place of slaughter, just as God granted them because of the people's sins.

This Worcester manuscript account has none of the detail of the battle offered by the Bayeux Tapestry or William of Poitiers, but it contains all the basic information of significance to the political history of the day and it avoids the portrayal of the duke himself as inspirational war leader which is so powerful a mark of particularly William's work. Certainly, this was a battle between two very different types of army, and the combination of (primarily) cavalry and archers did overcome the English infantry, but not without a ferocious struggle. The result was apparently long in doubt and never predictable.

The critical fact of the Battle of Hastings was not defeat, for many English kings had lost battles before against invaders and continued their careers. Armies could be raised anew from the thegns of England, and gaps left by death and disablement in the ranks of the elite housecarls could be filled. It was none of these things but the sudden and unexpected death of the king which was critical. This was a great psychological blow, and it is difficult to overestimate the impact of Harold's demise on the political climate of the day. The legitimacy of his kingship was built upon his ability to protect England and he had seemed to justify all expectations in the Stamford Bridge campaign against an enemy far more feared in England than the Norman duke. High morale – even overconfidence – was the likely consequence, and the royal councillors in London and others of the political community awaited the news of another massive victory delivered by God to their king and his forces over an invader. Instead, there came news of total disaster, a battle in which the king himself had been slain along with his brothers, many leading supporters and a large number of their men.

As the Worcester manuscript of the Chronicle suggested, the obvious conclusion to be drawn by a group dominated by clerics was that God had intervened against King Harold, raising him up in battle against the Vikings only to cast him down by the hand of the Norman. Hastings was not just a defeat, therefore, but the unpicking of all that Harold had striven to achieve; his political machinations and accommodation of the house of Leofric, the marginalization of Edgar's claim, the alienation and eventual death of Tostig, his marriage, his accession and consecration, his military leadership, were all revealed as unholy and against divine will. If that were true, then recovery of the aid of the Lord required that the English detach themselves from Harold's kingship and seek not an heir to that – and he had of course left sons by Edith Swan-neck who were now of an age to be militarily active – but a more appropriate and worthier heir to Edward himself. Such required an immediate return to the house of Cerdic, as the only rightful kings of the English.

THE RISE AND FALL OF KING EDGAR

The Worcester manuscript of the Chronicle recorded that Archbishop Ealdred and the garrison in London backed the candidacy of Edgar Aetheling in the crisis following Hastings. Ealdred's presence at London at this point supports but does not prove the suggestion that he was unlikely to have been at York during the campaigns against Hardrada. Rather, Ealdred's status as the most senior churchman in England whose consecration was uncontroversial is likely to have kept him at or close to the most important seat of government throughout much of the year, and particularly while the king and many senior laymen were absent from there, marching to war. Ealdred was arguably the nearest thing to a prime minister that Harold's regime had. At this point, therefore, the man who had negotiated the return of Edward the Exile, had probably only recently crowned Harold, and was in some nine weeks time to crown William, threw his considerable weight behind Edgar, grandson of the great Edmund Ironside and great-grandson of Aethelred II.

At London, his stand was supported by the armed men of the city, whose ancestors had played an important role in earlier succession crises such as those of 1013–16. London was arguably well supplied with armed men and its great fortifications made it the premier fortress of the kingdom, where the young Cerdicing and his supporters could feel comparatively safe from Norman attack.

William of Poitiers gave credit for the leadership of Edgar's party not to Ealdred but to Stigand, Archbishop of Canterbury. There seems every reason to suppose that Stigand was a core member of the group at London, but the subtle shift of emphasis to the primate whose own consecration was contentious and who had just been deposed when William wrote was presumably intended to weaken the legitimacy of Edgar's candidacy, and this compares with the claim that Harold was himself crowned by Stigand. Both William and the Chronicle did, however, concur with the view that the archbishops were supported by Earls Edwin and Morcar. William made passing reference also to other magnates but failed to name any.

Edgar, therefore, had the support of a wide spectrum of the political community, and more particularly its most senior figures both lay and ecclesiastical. The strongest feature of his candidacy was his royal blood, on which both the Chronicle and William of Poitiers separately remarked. It was 'his natural right' and he was 'of the royal race of Edward'. What is more, his name conjured up that of his great-great-grandfather, whose reign, in retrospect, appeared such a golden age of peace, security and ecclesiastical patronage, under divine protection. As William of Poitiers remarked, the English wished for a king from their own countrymen, and Edgar was the sole viable candidate. Widespread support for Edgar's candidacy represents a stampede back to the legitimate royal house following the traumatic defeat of a well-supported usurper – Harold Godwineson – in whose kingship all who now supported Edgar had hitherto invested. Commitment to Edgar was, therefore, not merely a political strategy for those involved but also had a providential dimension, as a means to regain the support of the Lord.

Although he is not known to have been crowned, Edgar was certainly active as king and should perhaps be accorded the title, particularly since very many late Anglo-Saxon kings reigned for months and even years prior to coronation. There is only a single example of his kingly deeds, but it is entirely consistent with this interpretation. It occurs in the Peterborough manuscript of the Chronicle, which records the fact that Abbot Leofric of Peterborough had been present on the Hastings campaign but fell ill and died on his return home, on 31 October. The monks then chose their provost, Brand, as abbot, and sent him to Edgar 'because the local people thought he ought to become king, and the aetheling happily agreed it for him'. This later brought down the wrath of William on the house, but it seems clear at the time that Edgar was both the popular choice as king and already dispensing royal patronage from the centre of power at London in early November. That near contemporary accounts refer to him as aetheling and not king reflects their composition after William had himself been crowned, at which point Edgar's brief reign was necessarily demoted to an interregnum.

Edgar's regime may have begun to organize a defence against William. If not, it had sufficient local support for a degree of local defiance to occur spontaneously, as William began his campaign post-Hastings. The duke's first priority was to assess the outcome of the battle itself and bury the dead. It is clear that the Normans knew that Harold and his two brothers had died in the battle, although the exact nature of their decease remains a matter of argument, as does the burial that Harold received. Both his mother, Gytha, and the canons of his refounded minster at Waltham Holy Cross are reputed to have claimed the body, and wild talk eventually circulated concerning Harold's survival of the battle and career thereafter. Hastings did not, however, produce any sudden change of heart concerning the Norman candidacy for the throne among the English elite, and none are known to have joined William even after the battle. There is a clear contrast here between the acceptability of William and Hardrada, whose claims found considerable support in Yorkshire after Gate Fulford.

According to William of Poitiers, the duke left a garrison at Hastings – presumably to guard his fleet and the retreat of his forces should that prove necessary – and marched eastward, first 'punishing' the men of Romney for their earlier treatment of his men, then moving on to Dover. Duke William had reputedly received intelligence that a great multitude had gathered there but many of these were probably non-combatants seeking the safety of the strongest defensive site in the area. Although Dover does not appear on the early tenth-century Burghal Hidage list of defensive centres it does seem clear that the castle site with its Roman lighthouse and Saxon church was by this date well protected by man-made ramparts as well as its considerable natural defences. William reported that: 'that fortress is sited on a cliff whose natural steepness has been everywhere artificially scarped, rising like a wall sheer out of the sea as high as an arrow can be shot'.

Dover was in no state to stand seige by the triumphant Norman army and its defenders negotiated surrender, although some of the Norman force began to fire the town. William felt obliged to keep face with the inhabitants by paying for the necessary rebuilding, and the vision of an ill-disciplined army which we are vouchsafed at Dover contrasts to great effect with William of Poitiers's earlier claims concerning the duke's iron control of his soldiery. William then reputedly spent eight days adding to the fortifications, and in all probability built another timber and earth castle. His interest in Dover again suggests concern to cover his line of retreat should that become necessary, and this was the stronghold which

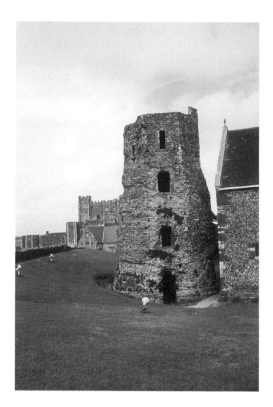

The Roman lighthouse, Dover. The lighthouse was the early focus beside which the Anglo-Saxon church of St Mary-in-the-Castle (far right) was constructed; indeed, the lighthouse was pressed into service as a western annexe to the church. The site was later fortified. William constructed a motte in the vicinity after Dover surrendered to him in the weeks after the Battle of Hastings.

had reportedly featured in the Bonneville Accord which the duke had earlier negotiated with Harold Godwineson, so was perhaps considered a crucial port of entry to England from northern France, then as now.

By this stage the Norman army was suffering from dysentery, brought on by foul water and bad food, but William pressed on. There is a brief mention in the Worcester manuscript of the Chronicle of reinforcements reaching William subsequent to his initial invasion, and these presumably joined him at some point during his sojourn either at Hastings or more probably at Dover. He left his sick at Dover with a garrison and then turned westwards, and the men of Canterbury were sufficiently overawed to come out to meet him, offer hostages and swear allegiance. The archbishop was not present, of course, but the fall of Canterbury was a major blow to Edgar's regime at London, and it was significant that it fell unfought.

At this point, William's victory over the mighty Harold Godwineson was the critical factor that discouraged resistance, and Edgar's regime badly needed to make an effort to shatter growing belief in Norman military invincibility. William of Poitiers supposed that Edgar was well supplied with armed men: 'Its [London's] citizens could themselves supply a numerous and formidable force, and they had now been joined by so many troops that they could hardly be housed even in this large town.' In the past, London had been crucial in sustaining English kingship in the face of invading forces. What Edgar did not have was experience of military leadership or credibility in this role. The aetheling is unlikely to have ever been in a battle, was still too young to take on the role of commander, and had no core of long-committed relatives, tenants and thegns to make up his military inner council and household. There is a great contrast in this respect between the position of Edgar in 1066 and his grandfather Edmund Ironside just fifty years earlier: both faced powerful invaders; both found themselves launching their candidacy for the crown from London, with the support of its citizens and leading grandees; and both could count on widespread sympathy. Only Edmund, however, was personally of an age and had already the experience and credibility to go out into Wessex and raise an army with which to relieve the city. This was a crucial difference, for London could not stand siege indefinitely, particularly with the numbers of its defenders swollen by incomers and its food supply threatened by Norman control of parts at least of the countryside around.

At this juncture, therefore, Edgar's candidacy depended heavily on the ability of his regime to mobilize an effective field army with which to counter the threat posed by Duke William. Only expectation of military relief and active support by the regime would embolden England's numerous fortified towns to close their gates to William and force him to risk his depleted forces in the open country and in siege warfare in an English winter. Edgar could not himself provide that military reassurance and leadership.

The senior lay figures within the regime were Earls Edwin and Morcar, and much depended on their military leadership at this point. They, however, were suffering from acute difficulties and seem to have been incapable of organizing an effective resistance. Both had been heavily defeated at Gate Fulford and had lost many men dead and wounded both in the battle and in the rout which followed. Their Mercian and Northumbrian affinities were, therefore, far less capable of independent military operations against an invader with William's resources in late October than had been the case in September. What is more, it is most unlikely that Morcar could have persuaded the Northumbrians to fight in the south in a war which at this stage can have seemed to have had little to do with themselves. The action against Harald Hardrada had been fought beneath the walls of York itself, where the earl was in a position to call out as many troops as possible. It is far from clear whether or not Morcar even retained his earldom after Gate Fulford and Stamford Bridge. Should the earls fight William, therefore, they had only the resources of Mercia at their backs.

The shortfall in terms of warriors could presumably have been made up by rallying the surviving thegns and housecarls of Wessex and East Anglia, but it seems most unlikely that Earl Edwin could have created a cohesive and effective force from such recruits. There had, after all, been deep and bitterly contested divisions between the affinities of Godwine and his sons and the house of Leofric over a period of thirty years. The marriage alliance forged by Harold and Leofric's grandsons in 1065–6 had accommodated their respective ambitions and harnessed their resources behind Harold's usurpation, but it would be naïve to imagine that it had healed the wounds of factional conflicts which had been a fact of political life throughout the adult lives of all concerned. Most of the bishops were allies of the Godwinesons, not Earl Edwin, and many of the more prominent landholders of England south of Hereford and Peterborough are likely to have had severe reservations about placing themselves and their military resources under Edwin's command and conceding him the kudos from any victory they might achieve.

Nor had the two northern earls much in the way of a military reputation. They had, admittedly, done well out of the Northumbrian rebellion, but that was resolved by political and military means. They had driven Tostig's Flemings out of Lindsey in the early summer, but when it came to major battles their record reads very differently – fought one, won none, lost one. Moreover, they had lost to that same Norwegian king whom Harold Godwineson had almost immediately then overthrown in a famous victory. Could Edwin and his brother be expected to succeed where Harold Godwineson had failed, against the Normans? There was, therefore, a serious problem of credibility to be confronted, which could only be faced down by an army built around the core affinity of the house of Leofric, therefore drawn from the Mercians and their Welsh friends.

It seems clear that the earls remained in London during the critical weeks of late October and early November, and this conclusion challenges that of John ('Florence') of Worcester, who portrayed Edwin and Morcar as abandoning Edgar and returning home with their forces. That rather hostile vision is impossible to reconcile with the final surrender of the earls along with the rest of Edgar's following, so should probably be set to one side. Perhaps they felt that their claims as the military leaders of a regime otherwise dominated by figures from the Godwineson faction required their continued presence at the political centre, but this meant that no field army was being recruited in the provinces to march to London's aid.

Despite being himself struck down by dysentery in Kent for a time, at an unknown place termed 'Broken Tower', William marched on London, apparently up the old Roman road of Watling Street, which is now the A2. His advance guard reached Southwark, and was attacked there by forces based on London, but the English were beaten back within the walls and the Normans fired 'all the buildings on this side of the river in order to inflict a double blow on the pride of their stubborn foes'. Whether or not the two earls had led the English troops is unknown but it does seem likely, particularly as there is an uneerie similarity between this affray and the battle at Gate Fulford beneath the walls of York. If so, the retreat of the English and the destruction of Southwark in full view of London will have done nothing to reinforce the morale of the English or confidence in Edwin's military leadership.

The Norman army then marched past London and further upstream, eventually crossing the Thames at Wallingford. At that point, the political cohesion of Edgar's regime began to buckle. With William poised to isolate London from its hinterland and with little prospect of effective resistance on Edgar's behalf, Archbishop Stigand abandoned the English cause, 'swore fealty and renounced the aetheling whom he had rashly nominated as king'. Stigand was a seasoned politician whose career had been built on an accurate reading of the balance of power. It should also be remembered that his diocesan see had already surrendered to William, so he was himself isolated from his affinity and also his income. His defection must, however, have dealt yet one more blow to the confidence of Edgar's adherents.

The final surrender occurred at Berkhamsted, and this event seems more accurately detailed in the Worcester manuscript of the Chronicle than by William of Poitiers. The Worcester manuscript reports that he:

> raided all that region he travelled across until he came to Berkhamsted. And there came to meet him Archbishop Ealdred, and Prince Edgar, and Earl Edwin, and Earl Morcar, and all the best men from London; and they submitted from necessity when the most harm was done . . . and gave hostages and swore oaths. . . .

William's forces were, of course, living off the land, and had been throughout their time in England, ever since their arrival in the vicinity of Hastings, but the duke seems to have used ravaging and destruction as a weapon of war as well. The firing of Southwark and of the countryside on the west side of London can only have further demoralized the Londoners and Edgar's regime within the walls. William of Poitiers had the Norman army operating in sight of London after the crossing of the Thames, and actually represented the surrender as occurring far closer to the city than seems to have been the case. The Normans were, therefore, demonstrating their control of the countryside and the inability of Edgar's regime to protect even the farms and villages close by the foremost city of England, following the defeat of his soldiery when they made their stand at Southwark.

The eventual surrender was clearly a matter agreed by the regime in London and was effectively co-ordinated, with all the relevant figures involved. Unanimity at this point offered the best chance for the survival of each, and responsibility was presumably collective. The location of the surrender is perhaps itself of some significance. Berkhamsted lies over 40 kilometres from the City of London, in Hertfordshire on the eastern edge of the Chilterns. It was a place of no more than local significance in 1066 – a borough with fifty-two burgesses in 1086 and a large manor stretching to twenty-six ploughlands owing geld on thirteen hides, in 1066 held by one of Harold Godwineson's thegns. However, the main routes out of London towards the West Midlands passed through or near the town, which therefore controlled access to the heartland of the power of the house of Leofric. Edgar's regime surrendered once it lost the option of raising an effective army from Earl Edwin's men. The earls had delayed too long in London, and William's presence north of the city made surrender inevitable. It was Berkhamsted's position on the road network that brought it briefly into the limelight at this juncture.

The surrender is undated, and any attempt to reconstruct a chronology rests only on the fixed points of the battle of Hastings on 14 October and William's coronation of 25 December. His march to, and occupation of, Dover arguably accounts for all October, placing the London campaign in November at earliest, but it is unclear how much time was lost by William when he himself fell ill. The surrender may have occurred some time in mid to late November, but an early December date is viable. There was certainly a gap between the Berkhamsted surrender and William's coronation, and this seems to have lasted for several weeks. The Chronicle complained that Norman ravaging continued even while the surrender was occurring and William's forces still presumably needed to live off the land. There is some evidence that the duke himself took the view that hostilities were not formally ended until his coronation had occurred, but this opinion was clearly not shared by the English, who were used to accession to the throne predating coronation by considerable periods.

KING WILLIAM

William of Poitiers portrayed the English as at this point importunate concerning William's acceptance of the crown and the duke as exhibiting misgivings, and persuaded only by his followers, but this reads too much like a further tribute to William's nobility, modesty and wisdom by his most eager apologist. Duke William had pursued the English throne long and hard and was hardly likely to have held back at this point from an early coronation, given the political value of that event to his cause. Thereafter, all opposition to him could be and was treated as rebellion. More importantly, he was busy taking control of London, and this involved the construction of a castle as well as preparations for his coronation. The primary phases of the Tower of London belong, therefore, to December 1066, and its building was intended to reinforce William's authority in England's greatest walled city, where he probably feared a change of heart among the citizenry which might still promote Edgar to the throne.

Indeed, there is some evidence that just such a change of heart actually occurred. William of Jumièges refers to a final and bloody stand by Edgar's men inside London after Duke William's passage of the Thames at Wallingford and presumably also after the English regime had come to terms. Recent archaeological work, as yet unpublished, suggests that this happenend between St Paul's and Cheapside and the discovery of several dismembered eleventh-century skeletons may give some substance to this interpretation. The English were defeated once more, of course, perhaps largely because of the dire lack of leadership by anyone of royal or even comital status.

The coronation occurred not in London but at Westminster, where Edward was buried and Harold had himself been crowned. The choice of location reinforced William's claim to be Edward's chosen heir, and avoided too the military dangers that might have been involved had St Paul's been utilized. The choice of Christmas Day invested the event with the dignity and solemnity associated with the nativity, and harnessed that new beginning to William's. Even so, the process was a shambles: Ealdred of York called upon the English to acclaim their new king and Bishop Geoffrey of Coutances did the same for the Normans, but the resulting uproar so unnerved the Norman soldiery standing guard outside the abbey that they fired the nearest corner of London, or more probably its western suburbs. That was the inauspicious start to William's reign.

This model of the White Tower, in the Museum of London, reconstructs what the Tower of London might have looked like in about 1100. The Tower has since become shrouded in ever more elaborate curtain walls, the most substantial built in the reign of Henry III.

William of Poitiers rounded off his account with a trenchant defence of William's title, which serves to reinforce its very fragility:

> The insignia of royalty became him as well as the quality of his rule, and his sons and grandsons by a just succession will reign over the English land. This land he has gained as the legal heir with the confirmation of the oaths of the English. He took possession of his inheritance by battle, and he was crowned at last with the consent of the English, or at least at the desire of their magnates. And if it be asked what was his hereditary title, let it be answered that a close kinship existed between King Edward and the son of Duke Robert whose paternal aunt, Emma, was the sister of Duke Richard II, the daughter of Duke Richard I and the mother of King Edward himself. . . .

William's claim by descent was, therefore, lamentably weak, and he came from outside to take the English crown without the support of any substantial party within England, be that English or French. Not even his acclaimed kinsman, King Edward, gave his candidacy support in 1066. He gained the throne primarily because of a series of accidents. These included military events but mostly without William's own participation, the cumulative impact of which was to render Edgar's regime incapable of withstanding the victor of the Battle of Hastings. If that great triumph was God given, then so too was William's ascent of the throne, and that view clearly persuaded some participants in the events of early winter 1066. On a broader view, William is revealed as a gambler, who risked much of what he had so far achieved in France on a very risky invasion of England. He won, against the odds, a victory which was far from predictable and was certainly unlooked for in England when Edward died, and his candidacy had therefore to be accommodated by an English elite who had already been battered by the traumatic events of the most turbulent year in English history. Five kings, therefore, but the spoils fell to the least likely successor to King Edward to enter the lists, who had begun the year with none of the principal characteristics which normally marked a candidate for the throne – royal blood, significant support among the English nobility, royal nomination and the support of the metropolitans and bishops.

Yet William's was not the first usurpation of the year, for it was Harold Godwineson's machinations which initially dispossessed the royal line and opened the door to the great power brokers from outside the dynasty, whose principal assets lay in the armies each could muster. Had Edward himself nominated Edgar Aetheling, and had the English rallied around his candidacy at the start of the year, then it may be that the Norwegian and Norman candidates would have had less scope to press their own claims. Harold's politicking in the last years – and particularly the last year – of Edward's reign generated a momentum behind his own candidacy which inevitably required the dispossession of the English royal line. A century earlier, young princes had been promoted to the crown without threat of disinheritance by non-royal claimants – although murderous power struggles occurred between the supporters of different aethelings. But in 1066, the political climate was very different to, say, that of 975. In the intervening years England had experience of regicide. It had experienced too a Danish kingship which had exploited disunity within the ruling house to seize and hold onto the English throne. The connection between Cerdic's descendants and the crown of the English had seemed immutable when Edgar the Peaceable died, but it was laid aside without apparent demur at the death of his last surviving grandson, Edward the Confessor, only to come rushing back just nine months and nine days later once Harold Godwineson was dead. It was the long-term fragility of the royal kin and the breakdown of its monopoly of kingship, as witnessed by their fathers and grandfathers, which made Harold Godwineson's succession possible in January 1066 and set in train the dramatic events of the remainder of the year.

Postscript

Two questions overshadowed 1066: one was 'who will be the next king of the English?'; the other was 'who should be king of the English?' At different points in the year, these questions appeared to have been answered in a variety of very different ways, and no fewer than five individuals were recognized as king of the English by at least some part of the political elite at different times: Edward, who died in January and Harold Godwineson who succeeded him; Harald Hardrada, who very briefly gained the backing for his candidacy of the men of York and two at least of the three ridings of the shire; Edgar Aetheling, at London during the few weeks following the Battle of Hastings; and lastly William, whose coronation occurred on Christmas Day. The succession was an issue on which military pressure could be brought to bear, of course, but it was not ultimately a matter which could be decided solely by war. Rather, it was a political issue which necessarily involved a wide sub-set of views about what constituted kingship and what legitimized any and every candidacy for that office. As late as October and part at least of November, William was still viewed by English leaders as an outsider whose candidacy they were determined to resist.

When the English leaders eventually made their peace with William, they acknowledged him as their king by performing fealty. They 'gave hostages and swore him oaths, and he promised them that he would be a loyal lord to them'. The mutuality of this settlement was then reinforced by the coronation ceremony at Westminster Abbey on Christmas Day, the terms of which included William's promise, reinforced by a hand-clasp with Archbishop Ealdred of York and an oath on the Bible, that he would 'hold this nation as well as the best of any kings before him did, if they would be loyal to him'. The Anglo-Saxon political classes thereby sought to reassure themselves that their new, foreign king would respect their role as the rulers of England beneath the crown, as the appropriate pool of candidates for promotion within the church of the English and as the owners of vast acreages of productive land, hunting forests, markets, churches and other assets too numerous to list. William's military achievements very obviously overshadowed the entire process of his enthronement. Indeed, it seems beyond argument that only his great victory and the absence of any other credible forces gave him the chance to be accepted as king by a people who were clearly unenthusiastic concerning his candidacy. Yet, even accepting the significance of his dominating military following in the short term, what occurred in the late autumn and mid-winter was not just a conquest but also an accommodation. William was accepted as king by the English leadership and crowned by an English archbishop and metropolitan in a ceremony conducted according to accepted English rites. In English eyes, therefore, William was to become an English king – if a rather curious one given that he seems to have had little or no knowledge of the language of his new subjects. The obvious parallels were the recognition as king by the provincial leadership of England of first Swein, in 1013, and then Cnut, in 1014 and then 1016, and the latter, particularly, may well have been in the minds of the English leaders as they journeyed from London to meet William at Berkhamsted. Some Englishmen did well under Cnut, clerics in particular, and that fact will have been well known in 1066. Another event to which contemporaries may have looked back was the coronation of Edward himself, who was hardly less 'French' in English eyes than William was, and under whom existing power brokers had retained a large share of effective power – if not always unchallenged by the king.

Despite all the bloodshed of 1066, therefore, there were precedents which will have encouraged those sections of the English leadership which had not committed themselves against William at Hastings to anticipate that they might find him a man with whom they could do business once he had been enthroned and the dust had settled. William's continental following clearly had other ideas, and it was largely their demands for power and wealth that began and then characterized the tenurial revolution of the next few years, and which witnessed the alienation then near annihilation and almost total replacement of the upper echelons of English society.

That eventual outcome was not, however, entirely predictable among those who enthroned William in 1066. Rather, most if not all arguably hoped to retain their own power and property under the new regime, and considered that acquiescence in the Norman candidacy offered the course of action most likely to produce that result. Indeed, William was crowned in order to bring to an end a period of severe dislocation and disturbance which threatened each and every member of the propertied classes – and others besides. The accommodation of the English and William was, therefore, perceived by those of the English nobility who participated as the most effective measure available by which to restore royal government and the peace and stability which could be provided only by an established king, and they hoped to be among the beneficiaries of that process.

The outcome of the Battle of Hastings was probably seen by many at the time as a judgement of God between two candidates for the throne, and William's apologists certainly thereafter exploited this perception of events so as to enhance his legitimacy as king. It was only in retrospect, however, when the hopes of those involved in the coronation had faltered, that the Norman Conquest came to be seen as a judgement of God upon the English race as a whole on account of their sins – something equivalent to the Viking attacks which Alfred had withstood and which Aethelred's England had likewise suffered. The Old English chroniclers' laments imply a vision of history indistinguishable from that of Aethelred's archbishop, Wulfstan, and expressed in his 'Sermon of the Wolf to the English'. They encapsulate a profound sense of betrayal and disappointment – yet resignation – among the English political community as their hold on the wealth of England rapidly dissipated in the years following a coronation which many lived to regret, and which some actively sought to undo. The loss was very real but the responsibility was God's alone, who was chastising His people for the sins they had committed. Their punishment would end only when He decided, and the matter moved from the sphere of active politics to one of prayer.

The Battle of Hastings and William's subsequent coronation stand out as critical events very largely because of political, cultural and ecclesiastical changes which they facilitated in subsequent years, even decades. Looked at within a narrower framework – and then, as now, it should be remembered that politics occurred within a short timescale – there are two things concerning William's victory which mark them out. Firstly there was the impossibility of predicting it at the beginning of the year. Secondly there was the sense of it being something which came late in a fast-moving sequence of events in a year of profound political change, only parts of which were determined on the battlefield.

In some respects, events at the year end were less radical than those which occurred in the January, when the succession had been detached from the patrilineal descent of the previous king quite peacefully and with his apparent consent. It is within that quite revolutionary political and ideological context that William's triumph should be interpreted in the first instance, as a part of a broader political process to which contemporaries brought pre-existing but mutable perceptions of what should, and what might, occur, and how they themselves should influence events and seek to profit from them.

William's coronation gave his kingship much needed legitimacy and forced his opponents thereafter into rebellion. The new king treated the principal leaders of the English as virtual hostages, detaining them at his court and taking them with him to Normandy in 1067, but this merely gave other magnates the opportunity to emerge as leaders of dissent. In 1067 in the continuing absence of Edwin from his earldom, Eadric the Wild, the nephew of Eadric Streona, raised parts of Herefordshire and Shropshire against William. That winter, the townsmen of Exeter revolted. This was probably part of a more general rising organized by the house of Godwine, since Harold's sons arrived with a fleet from Dublin before midsummer 1068 in the estuaries of the Avon and Taw but were driven off by Norman and English forces loyal to the king, leaving Exeter to make its own peace. William commissioned the rapid construction of Rougemont Castle at Exeter to secure this important provincial capital in the heartland of western Wessex, and the threat to his kingship from Godwine's grandsons faded as their failure let their credibility slip away.

A major problem which William's opponents failed to resolve was their disunity of purpose. While all wished to displace the Norman king, there was no agreement as to who should be his replacement. The Godwine family presumably looked to their own to provide a candidate, from among the sons of Swein or Harold. In Kent, local English nobility conspired with Eustace of Boulogne, King Edward's erstwhile brother-in-law, to supplant William while he was absent in Normandy in 1067. Copsig, Tostig's old lieutenant in the north, gained William's acquiescence for his own appointment to the northern earldom but was slain by the men of the house of Bamburgh. Edgar Aetheling, his mother and his sisters fled north to Scotland early in 1068, apparently in the hope that King Malcolm

The blocked-up gatehouse of Rougemont Castle, Exeter. The castle was constructed in haste on the outer edge of the town's defences following the rebellion of the men of Exeter in 1068. The style of the arch and other details betray the participation of masons more used to building English churches.

and his associates in the far north of Northumbria might offer a platform for effective resistance, but the Danish fleet which arrived to support the Northumbrian revolt in 1069 was led by King Swein of Denmark's brother and sons and inevitably sought to further their collective claim to the English crown by descent from Cnut's sister, Estrith. In the event, their divisions and inability to unite their forces behind a single candidate allowed William to destroy his enemies piecemeal as and when they took the field against him. His policy of building and garrisoning castles at key points gradually extended Norman control and made his kingship more secure.

Harold's mother, Countess Gytha, abandoned the struggle in 1067–8, taking refuge first on the Island of Flatholme in the Bristol Channel – where her grandsons were shortly to try their luck – and then removing to St Omer in Flanders and the charity of the new count, Baldwin VI. Archbishop Ealdred died in 1069, in a year which witnessed the wreck of his great minster at York as Danes, Normans and Northumbrians all fought for control of the city. Stigand was deposed in 1070 and Abbot Lanfranc appointed to replace him. In the same year, Eadric the Wild was reconciled to the king. Edwin and Morcar eventually escaped from custody in 1071 but too late to take control of the northern rebellions which had been suppressed with great violence during the previous year. Edwin was killed by his own men – the fate of his Welsh brother-in-law before him. Morcar joined the rebels gathered around Hereward at Ely but was recaptured later in the year and imprisoned for the remainder of the reign.

Of all the English leaders who attained prominence in 1066, only Edgar was still free by Christmas 1071. William had gone to considerable lengths to neutralize his potential as a hub of resistance following the Berkhamsted Accord and displayed a studied disinclination to harm this royal kinsman, whose death at his hands had some potential to damage his already poor reputation among the English. Edgar was, therefore, granted lands in 1067, but the pressures on him to pursue his own candidacy for the succession were considerable. By removing himself and his family from England in 1068, Edgar was necessarily distancing himself from the conqueror and renewing his own challenge for the English throne, but neither Malcolm of Scotland nor the Northumbrian rebels whom he joined in 1069 were primarily interested in his candidacy. When the Northumbrian rebellion collapsed in 1070, Edgar was merely the most illustrious of a stream of well-born exiles who poured into Scotland and Malcolm exploited his difficulties as a prince in exile to successfully demand the hand of his sister in marriage and so promote himself and eventually his sons as potential claimants of the English throne.

In 1072, William led an army and fleet into Scotland and Malcolm made his peace and did homage, giving hostages to guarantee his future behaviour and forcing Edgar to withdraw to Flanders, where the new count, Robert I, was far less amicable than his father had been towards his Norman brother-in-law. Even so, 1074 saw him back in Scotland. Philip I of France promised him his great stronghold of Montreuil as a base from which to harm William in that year, but the grand fleet which Malcolm provided foundered in rough weather off the English coast. At Malcolm's suggestion, Edgar once more made his peace with William and accepted a position in his court.

The Temple Pyx, of either English or German manufacture, c. 1125–50. It depicts three
sleeping soldiers who much resemble Normans. The pyx is barely more than 9 cm high and was
probably part of a Holy Sepulchre scene on a reliquary or shrine. It was reputedly found at the
Temple Church in London.

The fortifications of Montreuil Castle and town. Although these ramparts post-date Edgar the Aetheling, this hill-top site was an important fortress outpost of French royal authority towards the Channel in the second half of the eleventh century.

From late in 1074, Edgar's candidacy fell away and he was for the future little more than a peripheral member of the Norman royal family. He quickly became friendly with William's eldest son, Robert Curthose, and sided with him during the various disputes following William's death. The peace made by William Rufus and his elder brother in 1091 stipulated that Edgar be exiled but he quickly thereafter regained England and emerged as the protector of his young nephews, Malcolm's sons. It was stated by Orderic Vitalis that he participated in the first crusade as the leader of the English companies among the Varangians, but doubt has recently been cast on that claim.

By the marriage of Henry I and Maud, the daughter of Malcolm and Margaret, the Aetheling became uncle to the queen of England, but, predictably enough, he backed the losing side – that of Duke Robert – at the decisive Battle of

Tinchebrai in 1106. Thereafter he retired to his estates in England, where he is last documented in the 1120s. He cannot have been less than seventy when he died at an unknown date, still unmarried and childless, and in comparative obscurity. His death removed the last direct descendant of the house of Cerdic in the male line, more than fifty years after his candidacy for the throne of his grandfather was overridden by the military might and brutal opportunism of William the Conqueror, also called 'the Bastard'.

Many lesser men also fled England once it became clear that William was not to be unseated. By about 1080, numerous Anglo-Saxons had taken service in the Varangian guard of the Byzantine emperors. The later Icelandic *Saga of Edward the Confessor* suggested that the English had reached the eastern Mediterranean via Scandinavia and it may have been the ultimate failure of Swein's challenge for the throne that led his English allies to move on. Their leader was perhaps Siward Bearn, whose name occurs in the Chronicles as a prominent associate of Hereward at Ely. An English fleet variously described as of 235 and 350 ships eventually departed and sailed into the Mediterranean via the Straits of Gibraltar where their crews reputedly sacked Ceuta before arriving at Byzantium and entering the imperial service. They and their descendants were to be a significant element within the Varangian Guard for the next century and more, and they dedicated their own chapel at Byzantium appropriately enough to SS Nicholas and Augustine of Canterbury. The establishment of these English thegns, who refused to be reconciled to William's kingship, in the Near East provides a fitting end to our discussion of the death of Anglo-Saxon England.

Further Reading

PRIMARY SOURCES IN TRANSLATION

There are three major collections of sources for this period:

Whitelock, D. (ed.), *English Historical Documents*, London, Eyre and Spottiswoode, volume I, 500–1042, 2nd edn 1979, reissued by Routledge, 1996.

Douglas, D. and Greenaway, G.W. (eds), *English Historical Documents*, London, Eyre and Spottiswoode, volume II, 1042–1189, 2nd edn 1981, reissued Routledge, 1996.

Allen Brown, R. (ed.), *The Norman Conquest: Documents of Medieval History 5*, London, Edward Arnold, 1984.

The Anglo-Saxon Chronicle is available in several translations, the best and most recent, which is generally used here, being, Swanton, M. (ed.), *The Anglo-Saxon Chronicle*, London, Dent, 1996.

Other sources used include:

Barlow, F. (ed.), *The Life of King Edward the Confessor*, Edinburgh, Nelson, 1962.

Bosanquet, G. (tr.), *Eadmer's History of recent events in England*, London, Cresset Press, 1964.

Chibnall, M. (ed.), *The Ecclesiastical History of Orderic Vitalis*, Oxford, Clarendon Press, 6 vols 1969–80.

Jones, T. (ed. and tr.), *Brut Y Tywysogyon* or *The Chronicle of the Princes*, Cardiff, University of Wales Press, 2nd edn 1973.

Lowther, M.A., *The Chronicle of Battel Abbey from 1066–1176*, London, John Russell Smith, 1851.

Magnusson, M. and Palsson, H. (tr.), *King Harald's Saga*, London, Penguin, 1966.

Sawyer, P.H., *Anglo-Saxon Charters: an annotated list and bibliography*, London, Offices of the Royal Historical Society, 1968, provides a full bibliography and system of reference for the charter evidence.

Whitelock, D. (ed. and tr.), *Anglo-Saxon Wills*, Cambridge, Cambridge University Press, 1930.

Domesday Book is most easily accessible via the county volumes in *History from the Sources*, Morris, J. (ed.), Chichester, Phillimore.

SECONDARY LITERATURE

Barlow, F., *Edward the Confessor*, London, Eyre and Spottiswoode, 1970.

Barlow, F. (ed.), *The Feudal Kingdom of England*, Harlow, Longman, 1980.

Bartlett, R., *The Making of Europe: Conquest, Colonization and Cultural Change, 950–1350*, London, Penguin, 1993.

Bates, D., 'The rise and fall of Normandy, c. 911–1204', in *England and Normandy in the Middle Ages*, Bates, D. & Curry, A. (eds), London, Hambledon Press, 1994, pp. 37–50.

Blackburn, M.A.S. (ed.), *Anglo-Saxon Monetary History*, Leicester, Leicester University Press, 1986.

Brooks, N.P. and the late Walker, H.E., 'The authority and interpretation of the Bayeux Tapestry', *Proceedings of the Battle Conferences*, 1, Boydell & Brewer, 1979, pp. 1–34.

Brown, R. Allen, *The Norman Conquest*, London, Edward Arnold, 1984.

Campbell, J. (ed.), *The Anglo-Saxons*, London, Phaidon, 1982.

Campbell, J., *Essays in Anglo-Saxon History*, London, Hambledon Press, 1986.

Chibnall, M. *The World of Orderic Vitalis*, Oxford, Clarendon Press, 1984.

Clarke, P.A., *The English Nobility under Edward the Confessor*, Oxford, Clarendon Press, 1994.

Douglas, D.C., *William the Conqueror: the Norman impact upon England*, Berkeley and Los Angeles, 1964.

Fleming, R., 'Domesday estates of the king and the Godwines: a study in late Saxon politics', *Speculum*, 58, 1983, pp. 987–1007.

Fleming, R., *Kings and Lords in Conquest England*, Cambridge, Cambridge University Press, 1991.

Garnett, G., 'Coronation and propaganda: some implications of the Norman claim to the throne of England', *Transacations of the Royal Historical Society*, 5th series, 36, 1986, pp. 91–116.

Godfrey, J., 'The defeated Anglo-Saxons take service with the Eastern Emperor', *Proceedings of the Battle Abbey Conferences*, 1979, pp. 63–74.

Golding, B., *Conquest and colonisation: the Normans in Britain, 1066–1100*, London, Macmillan, 1994.

Grape, W., *The Bayeux Tapestry*, Munich & New York, Prestel, 1994.

Hill, D. (ed.), *Ethelred the Unready: papers from the milleniary conference*, British Archaeological Reports, Oxford, 1978.

Hill, D., *An Atlas of Anglo-Saxon England*, Oxford, Blackwell, 1981.

Hooper, N, 'Edgar aetheling, Anglo-Saxon prince, rebel and crusader', *Anglo-Saxon England*, 14, 1985, pp. 197–214.

John, E., 'Edward the Confessor and the Norman succession', *English Historical Review*, 94, 1979, pp. 241–67.

Kapelle, W.E., *The Norman Conquest of the North: the region and its transformation, 1000–1135*, London, Croom Helm, 1979.

Keynes, S., *The Diplomas of King Aethelred 'The Unready', 978–1016*, Cambridge, Cambridge University Press, 1980.

Keynes, S., 'The Aethelings in Normandy', *Anglo-Norman Studies*, 13, 1990, pp. 173–206.

Lawson, M.K., *Cnut: the Danes in England in the early eleventh century*, London, Longman, 1993.

Lewis, C.P., 'The French in England before the Norman Conquest', *Anglo-Norman Studies*, 17, 1994, pp. 123–44.

Mason, E., *Westminster Abbey and its People*, Woodbridge, Boydell Press, 1996.

Morillo, S., *The battle of Hastings: sources and interpretations*, Woodbridge, Boydell Press, 1996.

Raraty, D.G.J., 'Earl Godwine of Wessex: the origin of his power and his political loyalties', *History*, 74, pp. 3–19.

Reynolds, S., *Kingdoms and Communities in Western Europe, 900–1300*, Oxford, Clarendon Press, 1984.

Rumble, A. (ed.), *The reign of Cnut: king of England, Denmark and Norway*, Leicester, Leicester University Press, 1994.

Sawyer, P.H., *Kings and Vikings, Scandinavia and Europe: AD 700–1100*, London, Methuen, 1982.

Scragg, D. (ed.), *The Battle of Maldon*, Oxford, Blackwell, 1991.

Stafford, P., *Unification and Conquest: a political and social history of England in the tenth and eleventh centuries*, London, Edward Arnold, 1989.

Stenton, F.M., *Anglo-Saxon England*, Oxford, Oxford University Press, 3rd edn 1971.

Taylor, H.M. and J., *Anglo-Saxon Architecture*, Cambridge, Cambridge University Press, 2 vols 1965.

Williams, A., 'Some notes and considerations on problems connected with the English Royal Succession, 860–1066', *Proceedings of the Battle Abbey Conferences*, 1, 1978, pp. 144–67.

Williams, A., 'Land and power in the eleventh century: the estates of Harold Godwineson', *Proceedings of the Battle Abbey Conferences*, 3, 1980, pp. 171–87.

Williams, A., '*Princeps Merciorum gentis*: the family, career and connections of Aelfhere, ealdorman of Mercia 956–83', *Anglo-Saxon England*, 10, 1982, pp. 143–72.

Williams, A., 'The king's nephew: the family, career and connections of Ralph, earl of Hereford', in *Studies in medieval history presented to R. Allen Brown*, C. Harper-Bill *et al* (eds), Woodbridge, Boydell Press, 1989, pp. 327–43.

Williams, A., *The English and the Norman Conquest*, Woodbridge, Boydell Press, 1995.

Index

GHOST TOWNS & BACK ROADS

DONALD E. BOWER

Published by
STACKPOLE BOOKS
Cameron and Kelker Streets
Harrisburg, Pa. 17105

Price: $4.95

All rights reserved, including the right to reproduce
this book or portions thereof in any form or by any means,
electronic or mechanical, including photocopying,
recording, or by any information storage and retrieval system, without
permission in writing from the publisher. All inquiries
should be addressed to Stackpole Books, Cameron and Kelker
Streets, Harrisburg, Pennsylvania 17105.

ISBN 0-8117-2026-8

This book is a special, re-titled, paperback edition of the hardcover book
ROAMING THE AMERICAN WEST, published originally by Stackpole Books at $9.95.

Printed in U.S.A.

Library of Congress Cataloging in Publication Data

Bower, Donald E
    Ghost towns and back roads.

    First published in 1971 under title: Roaming the
American West.
    1. The West--Description and travel--1951-
--Guide-books. I. Title.
F595.2.B68 1974   917.8'043   73-16486
ISBN 0-8117-2026-8

fw
AEV 1875

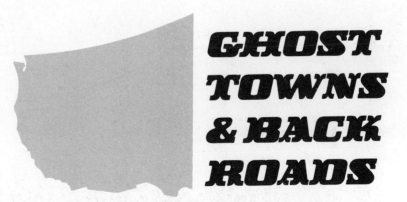

GHOST
TOWNS
& BACK
ROADS

adventure and activity guide to
110 SCENIC, HISTORIC, & NATURAL WONDERS

STACKPOLE BOOKS / Harrisburg, Pennsylvania 17105